2 October 1991

To Dick,

With thanks for being my adviser in all things literary!

Love [illegible] x

SHOOTING AT CLOUDS

Lauren St John

SHOOTING AT CLOUDS

INSIDE THE EUROPEAN PGA TOUR

MAINSTREAM PUBLISHING

EDINBURGH AND LONDON

For my parents

First published in Great Britain, 1991, by
MAINSTREAM PUBLISHING COMPANY (EDINBURGH) LTD
7 Albany Street
Edinburgh EH1 3UG

British Library Cataloguing in Publication Data
St John, Lauren
Shooting at Clouds: Inside the European PGA Tour
1. Golf. Competitions – Biographies
I. Title
796.3526

ISBN 1-85158-358-0

Author photograph on jacket by Peter Dazeley

Typeset in 10/11pt Goudy Oldstyle by Blackpool Typesetting Services Ltd, Blackpool
Printed in Great Britain by Billings & Sons Ltd, Worcester

CONTENTS

ACKNOWLEDGMENTS

Thanks to my agents Murray Pollinger and Sara Menguc for their support and encouragement; everyone at Mainstream Publishing, especially Bill Campbell my editor, without whom I couldn't have written this book, and Penny; the Simpson family and Dino for the garret with the carpet; my cousin Richard Bourne, for his invaluable advice; all members of the Association of Golf Writers, especially John Hopkins, Chris Plumridge and Norman Mair; Stuart Franklin of ASP and Phil Sheldon for their beautiful photographs; Mr Flower and the staff at Barclays Bank, Blackheath, for their patience. Lastly, and most importantly, thanks to the players of the European Tour, especially Simon Hobday, Mark McNulty and David Jones.

Introduction

A KIND OF MADNESS WITH RULES

Photo: Phil Sheldon

Masterstroke: Nick Faldo has got closer than anyone since Ben Hogan to mastering the game of golf

golf *n.* outdoor game in which small hard ball is struck with clubs into a succession of holes

I NEVER SET FOOT ON A GOLF COURSE UNTIL I WAS EIGHTEEN, and then for all the wrong reasons.

Before that day, I can only ever remember coming into contact with the game of golf on three occasions. I know I was transfixed by a tournament which Gary Player won and which I watched in black and white on our old farm television. Why it held my interest I have no idea, because I had never seen golf played before, I hadn't a clue what the object of it was and the programme was punctuated, as were all television programmes in Zimbabwe at that time, by the rolling of the picture – whereupon my dad was prevailed upon to go out into the garden and adjust the aerial – and extended musical interludes, all preceded by the notice: "We apologise for the break in transmission."

The second occasion was at boarding school. My two best friends and I discovered that we could skip up to half a day's lessons three or four times a week – employing the time more usefully by sitting discussing life in the sunshine, with our feet dangling in the pond on the edge of the 11th at Chapman Golf Club, Harare – as long as we produced the odd painting as evidence that these hours hadn't been wasted. Our art teacher, you see, was a great champion of our cause and a willing conspirator in these escapades.

Such was my lack of interest in the game of golf that, in all the years we did this, it never occurred to me to be more than slightly curious about those little groups of men who strode so briskly past us up the pristine fairways; or glowered at us as they entered the leafy glade at our backs and commenced beating at bushes and crashing among the branches; or even gazed hopelessly into the black depths of the pond. It didn't occur to me to be curious for the simple reason that I thought golf was a game – like bowls – which was only enjoyed by old men. No one I had ever come across played golf, not within our family or outside of it. At home, we did all the things that normal farming families in our area did. We rode horses, we fished, held braais (barbecues), swam, dipped cows, inspected tobacco barns and hunted with a spotlight in the dead of night. Golf was never included among our pastimes.

I was midway through journalism school when I had my third encounter with the game. I had met a man whom I was most intrigued by and asked him not long afterwards: 'What do you do in your spare time?'

'Well, I play rugby and I play golf.'

Now rugby is a respected pursuit where I come from, but golf was a different matter altogether. 'Golf?' I scoffed. He went down several notches in my estimation. I can remember laughing rather derisively, and then saying something inane like: 'What on earth do you see in a game which involves nothing except walking around for hours hitting balls with sticks?' It was the beginning of the end of that particular relationship.

Nevertheless, I was sufficiently interested to allow myself to be talked into going to Chapman Golf Club with a college friend of mine to watch her boyfriend play. We spent an exhausting afternoon in pursuit of his match, running unwittingly across greens and fairways, incurring the wrath of dozens of golfers, before being drenched by a sudden thunderstorm. We gave up the search and stalked sodden and sullen-faced off the golf course.

I suppose the fact that I went straight back for more just goes to show that the little streak of lunacy inherent in every golfer was lying dormant in me, just waiting for a chance to emerge.

It manifested itself at my very first golf lesson.

'This is a golf club,' said Andrew, a scratch golfer who had volunteered unwisely to teach me the game, 'this is how you grip it. Right you are, there is the fairway. No, no, not that way. This way. Good. Now hit the ball.'

I think he underestimated how little I knew about the game. The full extent of my golfing know-how at the time was that you should swing the club back as far as you possibly could and then smash the ball as hard as you possibly could. Then, of course, it would fly like an arrow several hundred yards along the fairway and you would go and hit it again. For 18 holes.

Ten air shots later, it was beginning to come home to me that there was more to the game than met the eye, and to Andrew that he had taken on a lost cause. This pattern continued for nine holes. I would flail with increasing desperation at the ball on the tee until I eventually made contact. Having watched it hurtle diagonally along the ground into the bushes, I would go and hunt for it, while Andrew played out the hole. I might have a putt or two and then we would repeat the whole scenario on the next tee.

And so began my love affair with golf. When I came off the course I felt three overriding emotions: humiliation, anger and astonishment. Golf was not like I expected it to be. Not at all.

Andrew shot away in a cloud of dust, anxious to escape before I requested another lesson. I wandered thoughtfully into the town centre where I found a second-hand bookshop and there, in amongst the Dick Francis, the Harold Robbins and the Mills and Boons, I found a battle-scarred copy of Brian Huggett's *How to Play Better Golf*. With the assistance of this, a box of golf books (containing everything from a complete collection of Jack Nicklaus, to Ben Hogan and Tommy Armour), given to me by a journalist whose father had been an addict, an antique five-iron, and a box of air-flow balls, I taught myself to play in the garden. Thrilled at the prospect of my taking up a hobby less dangerous than show-jumping or snake collecting, my parents immediately rushed out and bought me a set of golf clubs – Slazenger Lady Panthers. Within two months I was a member of Chapman Golf Club. My first handicap was 18.

I graduated from college; I cursorily scanned the appointments pages; I came to the conclusion that work would interfere with golf. Help came in the shape of an entrepreneur who owned a business which masqueraded as a promotions (mainly golf) company. I was recruited to run it. Our days went thus:

7.00 a.m. To the office. Brief, frantic burst of activity. Flying visits to printers, originators, clients.
10.00 a.m. Telephone tussles with clients, bailiffs and bank managers.
10.30 a.m. Golf.

I was very fortunate to live in a country where it is possible to play golf 365 days of the year, which I did (for up to eight hours of the day), where full membership of the best golf club in the capital city is less than £50, and where green fees for members are the approximate equivalent of ten pence. There was only one snake in this apparent Garden of Eden. My temper.

Nobody who takes up golf with serious intent does so without uncovering a side of their personality hitherto unknown to them. It may be that they are remarkably resilient in the face of adversity; they might find they have vast, untapped reserves of patience and determination; or they might, like me, discover that they are perfectionists with short fuses – two of the most completely unsuitable traits an amateur golfer could have the misfortune to possess.

I began playing with a group of low handicappers and scratch golfers who seemed to throw clubs as a matter of course. I watched and learned. Soon I could discipline a club with the best of them. Let me tell you, a recalcitrant three-wood sent soaring in a series of graceful somersaults over a fir tree is one of the most satisfying spectacles in the world. But the satisfaction gained from a horrifying display of temper on the golf course – where you might have broken every club in your bag, sworn in five languages, and taken a foot-long divot out of the green – is short and bittersweet, and all you are left with is a sick and guilty feeling in the pit of your stomach because you know you've violated a kind of sacred code.

I never really grew out of it though until I'd spent a season on the European Tour. Once you've watched a man with his whole life riding on a round of golf suffer seven kinds of disaster, and still observe the etiquette of the game and conduct himself like a gentleman, you tend to look at your own feeble efforts from a different perspective. You have to keep reminding yourself that you are only playing the hardest game in the world for pleasure; a professional golfer plays it for a living.

Henry Longhurst used to say that the way in which we are introduced to golf influences our attitude to the game for the rest of our lives. I agree. If I had grown up in a golfing family and had taken the playing of it for granted, I don't think I would have become as obsessed with it as I am, although I think I would always have enjoyed it because the whole idea of it appeals to me. I love it that you can play golf every day of your life and never master it. I love the complexity and mysteriousness of the golf swing, and I love it that you can play the same hole on the same golf course a thousand times and never play it the same way twice.

Sometimes, though, I think I'm attracted to the people in golf as much as I am to the game. Where else would you find top sportsmen with their livelihoods or dreams at stake, selflessly giving up their time to help chief rivals only moments before they go out onto the golf course? In what other walk of life is a man called upon to be his own judge? Where else is he asked to be so scrupulously honest that even when he has infringed a rule which no one else could possibly know he has, he will still call a penalty on himself? What other successful professional sport has retained the clean, wholesome image that this game has, and hung on through thick and thin to such old-fashioned values as honour and loyalty?

Nowhere else but golf.

I became a golf writer for all of these reasons. And I became a golf writer on the European men's professional tour because I wanted to work with the best players in the world.

The Professional Golfers' Association European Tour in 1991 boasts a prize fund of £20 million – an increase of more than £19 million since 1970. More than ten tournaments are worth over £500,000, and ten to 12 are worth between £400,000 and £500,000. But the Tour has grown long as well as rich. In 1991 the season begins in Spain in the third week of February and ends in Jamaica in November with a Johnny Walker sponsored tournament, where the first prize is £525,000 and the last place finisher receives £50,000. Every week on the European Tour, nearly 150 players of 14 different nationalities compete: some to win the tournament, a handful with the eventual aim of winning the Order of Merit, some merely to earn enough money to retain their cards.

I wanted to write the story of their lives. I wanted to go beneath the superficial glamour of the European PGA Tour, to know what made the best players as good as they are, where their motivation and talent comes from, what fuels their desire. What separates major winners? Why does a man who has never won a tournament and who only scrapes the most meagre living from the game want to play tournament golf so much? I wanted to write about everyone: about the rookies, the journeymen, the stars, the characters and the legends. What do they think about? Care about? Dream about?

So here it is, the PGA European Tour and the extraordinary people who populate it.

Chapter One

PARADISE LOST

Photo: Lauren St John

Waiting game: young qualifiers watch the scoreboard for the results which will decide their fate

LA MANGA, SUNDAY, 3 DECEMBER 1989. WHEN THE TOURISTS have gone and endless summer days have given way to the slow, wet Spanish winter, the 37 Bar at La Manga provides an unlikely refuge for a new, more solemn group of people: the players of the European Tour Qualifying School. The time they spend here is short – little more than a week in some cases – yet its importance cannot be overestimated. Many of their lives depend on its outcome.

The media have done well to furnish the glossy picture that is the European Tour. We see Ian Woosnam driving a Porsche; Nick Faldo, dressed in a Savile Row suit, standing in front of his Wentworth mansion, smiling his perfect smile, collecting his MBE, or kissing the Open Championship trophy; and more numbers after Seve Ballesteros's name on the career money list than there are in the London telephone directory. Seldom is it mentioned just how few succeed. Seldom do we read statistics of how many players never get as far as the Tour; of how short the period of grace is for most of those players who do, before they are forced back to the School by the strength of the competition coming behind them; of how many veterans find themselves washed up on the stony beach of life in middle-age, having devoted 30 or 40 years to the game – with nothing to show for it and a family to support. Reality, in professional golf, is harsh.

Still they come. And for every one that touches that big brass ring there are a hundred who don't. So, unlikely as the 37 Bar might be, refuge it certainly is: a sanctuary for souls bruised at La Manga, school of hard knocks.

Beneath fading portraits of Hogan, Snead and Palmer, players sprawl, killing time in between practising or playing. They come from every walk of life and a dozen countries. The only common bond between any of them is golf and a simple desire to be the best in a sport which accepts nothing less. The talk here is incessant. The players compare swing theories, swap Tour stories, offer one another consolation or advice when their rounds are done. All day long and way into the night they drink tall glasses of chocolate and milky coffee, play interminable card games and listen to the slow sounds of Anne Murray, John Denver and Don McLean's *American Pie*.

Some initiates have the white, pinched look of people who have bitten off far more than they can reasonably expect to chew. Others exude confidence and the fresh-faced optimism of youth.

Graham Whale, a young Essex county player turned professional, brushes his straw blond hair from his eyes and looks around him. 'This is a shit place,' he announces. 'I've decided that already. Don't wanna come here too often. Wanna get through and get going.'

Strange how one place can be so many things to so many different people. For young players, often just reaching La Manga can seem an achievement in itself. Poised on the threshold of their dream, they imagine that the School is only a short bridge which has to be crossed before they are home and dry.

For veteran Tour players it represents a low point in their career, a threat to their livelihood and a symbol of the demise of their game. To players who return year after year it can become a mentally insurmountable barrier.

Since Jeremy Bennett was made Rookie of the Year on the European Tour in 1981, he has been back to the School six times.

'Obviously it costs a lot of money,' says Bennett, who manages, nevertheless, to look like a walking advertisement for designer clothing, 'but yes, I get more nervous and just feel so bad the first round or two, than any other time of the year.

'I remember feeling exactly the same thing last year. I wasn't doing very well in the first round and I was thinking, I can't do this. I don't know why I'm doing it. I can't enjoy this pressure at all, I can't play properly. And then I got going again. I had been four over at one time in my first round and I finished one under so that wasn't so bad. But I didn't really play my proper game until the third or fourth round when I started getting more relaxed. I suppose it's the same for most people.'

Never has the examination hall of the European Tour been more full of chancers and dreamers and every other player who ever aspired to take over from Ballesteros, Nicklaus or Palmer. Twelve million pounds (Tour prize money will rise to £20 million in 1991) is an irresistible lure.

The PGA European Tour tries to weed out those unlikely to make the grade early on by making the entry requirements for the School as stiff as possible. Unless a player has exempt entry by virtue of finishing at the top of the Satellite Tour Order of Merit, or by meeting other conditions laid down by the Tour, it is necessary for him to pre-qualify at a selected course in Britain. If he fails there, he can have one more bite at the cherry – at Valencia in Spain – where the odds are even shorter. This year there were 588 pre-qualifying entries and 109 exempt entries to La Manga. Only 50 will win their playing cards.

The price of attempting to qualify is in itself a significant deterrent. La Manga alone can cost in the region of £1,500: £400 for the entry fee, £500 for a professional caddie and the remainder for flights, accommodation and food. Pre-qualifying adds another £1,000 to the bill – a lot to lose if you don't make it through.

Ultimately, the Qualifying School is the fairest test of a player's heart, but not necessarily of his game. The courses at La Manga demand little from a player compared to others used on the European circuit. Most golf courses on the Tour force the golfer to manufacture shots with every club in his bag; hence, the best shot-makers are the best players. The courses at La Manga are long and wide open and have a tendency to reduce the tournament to a putting contest.

Getting through La Manga is not confirmation that a player will succeed just as not getting through isn't proof that he won't. The School is just the first pinnacle in a game full of mountains. Each ensuing climb is higher and harder; majors are reached by way of cliff faces. Those who reach the top are those with one philosophy: winning isn't everything – it's the only thing.

At its best, La Manga is a depressing place. There is too little for the players to do and nowhere for them to go to escape from the pressure, from each other, or even from themselves. At its worst, it becomes a kind of cemetery – a place where dreams go to die.

'Colditz,' was how a caddie at the Portuguese Open described it when I mentioned I was going.

'Colditz?' I said in surprise, imagining stone walls and shell-shocked faces.

'Colditz,' he insisted. 'It's a nightmare, that place. Nothing there except two golf courses and a lot of depressed people.'

In the cold light of day La Manga was dank and gloomy. Grey sheets of rain fell on the empty villas whose inhabitants had taken their leave like snow geese with the coming of winter. I decided that the caddie hadn't been joking. When it slowed to a drizzle I walked down the hill to the 37 Bar.

It is possible to spend most of every day in its dim, smoky warmth, drinking endless mugs of coffee and listening to stories of past Schools. One such account recalls an occasion where several of the pros got together and paid another player to drive a car through the glass doors of his hotel, across the foyer and into the swimming pool.

Another, more infamous, tells of a player – a member of a recent Ryder Cup team – who missed his card one year when the School was still held in Portugal. He rushed straight up to his apartment and proceeded to smash every movable object and hurl it out of the window. Not content with that, he leapt into his car, raced down to the end of the pier and drove it off a ramp, smashing it down, turning it around and doing it all over again. The police, so the story goes, caught up with him in the end, and escorted him from the country.

Over the years pros have been known to break their golf clubs as well as their television sets, drive over their golf bags in cars, throw them off cliffs and even set fire to them. When veteran Danny Goodman failed to qualify, he and David Jones went to the top of the cliffs above La Manga and hit Goodman's entire bag of practice balls into the sea to the sound of the Allman Brothers' 'Hard Cross to Bear'.

Wayne Player, son of Gary, flew over from America in 1985 to prequalify at Foxhills golf club. He teed up in the most unsociable weather conditions Britain has to offer and hit a shaky drive down the first. Undaunted by a three-putt, he proceeded calmly to the second where he hit his tee shot into the rough. Having found the ball and played his approach shot, he discovered that it wasn't his at all. He was penalised two shots. His own ball came to light under a bush in an unplayable lie. He took a drop under penalty and carried on to the next hole, determined not to be beaten.

On the third hole, he hit a perfect tee shot. As straight as an arrow, it winged it's way down the fairway. But the flight of Player's ball coincided with that of 40 ducks. There was a small explosion of feathers in mid-air, then duck and ball succumbed to the forces of gravity. Under the rules of golf, such an occurrence is considered rub of the green. At the fourth, Player played the wrong ball again – and was penalised a further two strokes.

I could go on. Suffice to say that Player shot 84, 71 to miss the pre-qualifying mark by two shots.

Monday, 4 December. By mid-afternoon, the conversation in the 37 Bar has reached a pitch where it is no longer possible to hear the roar of the deluge outside. Condensation on the window panes obliterates the landscape outside.

Scotsman Gary Collinson, his black hair still wet from his round, looks as though he is on the verge of breaking down. His eyes are overbright, his voice unsteady.

'I feel I've aged about 20 years out here,' he says. 'Since I've been here I've had nightmares every night. I'm scared of flying. I keep dreaming about planes crashing.'

Collinson considers what he will do when he misses the cut tomorrow. It seems a foregone conclusion. He is lying 13 over par after three rounds and the cut isn't expected to be much higher than plus five.

'Give up.' He's not joking.

His brother Bob, who is caddying for him this week, came to the School once, missed his card by a shot and decided that if that was all there was to tournament golf he wasn't interested. 'I've got a club job now,' explains Bob, 'and I can still play the Scottish Tour, and that does me. If I have a good year I can make some money at that, and I can still get home every night and see my kids.'

For some players, getting a club job is an option they are prepared to consider. Others consider themselves tournament pros and wouldn't do it if they were starving. 'I couldn't do that,' Gary says disparagingly, snapping out of the reverie into which he has fallen. 'Selling golf balls.'

'That's the life they choose,' says Bob dourly, of tournament professionals. He clearly has little regard for it himself. 'It must be very soul-destroying, though. I mean, it's being able to cope with all the disappointments. There's certainly more downs than ups.'

Gary Collinson made what he feels was a tactical error by playing too many practice rounds. He played seven rounds of golf before the tournament started and wasn't over par once. When the gun went off, his game fell to pieces. In golf there are days when a player can get away with playing badly if he still manages to score well. 'But if you're swinging it bad and scoring bad . . .'

'What went wrong?'

'Just my head: it's gone. I haven't had a good meal in ten days. I've been out to restaurants but the food over here's crap. It's terrible.'

Between nightmares and mosquitoes, Collinson hasn't been getting much sleep. 'I've been bitten all over. Killed about 20 every night. Terrible. They keep going up into your ears. And the beds are so uncomfortable. Too small.'

The only plus this week, as far as I can make out, is that Gary and Bob shared with caddies instead of players.

'Some guys,' says Bob, 'you know, they have a post-mortem of their round and that's the last thing you want to hear – how every shot went.'

Rooming with caddies, they found time to have a drink and go out, not closeting themselves in their apartments the way that some players do, letting imaginings grow larger than life.

Gary Collinson smiles wistfully. 'The way I played this week, if I hadn't laughed, I'd have shot myself. I still think you've got to get out and have a few beers and try to relax.'

'Why change the habits of a lifetime?' agrees Bob.

The rain delays have caused a chain reaction. Every golfer here is playing two incomplete rounds a day: the tail end of yesterday's round and the beginning of tomorrow's. It plays havoc with your mind and your game. Richard Fish, who was supposed to tee-off at 8.46 this morning, didn't get away until nearly 11 o'clock and then in driving rain.

'Awful conditions,' he says crossly. His short blond hair is standing up in wet spikes. Out on the course he and his partners were just knocking the ball along, struggling to concentrate; just biding time, really, until an official came to stop play. Nobody came. Fortunately, Fish is more fatalistic than most people here. 'It's all part of this week,' he says, blaming himself for not playing well, rather than the PGA Tour or the elements. 'You just have to accept it and play the best you can.'

For some people, the European Tour School eventually becomes a way of life, an event which rolls around every December – like Christmas. Richard Fish holds the record for the most number of visits to the School. Eleven. On the surface, you wouldn't think it's the end of the world when he doesn't get his card. He laughs about it, shrugs it off and somehow survives until the end of the next year when he can try again. But La Manga takes a lot out of you each time you go through it. Nobody ever emerges unscathed.

'I enjoy playing,' he says when I question his perseverance, the extent of his self-belief. 'I think I'm a very slow learner – that's what keeps me going.'

This is golf at its cruellest. Perhaps it is ultimately easier on your soul if you come to the School a couple of times and finish nowhere. Eventually you could come to terms with the fact that you were never going to make it. But in golf there is no clear division between those players who are almost good enough to be tournament professionals and those who are. There are people who hover for years on the periphery of the Tour; some years they make it, some years they don't.

It can make you crazy. One pro I spoke to said that he resorted to a new ruse each year in an attempt to improve his golf. Out of season he had taken up weight-training, marathon running, experimented with anabolic steroids and changed coaches about as often as he changed shirts. He had made progress, but it was the slow progress of a man walking through a mire.

Talking to him I was reminded of something an American player said: 'You get to the point in your life where you keep trying to chase after this dream of getting on the Tour and making all this money everybody's making, and playing in front of all these people . . . and you've got to make a decision. Maybe it's time to give it all up and do something else.'

Tuesday is D-day. It is a day for shattered dreams, the abrupt dissolution of illusion, the end of a lifetime of hope. Today is the four-round cut. The players who miss it get nothing: no tournaments whatsoever. The more fortunate are PGA-qualified and have a club job or a sponsor to fall back on, but others have to make money any way they can; by working as labourers in warehouses and on golf courses.

'I've done some incredible jobs,' remarks Nick Mitchell, a Satellite Tour player. 'I've sold roof-sheeting, cleaned toilets, done night jobs . . . *anything* just to keep playing.'

The rain does nothing for those players who still have a chance to make it. They mill around uneasily, watching for a break in the clouds. Players without a prayer look pale and exhausted. Their eyes are full of the fear of facing their friends and families back home. One pro's mother sold her flat to send her son to the School. He never made it.

Everyone has a different approach to the School. Some players like to arrive just the day before, believing that familiarity breeds contempt and creates swing problems at La Manga. Others are only happy if they can play both courses in their sleep. Tour player David Ray prepares for La Manga just as he would for any European tournament.

'Some people,' says Ray, who is dressed rather strangely in a golf shirt and a blue-striped tie, 'come out here and they hit thousands and thousands of shots, and they're just not used to doing that. I know two guys who arrived eight days before the first round and they played every day. By the time you tee it up on Saturday you're cuckoo, really.'

Disadvantaged by the 'psychological blow' of returning to the School for the third time – after having won it in 1983 – Ray has resorted to eating two raw carrots a day; one on the practice ground and one on the tenth tee. Carrots contain a substance called Carotene – also found in Beta-blockers – which is supposed to calm the nerves. Sam Torrance started the trend after finding carrots immensely beneficial to his nervous system during the 1989 Ryder Cup, and Ray claims they have cured his yips. He brought 60 of them with him to La Manga.

Later I walked down to the practice ground.

Richard Fish tips another ball miserably from the bucket as I go by. 'Know anything about the golf swing?' he says to me, then answers his own question. 'No.' He calls over Stuart Smith.

'Am I too inside?' he asks.

'A little bit,' says Smith, examining his backswing critically.

'Fucking game,' says Fish.

On the wall behind the scorer's table back at the clubhouse, someone has taped a message. It is crudely printed in red ink and it says: 'THE CUT +4'.

Wednesday, 6 December. Graham Whale is the picture of dejection, balanced on a bar stool and hunched over the grand piano. His face, propped on his elbows and reflected in the shiny black surface, is wan, his manner devoid of its usual arrogance. Whale missed the cut by two shots, which is one situation he has no intention of getting used to. He feels that there has to be a cut-off point, that you can't keep coming back to the School every year chasing a hopeless ideal.

'You can't keep going and you've got to be realistic,' says Whale, with players like Richard Fish, who has missed his card again, in mind. 'That's what separates me from a lot of people, hopefully – I'm realistic. I've got my feet stuck firmly on the ground.'

Golf has long hours of enforced boredom in which to dwell on lost opportunities. At the School, a momentary loss of concentration, a single bad lie, a putt that skips out the back door, these are the things that could cost you your dream. Graham Whale has no such excuses. When it really counted he lost his nerve.

'I lost the control I had. I was cruising, no sweat. Hit it nicely, good rhythm. Three-putted one hole – I missed a putt of about 18 inches – and it threw me, completely threw me. All of a sudden it became emotional. Everything became an effort, rather than being simple.'

Perhaps there is no other week in golf where players are forced to be so selfish, so abstemious, so tunnel-visioned as the week of the School. It can have an adverse effect. The result of each shot can begin to prey on your mind until it eats away your concentration altogether.

'If you hit a bad shot here you feel it more,' says Whale, 'because it's that much more important. It's harder to chip it close and the hole gets a little bit smaller. I just got too anxious over it. I had plenty of chances on the way in to get out of it, I just never really got it going for me.'

For most of his life things have come easily to Whale. Having prepared for the School by playing on the South African circuit, he was confident it would fit smoothly into the same pattern.

'I never thought I was going to miss the cut until the last ten holes. Always thought I was in. If you're worried about making the cut, you're not worried about playing the tournament. I came here to win it. Didn't come here to make the top one hundred.'

Whale smiles self-consciously.

'You see, I've got this thing. I'm not in golf for the money. I'm a glory seeker. I love the attention, love it. I can't help it. Out there in Africa for the first time, signing autographs for little kids, talking to spectators; I've got no hassle with that. And I come down here and for four days I was in there and fighting, when I could have shot 80 in the first round and been out of it.'

His laugh is ironical. Whatever else he might be, Whale is a survivor. 'You live to fight another day,' he says philosophically. 'I mean, I shed a few tears about it, sat in a corner and cried. But you come back and you fight – you've got to. The only hard thing about it all is you've let people down. I've let my father down. I've got nothing to feel ashamed of because I put everything on the line and it didn't come off . . . That hurts, knowing that you weren't good enough. I wasn't good enough because I wasn't experienced enough.'

Not every story told at La Manga is a sad one. After two years in the wilderness – recovering from short game yips and the doubtful policies of too many teachers – Michael McLean finally reached the other side. He won back his playing card.

McLean, who is nicknamed Nobbie on the Tour, is one of the most likeable people in pro golf. He's so small and appears to be so shy that you wonder where he finds the courage needed to make it in this sport (in reality, he is one of the wickedest – in the nicest possible way – players on the Tour!). But his motivation is his hatred of losing, his inability to accept mediocrity. 'Something in me always makes me fight back.'

The School was his last resort. If he hadn't won back his player's card this year, he would have had to give up the game. What he would have done then, McLean has no idea.

'You cross that bridge when you come to it,' he says quietly. Golf is the only thing he knows.

'The hard thing about this week is concentration and doing it under pressure. Because under this pressure you could play around the easiest golf course there is and it would be difficult. It's a test. I mean, I was really wound up about the whole thing. I was really unsure of myself. I didn't know whether I'd be able to get it back. Whatever happens now I feel I've achieved my goal.'

Thursday, 7 December. There is an ancient truck with no sides at La Manga – more suited to game viewing in Kenya than to the transportation of professional golfers – which is known as the Gua-Gua (Wa-Wa) bus. It keeps a schedule familiar only to itself and makes a tortoise-slow journey from the hotel and golf club to the apartments at Bellaluz and back. Bad weather of any description renders it more or less useless, so you spend a lot of time walking. That was how I met Mickey Yokoi.

Yokoi, a Californian of Japanese origin with a keen line in card tricks, had decided it might be fun to try and qualify for the School this year. He was confident that he'd breeze through, and that he and his wife could spend the following year getting to know Europe in between tournaments. He didn't anticipate missing the cut, or the heartache that comes with it.

'If I'd known it was going to be [as lonely as] this,' he says, 'I wouldn't have roomed by myself. To try to qualify, usually, you've got to be away from people, because if you've got a room-mate that's not doing too well, then he kind of drags you down with him. They talk about how bad they're playing – everything's negative – and I hate to be around people who are negative. But I'm all by myself and there's no television in the room.' He holds up his walkman. 'If I didn't have this music to listen to [Kenny G], I'd just drive myself crazy in this room. I never read, but I've read over a thousand pages this week.'

Yokoi missed a lot of putts in the third and fourth rounds and they cost him dearly. Five holes into the last round he began to think he was out of the tournament but managed to claw his way back. 'I got myself so I was five over with four holes to play. I figured if I just parred in I'd make it . . . I had no idea the cut was going to go down that low. The first person I talked to was a friend of mine and he said four over made it and my heart just went down. I thought, "Oh no!"'

If they miss the cut, some players sit around with their head in their hands. Yokoi is a 30-year-old bundle of frenetic energy and has to work it out of his system. On different days he has pumped iron down at the gym, driven around some of the poorer surrounding areas and gone go-karting.

'There are worse things going on in the world than me not qualifying,' he points out, and cites the fate of an American player as an example. In the fourth round, the player was even par with three holes to play. He three-putted the 16th, three-putted the 17th, and hit his drive out-of-bounds on 18 to miss the cut by a shot.

'You're always thinking about qualifying,' comments Yokoi, 'and that's not what you wanna think about. You wanna think about playing really well. In a tournament, you're always looking to win, but in the Qualifying you're always looking to be ahead of the last spot. So your whole idea's different.'

Thursday p.m. As soon as the four-round cut is made at La Manga there is a perceptible change in atmosphere. The players who miss it often break down and cry publicly. They either feel suicidal or they feel enraged. Anybody who can escape flies away from La Manga on the first available plane. Those that can't are trapped here – reluctant witnesses of the triumphs and failures of the remaining players.

On Wednesday, you can feel rebellion brewing in the air. But it is still a day of mourning, of coming to terms with grief. On Thursday there is a revolution. All the pent-up emotions and frustrations of every player who ever fantasised about winning the Open Championship explode like a cork from a champagne bottle. From that moment on they party.

West German Heinz-Peter Thuel won the School with a record 15 under par, so the Germans and the Swedes took over the steak-house and celebrated raucously in one corner of the room. After spending much of the evening running in and out of the restaurant consulting sheets of paper, spraying each other with champagne and almost setting the place alight with flaming kebabs, they burst into song. It is traditional, Mikael Krantz informed us later, for the Swede who finishes highest at the School to be made to sing solo at the dinner given by the Swedish Federation.

Back at the 37 Bar, a party was in full swing. The pianist who had been hired for the week struggled to keep pace with her requests. She was completely surrounded by players in varying states of inebriation, and the banging on the piano drowned out all but the occasional note of music. By the time she had sung 20 renditions of *American Pie*, her voice was showing a distinct lack of emotion. David Ray's caddie annoyed her by seizing the microphone and treating us to his own version of *Candle in the Wind*, then David Ray sang *Allouetta* (a French song), which wasn't really in keeping with the occasion.

Mikael Krantz wove an erratic path over to the table where I sat talking to Paul Carman and a couple of other players. He and two fellow Swedes were given a fortnight's release from the army to attend the School and he has managed to win back his card.

'I'm so happy,' he says to Paul Carman. 'I'm just so happy.' He looks around the bar at the players trying to exorcise the demons of this week, and shakes his head. 'This place is a fucking nightmare,' he observes.

It is after midnight and the bar is full of people sharing that exact sentiment.

Friday, 8 December. From first light on the final day a nervous crowd gathers around the scoreboard. Forty-eight cards are awarded automatically but the last two have to be fought for in a play-off. Nobody wants to be on the borderline. It is a situation comparable to that of a runner reaching the finishing line of a marathon, only to be told he has to run another mile before the outcome can be decided.

Of the 50 players who win Tour cards, only a handful will retain them. At the end of every season the top 120 money winners are exempt for the following season. The rest have to return to the School. To find the players with a fighting chance of success you don't need to look much further than the top ten finishers at La Manga because, the lower down the ladder you go, the less the number of tournaments allocated to each player.

When Jeremy Bennett won the 43rd card a few years ago, it entitled him to seven tournaments, only three of which he had practice rounds for. Bennett calculated that he would have had to finish 30th or better in every tournament he played to make the top 120 in the Order of Merit. The mental and financial strain of playing the Tour under those circumstances can be crippling. As Bennett says, 'You must be hungry, but you mustn't be desperate.'

Sudden death is the most appropriate term in golf. At La Manga, it gives the play-off the sinister significance of a Russian Roulette game. The nine players tied on two under par competed for the final two places. José Rozadilla and Scotsman Russell Weir walked back after the first extra hole – victor and victim respectively. Rozadilla birdied and earned his card. Weir bogeyed to miss it.

On the second hole, Carl Stronberg leaves a five-foot birdie putt for his card short. Having traversed their way safely through the traps laid by the Qualifying School, some players lose their nerve. One by one, like the storyline of an Agatha Christie novel, they are eliminated. At the last green only Spaniard Santiago Luna and Keith Jones, a supremely confident young Englishman, are left standing.

Luna makes his putt. He stands under a palm tree on the fringe of the green and closes his eyes. Jones ignores the fine mist rain which has begun to fall and walks over to his putt with cat-like grace. The ball rushes towards the hole, teasing him, and then slides on by. For a split second his composure slips and agony crosses his face. Then he picks himself up, congratulates the speechless Luna and walks away without a backward glance.

Perhaps the only way for a player to survive the blows that professional golf inflicts is to use them to strengthen himself, to make him more determined. 'You almost have to go through this pain before you can get to the ecstasy at the other end,' said Irishman Des Smyth once.

The Qualifying School might be the hardest lesson in professional golf, but it's only the first.

In the grey light of evening I stood on the balcony of the 37 Bar and looked out over the rain-scarred courses and the silver strip of sea on the horizon. Of the events of the past week no visible trace remained. The souls of those players who died on the killing fields of La Manga had been blown to the four winds.

Chapter Two

CONQUISTADOR

Photo: ASP, Stuart Franklin

Seve Ballesteros: 'I think you have to make mistakes and you have to struggle. This will make you more hungry to win – in anything in life, I think'

'The longer you play the more certain you are that a man's performance is the outward manifestation of who, in his heart, he really thinks he is.'

Hale Irwin in *Strokes of Genius* by Thomas Boswell

MAJORCA, SPAIN, MARCH 1990. TODAY IS ONE OF THOSE cobalt blue spring days where the sunshine has the hard brightness of a mint coin and the air is so bitingly cold that it hurts you to draw breath.

On such days even my boundless enthusiasm for the practice ground tends to wane and this morning, a practice day, so has that of a large group of players. Instead, we sit huddled before a video in the rustic warmth of the Son Vida clubhouse, watching highlights from past US Masters Championships. Between them the players can anticipate every shot so they provide a running commentary.

'Nicklaus takes an eight-iron here,' Rodger Davis says. 'Hits it back left of the green.'

'He holes a ridiculously difficult putt here,' supplies a caddie. 'Watch this . . . There! . . . Did you see the borrow on that?'

Out of the corner of my eye, I see Severiano Ballesteros enter through the distant clubhouse door. His handsome countenance is customarily dark and brooding, and he wears the absorbed expression of a man intent on his own affairs. His is a strong face, one that would not look out of place on a statesman, a lawyer or a successful businessman. It has an actor's capacity to dramatise expressions, looking by turns stricken, enraged or joyful, and it reflects the climate of his mood with the accuracy of a weather barometer.

Right now, as I watch, it softens. Ballesteros drops to his knees beside an old armchair in the lounge outside. A fat tabby cat, warm from the fire, rolls on her back so he can rub her furry belly. After a time, he stands up and comes quietly into the room where we are gathered. He watches the clips from the 1987 Masters.

'That was a very conservative shot for Greg,' he comments, watching the Shark's approach to 11, the play-off hole where he lost to Larry Mize's 40-yard chip-in. 'That really cost him the tournament.'

'He should have gone for the pin,' agrees Davis.

'That's what I mean,' says Ballesteros. 'It was too conservative. It was the same when he played Bob Tway.'

His own image flashes on to the screen. Ballesteros watches himself hit that fatal four-iron into the lake on 15 in 1986. Covertly, everyone watches him for reaction.

'That shot saved Jack,' observes Ballesteros casually and without embarrassment.

Strange how the effects of a single shot can last a lifetime.

They say that Tony Jacklin was never the same after Trevino holed his chip shot at the penultimate hole of the Open in 1971 to snatch certain victory from his grasp. They say that when Tom Watson chipped in at the 17th to defeat Jack Nicklaus in the 1982 US Open at Pebble Beach, the Golden Bear took the best part of four years to recover. There are those who will tell you that Hubert Green still loses sleep over the three-foot putt he missed for victory at Augusta in 1978. Green went back to that green after it was all over, leaving Gary Player – the winner on the second play-off hole – to his celebrations, and played that putt again. When it didn't count, he made it easily.

Green, and the rest of that sad band of players more famous for the way they lost a major than some people are for the way they won, know how one stroke can sear the mind. Sometimes the scars inflicted take years to heal. Sometimes they don't heal at all.

On that fateful Sunday, 13 April, Ballesteros waited on the 15th fairway at Augusta National with a four-iron in his hand. Ahead of him, Bernhard Langer took an age to putt out on the green where Jack Nicklaus had just carded an eagle to move within a shot of him. How long he waited for the green to clear, Ballesteros has no idea, but it was a long time. Long enough to break his rhythm and interfere with his concentration.

When he finally played his shot, Ballesteros did something which cost him dearly in previous and subsequent majors. He pull-hooked – into the creek. An audible gasp accompanied the curved flight of his ball into its watery grave. A deathly hush followed. As the ripples spread across the glassy surface in ever-decreasing circles, Ballesteros made bogey. Then he bogeyed the next. The fire which had burned bright in him at the start of the day had been doused. When Nicklaus came after him with an inward half of 30, one of the greatest back nines in the history of golf, Ballesteros had no reply. He finished fourth.

And so began a four-year-long dry season. The next year, Ballesteros three-putted the first extra hole of a play-off for the Masters against Norman and the ultimate winner, Mize. In the Open Championship he fared no better. He tied for 38th place in 1985, finished sixth in 1986, and 50th in 1987.

It was a time when the majors seemed beyond the reach of Ballesteros; when it began to look as though the greatest player in Europe had gone into an early decline. Newspapers and golf journals began to print articles under headings such as: 'Is there a way back for Ballesteros?'

Those were years when the Spaniard became increasingly moody, prone to frequent outbursts on and off the course. The greybeards shook their heads and pondered the problem. It was true that Ballesteros had been devastated by the death of his father, Baldomero, and it had taken its toll on his game. But was it also the fault of his brothers who caddied for him and with whom he had constant heated rows? Was his tempestuous relationship with Carmen interfering with his golf? Had he lost his putting stroke? Or had he tempered his game so much that he was in imminent danger of playing too cautiously?

All these things might, in part, have been true, although none of them prevented him from winning titles throughout the world all the while. But golf is a game where a player is measured by major victories alone. And because Ballesteros measures himself in much the same way, doubts began to gnaw at his mind.

'Really, I lost a lot of confidence,' he says in retrospect, 'because once the time goes by, you know, it makes you think a little bit. And you say, well, it's been four years without winning a major championship, maybe I'm not going to win anymore.'

His laughter now holds a note of incredulity as though he can scarcely believe he ever thought such a thing. He shrugs. 'It happens. It's like when you're playing badly for long periods of time, you start to think, "Have I lost my form?" '

Shoulders hunched, dark forearms placed together on the wooden table-top, Ballesteros's stare is hawk-like in its intensity and makes one experience feelings similar to that of a rabbit hypnotised by headlights. Under this penetrating gaze, questions threaten to vanish from my mind without trace and I have to make a conscious effort to grab them by the tails, like eels, and hang on to them.

Ballesteros has not the slightest intention of being intimidating. On the contrary, he is relaxed and amiable as he discusses the arduousness of winning majors in the modern era.

'There are four majors a year and there's a lot of good players today. You watch Norman. Norman has been playing great for the last six or seven years and he has won only one major. Norman has been the favourite in every [major] tournament for the last three years and he hasn't won one yet. That tells you how difficult it is.'

In professional golf there are two kinds of pressure. There is the kind a young player feels when he's starting out on Tour, when he's struggling to survive financially and competitively. Then there's the kind of pressure that follows a major championship victory: pressure to maintain that level of play, to be a contender in every major championship thereafter, to win another major, to prove yourself time and time again.

Before he won the Open Championship for the third time at Royal Lytham in 1989, Ballesteros was bowed under the weight of the latter. 'The first one was difficult, but I think the second one is much tougher. Much tougher. There's no question.'

For that reason, his victory at Lytham, his fifth major, was as much over himself as it was over the Zimbabwean, Nick Price. 'It was very important for me to win,' said Ballesteros, who rated his last round 65 as one of the best of his career, 'because I can now remember how I played today and forget about that shot at Augusta.'

Immediately afterwards, having cast off the shroud of public opinion which had threatened to smother him, Ballesteros became a changed man. He no longer looked sullen and bad-tempered, glowered at spectators or snapped the heads off reporters and caddies. He was no longer at odds with the universe. He began to rejoice once more in his own ability and it showed in his game. The old Ballesteros magic came back: the swashbuckling play, the daredevilry, the arrogant assumption that anything in golf was possible, however improbable.

In 1988, in only 24 outings, he won an incredible seven titles (including the Open) on three continents, and finished in the top ten in eight other tournaments, topped the Order of Merit, and knocked Greg Norman right off his perch as number one in the Sony World Rankings. A further three European victories in 1989 took his total number of titles to 62.

Now, confidence restored, Ballesteros says: 'I think if I can get ten majors, that would be good. I'd be happy.'

Contemplating the probability of any contemporary player winning as many majors as Nicklaus has (20) seems to afford him some amusement. 'Well, it's possible but it's not likely,' Ballesteros says, black eyes crinkling at the notion. 'I think there's more pressure in the majors today than there was maybe 15 or 20 years ago, and also the competition is more close. That's why it's become more difficult. If you look at the record, in the last ten years there have been only two or three players that have peaked and that proves how tough the competition is now.'

Severiano Ballesteros Sota was born on 9 April 1957, in the tiny Spanish town of Pedrena. The youngest son of a peasant farmer, he grew up running barefoot and free in the wild and ruggedly beautiful country of Northern Spain. Times were hard, but they instilled in him the strength of character and resilience in the face of adversity that such beginnings often do. His education was rudimentary.

At the age of seven he was given his first golf club. Made by Manuel, one of his three brothers – all of whom became golf professionals – it was fashioned from the head of an old three-iron and a stick which served as a shaft.

Ballesteros's love affair with golf was instantaneous. Forbidden to play at the exclusive Real Club de golf de Pedrena, which adjoined his father's land, he taught himself the game on the beach along the Bay of Santander. As soon as he was able, he began caddying. In his free time he and the other caddies held fierce competitions along the sea front, using pebbles for golf balls. Playing and practising off impossible lies over near insurmountable obstacles, Ballesteros learnt to imagine shots and then manufacture them. Armed with only his makeshift three-iron, he learnt to see and play more shots than most professionals could manage with a full set.

His most precious childhood memory remains, to this day, that of stealing away, aged 12, from the tiny, windowless room where he slept and playing the empty golf course at dawn.

His aspirations then were simple. 'When I was small I never thought about winning. I was never even thinking about the majors. I was thinking I'd like to be the best.'

Such attitudes are as often inherited as they they are inherent. Ballesteros's father was a champion rower, renowned for his strength and courage. His uncle, Ramon Sota, was Spain's best golfer. Sadly, Ballesteros rarely had a chance to play with him because their careers took diverging paths. While Sota was away playing tournaments his nephew was still caddying, and when he retired Ballesteros's own career was just beginning.

It wasn't so much a beginning as an explosion.

At 19, in his third year as a tournament player, Ballesteros entered the final round of the 1976 Open Championship at Royal Birkdale two strokes ahead of Johnny Miller, whom he had led for three days. At that age his game was less tempered, almost uncontrolled. He worked on extremities: wild drives, Houdini-like escapes, bold, attacking iron play and superlative chipping and putting. He fought like a tiger for four days, only faltering at the last through misadventure. He finished runner-up to Miller and tied with Nicklaus.

Those were the days when tournament golf was as slow and primly conservative as a Renoir painting. Golf clubs were the domain of the rich and the landed gentry, major championships were the preserve of a handful of great players – Palmer, Nicklaus, Player, Watson – and tournament fields were made up of nameless, faceless golfers with indifferent golf games and few distinguishing features.

Ballesteros was an entirely new entity. Fiery and brilliant and as darkly good-looking as a movie star, he refused to conform to the existing mould of a tournament professional. He couldn't and wouldn't play the odds on the golf course. He played to limits – his own limits – far beyond the comprehension of most other golfers. He had colour, vibrance and irresistible charm, and he arrested the attention of a complacent public.

But he carried the legacy of his poor background with him like a burden. He had a roughness about him; he was gauche. He had a social chip on his shoulder, accentuated by his struggles with the English language, which gave rise to many misunderstandings. At that time there were a lot of other Spanish players on the Tour with only a very basic grasp of English, all of whom had the same problem. They developed an intriguing system of coping with situations such as interviews, ordering in restaurants, and asking chambermaids about the laundry service. Whichever Spaniard was highest on the Order of

Merit in a particular group would speak, and the rest would act dumb. Which was all very well until they changed positions on the money list.

Willie Aitchison, Lee Trevino's caddie, remembers going out for a practice round with Seve and his elder brother, Manuel, around that time. 'My first impression of Seve was this scruffy kid. He hit the ball all over the golf course. But whenever he got to the middle part of his game and his short game, it was magic. You could see there was something different about the way he stroked the ball on the green and the way he played chips.'

Just how different, Ballesteros was to prove. For three successive years, 1976 to 1978, he was leading money-winner in Europe. Then in 1979 at Royal Lytham, aged 22 years and three months, he won the Open Championship.

Cruel winds sucked and swirled and tore at the links of Royal Lytham that week, lending her the means to flaunt all her wiles. Ballesteros went out in the worst of the conditions on the first day and shot 73. On the second day, he recovered with a 65 to move to within two shots of Hale Irwin, the tournament leader. 'He did what?' was Irwin's disbelieving response on hearing this news. But the third round brought rain and it was all the pair of them could do to shoot 75s.

Ballesteros hit the ground running on the final day. He birdied the first hole and watched Irwin three-putt the second to take the lead. He played with reckless abandon, gambling with certain disaster and staking his life on an almost occult ability to escape from the inescapable. He went to the turn in 34. Irwin trailed in his wake with an outward half of 37 and an eventual tally of 78.

All week at the 339-yard 13th, Ballesteros had been trying different clubs. To reach the green with a driver it was necessary to fly the bunker, a carry of 300 yards. This time he just turned to his caddie, Dave Musgrove, and said: 'We'll go for it today.' By now Ballesteros was flying. Veins coursing with adrenalin, he hit a drive which was unlucky to catch the top of the bunker and go in. His recovery spun off to the right of the green. From there he holed out for a birdie three. Irwin watched open-mouthed.

Then came the 16th. At this stage in a major championship, most players would have thought it prudent to observe caution and take an iron off the tee at this treacherous hole. Not Ballesteros. He took a driver and smashed his tee shot 40 yards off line and into a car park. But according to Musgrove, Ballesteros had planned his round much more carefully than it would appear. He had studied the rough on every hole. Playing from the car park meant he was coming back into the wind. From the fairway it was nearly impossible to stop the ball on the green where the pin had been positioned. Given a free drop from an Austin-Healey, Ballesteros landed the ball 20 feet from the flag and holed the putt for birdie. He finished with a score of 70 for an aggregate of 283, winner by three shots, and in so doing, became the youngest Open Champion this century, and the first Continental to win the Championship since Arnaud Massy of France in 1907.

'Why do I want to win?' says the mature Ballesteros in the manner of someone who has never known what it is not to want that. 'Well, it's difficult to describe how much satisfaction you have inside when you beat everybody. It's the goal. It's just what you try to achieve.'

In the spring of 1980, Ballesteros became the youngest winner of the Masters and the first European champion. Two years later he claimed that green jacket once more, overcoming the formidable trio of Watson, Stadler and Floyd in the process.

'When Seve gets going,' Ben Crenshaw said famously, 'it's like matching a model T Ford against a Ferrari. He plays shots that the rest of us can't even imagine.'

It was at this point, speaking from his position at the pinnacle of world golf, that Ballesteros approached the US Tour Commissioner, Deane Beman. He wanted the requisite number of tournaments foreign players had to compete in to be lowered to 15. Beman complied. Then came St Andrews and the Open Championship. Ballesteros won there in 1984, dashing Watson's hopes of a Scottish hat-trick and of matching Harry Vardon's record of six Opens. Subsequent demands on his time were such that Ballesteros decided to ignore his 15 tournament commitment and to play in just eight US events. Enraged at having his authority flouted, Beman banned him from the 1986 PGA Tour season.

That was the year fate struck its cruel blow at the US Masters; the year that Ballesteros's reputation in the majors went into a sharp decline; when he became sulky and irritable, convinced that everyone and everything was conspiring against him.

Ballesteros dismisses the memories of that low period in his life with a lift of his shoulders.

'I think you have to make many mistakes and you have to struggle. This will make you a little bit more hungry to win – no question. In anything in life, I think. If things come very easily you don't appreciate them. I know some players that have the potential and the ability, but because they're making the [good] life so easily and they're making so much money, they just . . .' He purses his lips in a characteristic expression of contempt. 'You know.'

'There are many good players but they are not champions in their hearts. To be a champion it has to be inside. Some people they have that naturally and other people they don't. That's why they don't become champions.'

Events, seasons and years rush by at such speed in golf that they are almost self-effacing. Only the majors stand out as yardsticks, recognised measures of greatness. In such a protean environment, the players who leave an indelible mark on the game are people with a single work ethic: 'To be a champion you have to live for what you do. For golf or football or any sport, you have to think and you have to live all the time for that, otherwise it's impossible to be a champion. And you must like it.'

Ballesteros's words hang in the air, heavy with the weight of conviction.

'Some people,' he continues, 'want to become champions, and when they become a champion – once they have that and all the tension and the pressure that comes with it – they cannot take it any more. So they escape from it. That's why they come down.'

But there is a price to be paid for becoming a world champion. No one reaches the pinnacle of any sport without paying for it. Not ever. To Ballesteros, an intensely private man, giving up his personal freedom and any semblance of a normal life was the ultimate sacrifice.

'I went through a very tough time. I think when I became famous I feel like I lost a big part of myself. This is the most difficult thing that could happen to anybody . . .' He pauses, searching for words to express the hurt that it has caused him.

'It's not good to be famous,' he says at last. 'I think it's good to be recognised but not too famous, because it's like carrying a big stone on your shoulder all the time. Now I beat the pressure but before that I went through a very tough time.'

In that respect, marriage to Carmen Botin, the daughter of one of Spain's wealthiest bankers, has helped him enormously. Ballesteros, you see, is a man to whom family means everything. Throughout his brilliant career, his brothers have been there for him, watching from the wings. Manuel was the guiding influence in the early stages of his playing life, Vicente has coached him and caddied for him, and all four of them are heavily involved in the family firm. After all these years, Ballesteros will still go to his brothers for advice on his game before he goes to anyone else.

'My brothers help a lot. They are the only ones that know my swing because they saw me grow up. Everybody else, they don't know my swing. To teach someone that plays good golf is very difficult unless you know their swing.'

Like his brothers, Carmen is always there behind the scenes, calmly supporting him, as far removed from the stereotype of a golfer's wife as is imaginable. Her hair is dark and straight and her face, like Ballesteros's, is more striking than conventionally good-looking. When she smiles it lights up her whole face, just like it does his. Ballesteros was denied her hand for 12 years because her parents didn't think a man with his peasant background was good enough for her. Only when he had amassed a fortune and earned a reputation consistent with their own high standards, did they relent. Seve and Carmen were married in November 1989.

'Marriage helps in many ways, no question,' observes Ballesteros, whose leisure time is spent pursuing his passion for cycling, fishing, playing cards with his friends and watching television and videos. 'I think,' he says, 'it settles you down a little bit. It's much better.'

Of all our modern players, Ballesteros most exactly embodies the spirit of the game.

'As a golfer, as a striker of the ball, Seve's supreme,' said Tony Jacklin. 'You can see that without knowing anything about golf. It's his balance, his poise. He's exciting . . . The game lives in him. He can create atmosphere wherever he is. That's what charisma is about.'

'Seve's a great inspiration,' enthuses Rodger Davis. 'I think his attitude and charisma are fantastic. Myself, I think he's the best player in the world at the moment. He's the complete golfer . . . I think you just get a guy that comes along once every ten years that has that indefinable "it". You can't teach it – someone just has it. Now that's not saying that guys like Faldo or Greg Norman aren't great players, but there are certain people – Nicklaus had it, Hogan, Palmer – they just have something. It's hard to put your finger on what it is.'

'Let me tell you something about Seve,' said ex-journalism graduate, Chip Beck, at the 1989 World Match Play. He was collapsed against a radiator in the press tent, recovering from a severe Ballesteros mauling (Ballesteros won 9 and 8). 'He's a tough competitor; he's a great competitor. He could probably play hurt and beat most people in the world.'

It is as much the myth as the man which intimidates his foes. 'Everybody gets nervous,' says Ballesteros of his apparent invincibility on the golf course. 'I think that anytime you don't have any nerves out on the course it's because you aren't interested in the game. Sometimes it helps. Not every shot, every hole, but sometimes. I think especially when you play the last few holes and you're close to winning. I think a little pressure helps. But it's the kind of pressure everybody is looking for. It's sweet pressure, you know. I like that. I don't know about the others, but I like it.'

In years to come, in the annals of golf, Ballesteros is the criterion against which all others will be judged. Who else in today's uniform ranks of up-and-coming players is likely to take every facet of the game to its nth degree the way he has?

In the players' lounge at Son Vida, I put the question to Ballesteros. 'I know one,' he replies with a twinkle in his eye, 'but I think I'm not going to tell you.'

'In that case,' I say, 'how much longer do you intend to keep playing before you start thinking about retiring?'

'*Retiring?*' Ballesteros says, horrified. 'What else can I do? I don't know. I don't have any . . .' He laughs and shakes his head vigorously to dispel the image. 'No, no, no, I don't want to think about that. I like to play forever.'

'Like Gary Player?'

'Not like Gary Player. No, no, no, that's not my way. Because I think one day I will like to stay home and not travel so much. Travelling is very tough. But definitely, I will like to play for as long as I can.'

At length, Ballesteros strides from the clubhouse on his way to practice, frowning at some private thought.

'Seve,' shouts Harry Pichannick, a tiny white-haired Irish caddie. The Spaniard stops in his tracks, his face relaxing into a grin. 'I'm going to put money on you to win the Open this year,' HP tells Ballesteros, 'but not the Masters.'

He speaks to Seve as though he doesn't think the man can understand English. 'Your putting – no good.'

Ballesteros assumes a menacing scowl. 'Why not the Masters?' he demands in mock annoyance. Ian Wright, his caddie, stands behind him like a bodyguard, legs astride, hands on hips. He listens to the exchange with amusement.

'Oh no,' says HP, 'Those greens – too slick for you.'

Ballesteros turns on his heel and starts to walk down the steps. 'HP', he says sternly, 'in a few months, I quote you back.'

World Match Play, Wentworth, September 1990. But Ballesteros didn't win the US Masters. He wound up a forgotten sixth. And at the US Open, after shooting 73, 69, 71 in the first three days to enter the final round only four strokes behind the leaders, Ballesteros sank his tee shot in the lake at the second and blew out with a 76. At the Open and US PGA Championships, he never even made the weekend. His European Tour appearances have been erratic, to say the least. Out of 12 starts he has had just one victory (in the Majorcan Open), two missed cuts and seven top ten finishes.

It has not been a year upon which Ballesteros will look back with fond memories. From the start it was dominated by a multitude of distracting dilemmas. The first thing that happened was the announcement that Carmen was expecting a baby, after which Ballesteros became increasingly preoccupied and progressively less attentive on the golf course.

Then there was the business of the venue for the 1993 Ryder Cup. Ballesteros led the bid for the event to be held at Club de Campo in Madrid, using tactics which those familiar with his arguments with Beman would recognise ('If the Ryder Cup doesn't go to Spain, I might lose interest in the game' and 'if Samuel Ryder was alive today he would be for Spain'). But in the end, although everybody agreed with Ballesteros that he had done more than any other player to promote golf in Europe, it was decided that the Ryder Cup should return to the Belfry in 1993, with Club de Campo pencilled in as a possible venue for 1997.

After that there was an announcement of a swing change which would be implemented under the guidance of Vicente in the months following the Madrid Open in April. This statement was as good as retracted at the Open Championship. And then finally, he and Ian Wright, his caddie, parted company at the English Open.

Ballesteros came into the press tent to be interviewed at the start of that week, looking like a man with the weight of the world on his shoulders. He sat down behind the microphones and stared fixedly at the table cloth, dejection in every line of his body.

'My concentration is not good,' he said in reply to a question about his game.

'Why is that, Seve?'

Ballesteros cleared his throat. He shifted in his chair. His expression was hunted. 'Well, I don't really want to go any farther about that,' he said at last. 'That's all I want to say. I don't really like to think about why this and why that. It's not necessary. Let's concentrate on the English Open. It's the only important thing right now.'

'Apart from the concentration problem, are you happy with the way you're playing?'

Ballesteros eyed his persecutor miserably. 'I say-a that I just don't want to go over that.'

He refused to talk about the US PGA, or to discuss past events in any shape or form. We proceeded along the narrow route of the English Open. We exhausted topics such as the weather and the golf course. When a reporter tried to get him back on to the subject of his poor form, Ballesteros snapped: 'Listen, I come here to play and to enjoy this golf tournament . . . I always play the best I can. It's important to win, but it's not the aim of my life and it will not be the aim of my career.'

'You seem unhappy,' someone else tried, after further attempts to get a dialogue going had been foiled.

'Unhappy? I'm not unhappy. I'm just not happy with the way things are going for me in golfing matters.'

Unable to advance or retreat, we eventually reached stalemate.

As the year has gone on, people have begun to talk about Ballesteros in the past tense, in the way that they have about Sandy Lyle through his slump, Bernhard Langer in the throes of the yips, and the Spaniard himself before he won at Royal Lytham. Even the players are beginning to talk in the same way, which is a bad sign. At the Belfry, Sandy Lyle said, 'Seve is a very proud man and he wants to dominate golf like he did through the eighties. He's struggling to come to terms with the fact that Faldo is the man of the moment.'

'He's lost his aggression on the golf course,' observed Wright, 'that natural sparkle. That will to play golf wasn't there this year.'

By far the most interesting theory I've heard on the subject is that of Ted

Pollard, martial arts expert and fitness adviser to the Tour. Pollard believes that the deterioration of a major golfer starts with his eyes. He says that once you reach a certain age your eyesight becomes impaired, and unless you correct it immediately by getting glasses or contact lenses, your brain gradually adjusts itself to cope with this new visual information. And if all of a sudden, the visual information that a golfer gets, with regard to club selection, lines of putts, etc., begins to alter, then he cannot continue to play in the same way.

But now at Wentworth, regarding us genially from his roost on the press conference platform, Ballesteros (blissfully unaware that his eyesight may be worsening by the minute) appears to be in quite the best mood I've ever seen him. It may well be the product of his new-found status as father, bottle washer and nappie changer – his son was born on 20 August – but whatever the cause, this new sunny disposition is infinitely better than the state of depression he has been in for much of this year.

Two things have come out of the arrival on earth of the Ballesteros baby. One is the rather odd rumour that Seve calls him Baldomero (the boy's official name and that of Seve's father) while Carmen calls him Xavier which I haven't placed too much store by. The other is the joke:

'Why did Carmen take so long in labour?'

'Because the baby was demanding appearance money.'

Oblivious to such idle chatter, Ballesteros watches Tony Greer, the World Match Play press officer, shuffle his papers and pens.

'Your thoughts?' asks Greer, peering at Ballesteros through the milk bottle thickness of his glasses.

'You want my thoughts?' Ballesteros asks the attendant press corps. 'I don't really have anything to say.' He pauses to let the comment sink in and then relents. He smiles widely. 'Well, it's always nice to play match play, and of course I like Wentworth.'

'Could we have the Ryder Cup here?' a reporter asks, goading him.

Ballesteros refuses to rise to the bait. 'We can have the 1997 Ryder Cup at Wentworth.'

'Is it important to you to win the World Match Play this year?' Ballesteros has won this event four times, one short of Gary Player's record of five. 'I would like to win it anytime . . . To win the World Match Play is difficult, but to win the World Match Play five times like Gary did is something more difficult.'

'Are you playing well enough to win?'

'I played good enough last week (the Lancome Trophy) to win, and I played good enough at the Belfry (the English Open) to win.' In fact he won neither.

'The odds are 11-1 against you,' a scribe tells him. 'Is that good?'

Ballesteros shrugs, half-amused. 'Maybe.'

He is in a playful mood. We throw conversational tennis balls at him and he bats them merrily back.

At intervals our eyes drop below the level of the table, where he performs an intricate juggling act with a small brown ball, mauling it, stretching it, tossing it. Eventually he throws it at Tim Glover (the *Independent* correspondent), who gives it to me as a souvenir. I examine it closely. It turns out to be a piece of bread kneaded, the way a child does, into a dough-ball.

Ronan Rafferty, whom Ballesteros meets in the first round tomorrow, is playing very well and the Spaniard knows it will be a tough match. We remind him of his opening draw in the 1983 World Match Play when his opponent was Arnold Palmer. The match went to sudden-death after 18 holes and Ballesteros won at the 21st.

'Of course,' said the journalist who raised the subject, 'he was young then.'

'Who?' Ballesteros asks with a grin. 'Arnold Palmer or me?'

Ballesteros has an outstanding record in the World Match Play, having won all four finals he has played in. 'Better than Sandy Lyle,' he says wickedly when it is mentioned. Prior to his victory in this tournament in 1988, Lyle had the unfortunate record of having played in four finals and lost every one.

'Do you think that you should have been seeded,' asks a reporter, raising a controversial issue. Ballesteros is unseeded for only the third time in 15 consecutive starts in this event.

'Well,' says Ballesteros, 'if you go by the record, I've won this tournament four times. Some people should think about that. But I'm not upset about that. I'm just hurt.'

A tabloid reporter captures his attention. 'Do you get upset when you read in the papers that people think that you are finished, that you might never win again?'

There is a moment's horrified silence, the kind that always follows the voicing of the unthinkable.

'What?' says Ballesteros, doubting his own hearing. Unbelievably, he takes it with perfect equanimity. He even smiles at the man who asked the question. 'I don't get upset, no. I say that they don't have any idea what they are writing about. This is what I say.'

Emboldened by his calm response to this polemic the reporters become more and more daring. What is the matter with him in that case? they ask. Why hasn't he won a tournament since the Majorcan Open in March?

'I'm quite confident that I'm going to win before the year is finished,' replies Ballesteros. 'I have that feeling.'

But they persist. What has been the problem? Why hasn't he performed well in the majors?

'I don't have to prove anything to anybody,' says Ballesteros, letting their taunts slide off him like water off a duck's back. 'I have to prove it to myself. My record speaks for itself . . . I think over the years I have proved to everyone what I can do when I play well. I have nothing to prove anymore.'

'What do you have to prove to yourself?'

'Well, my career's been very steady and quite good over the last fourteen years, and I feel that I have to win over the next few weeks to continue that, that's all.'

'What happens if you don't win?'

'NO!' shouts Ballesteros (but not angrily), cutting the question short. "I *will*. I *will* win. You want to have a bet with me. I'll give you four to one.'

Go on, Brian,' chorus the press in unison. 'No,' cries the Reuters reporter indignantly. 'I want him to win.'

Ballesteros's face is alive with merriment. He looks down upon the man as indulgently as a headmaster who has had to reprimand a favourite pupil.

'I know you do,' he assures Brian.

Chapter Three

NOMADS

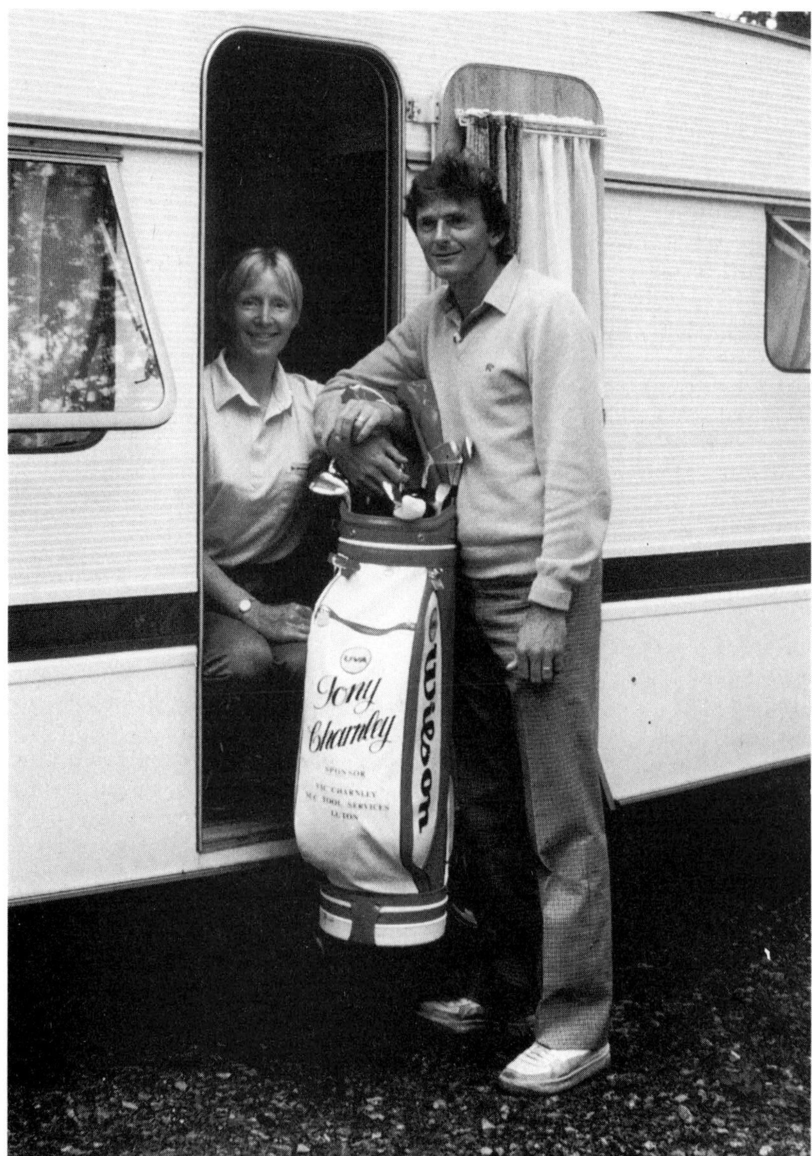

Photo: Phil Sheldon

On the road: Tony and Lucienne Charnley –
'The only good thing about being in a hotel is they make the beds'

D. A. RUSSELL PLAYS THE BLUES.

The soulful sound of his harmonica filters into the antiseptic atmosphere of the airport lounge. On this grey, still day, the gods have conspired to delay us. Other people throw up their hands in despair or erupt into towering rages when the television monitors confirm this. The pros, all veteran travellers, ignore the coughs and squeaks emitted by the loudspeaker – alluding vaguely to air traffic controllers and high winds in distant places – and head up the stairs to the smoky innards of the bar.

Russell occupies centre-stage. He holds a captive audience. The faces of John McHenry, Stephen Hamill, Wayne Riley and Steven Bottomley are enraptured. A ragged line has formed around them as people press forward to pay for drinks and the air is heavy with the mixed aromas of strong coffee, cheap liquor and Continental cigars. Riley whoops and dances a jig, stamping his feet on the floor. Here, freed from the pressures of the tournament environment and out of their work clothes (lambswool sweaters off the golf course are taboo), the pros seem much younger; in their jeans and sweatshirts they look like students.

Fellow travellers give them a wide berth. 'Hooligans,' I suppose they must be thinking. They can't know that some of these players have known more heartache and hardship than many people twice their age; that sometimes the only way to stop yourself crying in professional golf is to laugh. Moments like this are their release.

Riley, for instance, has good cause to celebrate. He came within one shot of losing his Tour card this week (Portuguese Open 1989). After the first round he was four over par, when it was unlikely the cut was going to be more than one over. I found him down on the range one night, alone except for the mosquitoes. Illuminated by the floodlights, he stood hitting balls like shooting stars into the darkness. 'Can I tell you something?' said Riley stopping suddenly, his face rigid with determination. 'If I miss the cut tomorrow and I lose my card it doesn't matter, because I know that every week I've gone out there and I've done my best.'

He shot 66 the next day to make the cut and keep his card.

Other members of this happy group were not so fortunate. Russell, McHenry and Bottomley might be enjoying themselves now, caught up in the general end of term spirit (this is the last tournament of the year for most players), but all three have lost their playing cards and will have to return to the School. At the back of every mind lurks the fear, however subconscious, that this time might be the last time.

France, April 1990. If it's Wednesday, it must be Cannes.

After a while on Tour, you begin to think like that. Each week partially erases the last so that all you are left with is fragments; colours, faces and places blur in your mind like a kaleidoscope. You reach the stage where you have to go through a kind of ritual every morning to establish where you are and what day it is. Weeks are no longer divided into weekdays and weekends, but travel days, practice days, pro-am days and tournament days.

But when I look from my window this morning, there's no mistaking the blue of the Côte D'Azur, the rows of designer shops and, in the distance, the theatre where the film festival is to be held in a fortnight's time. Location: Carlton Hotel, Cannes. Pro-Am day.

Tour travel is not real travel. It's an endless succession of views from windows: from the plane, the bus, the hotel room. Paris, London, Rome – we could be in any one of them for all the impression we get of each place. The way in which we travel screens us from the real world; the problems that the ordinary tourist encounters pass us by. For the most part, we go on packages organised for the Tour by three companies: Traveleads, Randy Fox and Golf Tours International. We are met at the airport, whisked by coach or courtesy car to our hotel, and fetched and carried daily to and from the golf club. The hotels we stay in are uniformly large and splendid.

The price of Tour travel is not low. A player's expenses per week, including accommodation, food and caddie, average out at around £1,000. Australian, African and American players have to bear the extra cost of long-haul airfares and maintaining second homes. Australian, Peter McWhinney, says that it costs him approximately Aus $100,000 (around £40,000) a year to play the Tour. Most tour pros play between 18 and 30 tournaments a season, over 150 players following the circuit to some 14 countries. Package prices vary from week to week. The Desert Classic trip to Dubai costs around £600 for flight and accommodation, which wasn't particularly expensive given the distance to the United Arab Emirates and the quality of the hotel we stayed in. Traveleads' quote for two weeks in Madrid for the Madrid and Spanish Opens was £1,600 for a single room, which was unusually high. Randy Fox's charge of £250 for the Dutch Open, based on shared accommodation, transfers and flight was exceptionally low.

Ten years ago, half the Tour travelled by car or caravan. Ian Woosnam did, so did D. J. Russell, D. A. Russell and Denis Durnian; David Jones slept in the back of his van. Tony and Lucienne Charnley are about the only people who still prefer to take a caravan to British and Continental events. 'The only good thing about being in a hotel,' claims Tony Charnley, 'is that they make the beds.'

The Charnleys' caravan has all the basic amenities of a small home, including a television, radio cassette player, books and Lucienne's knitting. 'I had a discussion with Ronan Rafferty who said he'd never ever go in a caravan,' says Charnley. 'And basically, I proved to him that what he has in his hotel room is less than what I have in my caravan. But it's just a case of people like that, unless they're spending £1,000 a week, they don't feel they're doing their job properly.'

Continuous travel requires a certain hardiness and a great adaptability to changes in climate, language, food. Even by taking adequate precautions you are always vulnerable to colds, viruses and stomach bugs. In Majorca earlier this year, about 20 players ended up with severe food poisoning after eating chicken sandwiches on the practice ground. Peter Smith had to be rushed to hospital, haemorrhaging from the stomach, and Jamie Spence collapsed on the golf course.

Partly for this reason, we tend to stick to familiar restaurants. Half a dozen of the best in every town tend to be common knowledge – McDonald's in the centre of Madrid is one such place – and most of the players will eat there. Personally, that's one of the things I like best about Tour life, but there are people who will make a point of eating or staying in places where they know they won't find anyone connected with the Tour.

The good side of life on the European Tour far outweighs the bad. There is the golf, the good humour and the companionship and, although we seldom see the cities we go to, the opportunity is still there. In Monte Carlo, for example, we are annually invited to the palace to meet Prince Rainier, Princesses Stephanie and Caroline, and Prince Albert. This year (as usual) only a handful of players went, most people passing up the opportunity in favour of watching the World Cup on television.

Each place has its own accompanying rituals. In Dubai, we went to the market and bought fake designer t-shirts, watches and cassettes, and walked through the Gold Souk alongside black-veiled women, Arab sheiks, expatriates and poverty-stricken migrant workers. In Dusseldorf, we ate chicken with our hands at a street cafe. In Valencia, we drank bitter coffee in neon-lit dive bars, sampled every ice-cream on their grubby menus, and shopped for porcelain figurines.

It is a strange, nomadic existence, enjoyable in its way, but also very artificial and very insular. The Tour is an environment which encourages reclusivity and selfishness, because if you choose you need never have any other life. If you are not the type of person who keeps abreast of current affairs, world wars could literally pass you by.

'Things happen in Britain,' says Yorkshireman Gordon J. Brand, 'and we miss them completely. Six months later, someone will mention something and I'll say, "I don't remember hearing about that. Is radiation fatal then?" I don't particularly go and find newspapers when I'm away. Some players do but they keep them to themselves because they're so expensive.'

At any one time on Tour there doesn't seem anything more important in life than who is leading the tournament. It is a life that doesn't require a lot of thought. Get on the plane, go to the tournament, go home, pack, catch another plane. Your years are mapped out for you, so are your weeks and your days.

David Llewellyn, conditioned by years of travelling to do things automatically, once even managed to get on the wrong plane. It was only because one of the other players spotted him disappearing through the wrong exit gate that he was rescued at all. Otherwise he would have found himself in Cyprus on arrival, an altogether different destination from the one where he was headed.

German Open, Dusseldorf, August 1990. Randy Fox describes himself as 'a baby-sitter, cook and bottle-washer, priest, rabbi, psychologist and pimp'. Others might add to the list. In truth, he is a Jewish-American, one-man travel operator, with a round, pale face with spots of high colour on the cheek bones, an excitable nature and scarcely any hair.

Fox has, he says, always been a golfer by profession, but never a player. In the hippie days, he used to tuck his hair away and teach golf at night to get himself through graduate school in Buffalo, New York. What was he doing there? Many, many things. Avoiding the Vietnamese war, but mainly studying what we call English. A Masters degree in English and education led to an associate professorship at the university, until things got 'very hot and frustrating in the ivory tower' and Fox went back to being a golf pro. When he tired of the sterile atmosphere of American clubs, he became a travel guide for a Californian who was bringing American players over to Europe. Eleven years ago he started his own company, Pro Travel, on the European circuit.

Of course, Tour travel was different in those days. The players used to stay on the Continent for five weeks at a stretch; they didn't come home every Sunday like they do now. The old system of prequalifying for every tournament was still in existence then, so that players failing to qualify on the Monday of each week would be forced to spend the days in between incarcerated in the hotel.

'They went crazy,' recalls Fox, with a slight shudder. 'I remember my very first trip – they ran out of natural gas and there was Tony Jacklin needing a shave and looking like he hadn't had one in weeks. The airlines were on strike, so we chartered a plane to Malaga and the great three – Simon Hobday, Bobby Lincoln and [the late] Vinnie Baker – had a little bit too much to drink and the pilot threatened to put the plane down if they didn't behave themselves. When we landed, we lost Baker and I found him two or three days later sobering up somewhere.' Baker had got himself into trouble in a bar and had to be bailed out of jail.

'We got to Spain and the hotels were on strike . . . There was no food. We ate shredded lettuce for three days . . . From there we flew to Italy, and from Italy to Leone. We had a young German player with us, who was a prequalifier and who had no money in those days. His name was Langer. I remember checking in at Leone and they wanted to overweight us. Instead, I talked them into averaging the player's weight with that of a group of 40 nuns. But it was

Langer's ticket that they had held back. He was the one that would have had to pay all the money.'

If stories like that don't convince prospective clients of Fox's attributes as guardian angel abroad, he pulls out the old Tour favourite – Brian Sharrock's incredible journey – which has, he says, done more than any marketing campaign to demonstrate to young professionals the pitfalls of travelling alone.

Brian (Save a Shilling) Sharrock was a Tour player in the mid-seventies. He was scrupulously careful with money; so much so that, given the choice of flying or driving from Madrid to the south of Sardinia for the Italian Open one season, Sharrock decided to drive. He set off for Marseille on Friday afternoon, only to discover on arrival that there was no ferry to Sardinia for three days and he had to fly after all. The only flight available by that time was one to the northern tip of Corsica, which he had no alternative but to take.

In Corsica he hired a car and drove like Ayrton Senna the length of the country. He spent Saturday night in a hotel and went down to the harbour at the crack of dawn the following morning to try to get a boat to Sardinia. A surly French-speaking sea captain seemed to be the only living soul in existence. The language barrier was prohibitive and at one point threatened to put paid to the whole expedition. But eventually Sharrock's rantings and gesticulations won through and the man agreed to take Sharrock across the water – for a price.

When they reached the other side, the captain flagged down a passing mini, engaged in an animated discussion with the driver and proceeded to load Sharrock's luggage into the car. Sharrock followed it gratefully. The driver then got behind the wheel, drove 600 yards down the road to a bus stop, dumped a surprised Sharrock, his suitcase and his golf bag on the roadside and hurtled away. When the bus finally came, some three hours later, it only took Sharrock as far as the town centre. He then caught a train to Is Molas, the tournament venue, where he arrived at 11 p.m. having spent a small fortune. The luckless Sharrock took a wrong drop at a water hazard in the first round of the tournament and was disqualified.

Fox talks rapidly in an American twang, reeling off ten stories in the time it takes most people to think of one. A party was thrown in Barcelona to celebrate a Scottish player's second-place finish, which resulted in a room being trashed at the Ritz, and a Jaguar being damaged by a milk bottle flung from a window. Mark James and Ken Brown, who were sitting innocently in their room while all this was going on, lit a fire in the artificial fireplace because they were cold, and ruined the wallpaper. Buses have also broken down and drivers have fallen asleep, and Fox has arrived in countries at midnight on Easter Monday with his group, to find no coach waiting there to collect them.

'We found Mac O'Grady and Danny Goodman [who broke 28 putters and his caddie's ankle one year] riding in the undercarriages of buses several times.

I don't know what they were doing . . . Mac once raced us from the airport in Madrid back to the hotel (12 kilometres) and beat us. He was a jogger in excellent shape . . . Another time in Madrid, we were going round a roundabout near the Palace Hotel and the undercarriage of the bus opens up and a golf bag falls out. Sure enough, it's Tony Johnstone's. There's clubs all over the street. So Tony jumps out and starts yelling and screaming as Tony was prone to do in those days.'

Fox goes on and on without pausing for breath.

'The Tour has,' he says, 'evolved into a high pressure [big money] business with a lot of very serious young players who are born into playing pro golf . . . who are very alike and get more clonish every year. When we started, a lot of them were club pros and there were a couple of hell-raisers who got fined thousands. There was Ken Brown and Mark James, who got fined for every conceivable thing, from refusing to salute the flag, to wearing jeans at the official Ryder Cup dinner, to refusing to sign autographs. There were others and there was action on the Tour. I'm not saying it was better; it wasn't. But there was a lot of hell-raising, a lot of girl-chasing, a lot of groupies, a lot of drinking.'

There are no groupies now – unless you count the adolescent autograph hunters who sometimes hang around the practice ground – and little or no revelry of any kind.

Only one recent incident stands out as being particularly unsavoury. Mikael Krantz, a young Swede, went out one night at the Irish Open (June 1990) and had quite a bit to drink. No one, including Krantz, is entirely sure what happened next, but he allegedly left a bar at midnight and then was seen leaving it again at about 3 a.m., which would seem to indicate that he went back again. In any case, when he turned up the next morning to play with John Morgan and Keith Waters, he was clearly still inebriated. But he did, according to Waters, manage to play 18 holes without inconveniencing his partners in any way.

But Morgan felt that his own round had been disrupted and duly reported Krantz, thus breaking a time-honoured code of loyalty between players. The story was blown out of proportion in the papers, particularly by the Swedish press, and Krantz lost his sponsor. Morgan was strongly criticised by the rest of the Tour for being, among other things, a hypocrite, although he continued to insist – without a shred of evidence – that he had believed Krantz to be high rather than drunk.

The fact that the episode aroused such a furore just goes to show how quiet it is on Tour these days.

'There's nothing at all,' agrees Fox. 'They're very homogeneous; to an outsider, very boring unless you know them. Players nowadays are really concerned with making money . . . and with planning and preparation. The top priority today for staying in a hotel is satellite television in English. McDonalds is a high priority: if Mickey D's is close by, they'll stay at the hotel. Things have changed. Most guys don't go any further than the bar, whereas in the old days – the pre-AIDS days – they used to chase around the red light districts looking and messing around.'

It's been suggested that Fox has on occasion put players in hotels in close proximity to the less salubrious areas of certain towns in order to keep them entertained.

'Categorically untrue,' denies Fox emphatically. 'Whatever hotel we chose, people would find the red light district . . .

'There used to be a lot of hell-raising and parties. Now, the only place where the players go out at night is Sweden. We had kids from the hotel there jockeying us back from the Cafe Opera [nightclub] at two or three in the morning. Yes, the guys get involved in Sweden, but it's a dating-type thing, not a heavy thing. In Switzerland, there's a traditional insane party on Tuesday night at the members' bar. It just started spontaneously two years ago. But generally it doesn't happen anymore. To be honest, the hotels are dead at 10.30. Everybody's watching TV.'

A camaraderie not found in any other sport exists on the European Tour, born of the unique, nomadic lifestyle of the players. It stems from the constant insecurity of playing a game as unpredictable as golf and from spending a lifetime in the company of others in search of the same dream, and it has the same strength and moral support system as a large family.

'One thing I do like about Europe is that there's no caste system on this Tour,' says Fox. 'You can find Sandy Lyle talking to Wraith Grant about cars, you can find Seve having dinner with rookies. Nick [Faldo] too, hard as that is for people to believe; Nick's best friend on Tour was Peter Thomas many years ago and two more unlikely friends you'd never see. But there's no caste system, which I've heard there is in America. If you win a tournament, you eat in one place; if you win a major, you don't talk to this one.

'However, the caste system among nationalities here is destructive. The Swedes *will not* go out to dinner – with a few exceptions – with anyone else. They *refuse* to stay in a room unless it's with another Swede. The Spaniards have never ever made any attempt to communicate with anyone else. The Italians are the same way. [Alberto] Binaghi and his friends eat Italian food at the same restaurant at a tournament every night. There's no attempt at variance whatsoever. The Americans are just *so* tight. And even among the British players, the Welsh don't want to room with the Scottish and the Scottish don't want to room with the English. The Aussies and the South Africans will sometimes get together. You know, it's more than which football team you like. They thrive on it.'

But you have to balance that against the complete lack of snobbery or bias among the players. Everybody, no matter who they are, looks out for everyone else. 'If you're stuck you can always turn to someone,' grins Gordon J. Brand, 'which I often tend to do because I'm not an organiser. I'm a follower. I hate it when I catch a plane that no one else is on. I don't know what to do. Where do you get the baggage? How do I get from the airport to the hotel when there's no bus there with Traveleads on the front?'

In general, everyone gets along. Real arguments or fights are rare. As Mark Roe says, if you took a survey among the players, you would find that only about two per cent of the players aren't popular and that everybody dislikes the same few people. But for the most part, professional golfers have an acceptance of each other, regardless of their colour, nationality or beliefs, that we could all learn from. On the US Tour, I've heard it said, you could go into a restaurant with 52 tables, and there would be a player at each one. On the European Tour you don't ever have to be alone unless you want to be. 'You can be a loner or an extrovert,' says Brand, 'and it doesn't really matter, because there's always someone to suit your needs.'

Chris Moody can be slotted firmly under the category of extrovert. Donald Stirling, a Satellite Tour player, has a story which he tells about the time he bumped into Moody in a wine bar in Barcelona. After exchanging a few platitudes they sat down for a drink. The focal point of the bar was a huge magnum of champagne.

'Christ,' said Moody suddenly, 'I could nick that.'

'You're joking,' said Stirling, startled.

'If I get across this bar and take the champagne,' said Moody, 'you have to buy dinner.'

'Fair enough,' said Stirling, feeling that his money couldn't be safer in the Bank of England. In due course, first one barman, then the other, disappeared. In a flash Moody was round the bar and had the champagne tucked under his leather jacket. Stirling, who is a very serious pro with a habit of talking in a sort of half-whisper, couldn't believe his eyes.

Now over in the opposite corner of the room, oblivious to all of this, were three Irish professionals. 'Watch this,' said Moody gleefully. He strolled over to their table.

'Well, Eamonn,' Moody said to Darcy, 'we've had our differences in the past but I'd like to show you that there's no hard feelings.' And with that he produced the champagne and handed it over.

'Now the fun begins,' said Moody to Stirling when he returned to his chair.

The Irishmen were stunned. They stared at the bottle for several moments and then began to pass it around the table, trying to decide who should open it. Some time elapsed before the barmen caught sight of their prized possession, which was by then in the process of being opened. As one, they dropped what they were doing and raced around the bar, shrieking profanities in Spanish. An almighty row broke out. 'It's mine,' cried Darcy, clutching the bottle to his chest. 'It's ours,' screamed the barmen trying to wrench it from his grasp.

'Chris,' said Stirling, 'you'd better say something . . .'

But Moody was nowhere to be seen. As he well knows, when the going gets tough, the tough get going.

A lifetime spent on the road makes most players philosophical, resigned to a multitude of fates. As a group, they are quite extraordinarily patient (David Grice, the long-suffering Traveleads rep, would disagree), the result, I suppose, of years spent playing a game which requires so much of that virtue.

'There are people who aren't patient,' comments Brand, the winner of the 1989 Belgian Open and six Safari circuit titles, 'and they tend to stand out like a sore thumb. I always just sit and wait. Occasionally I'll have a ding dong with someone, but it's a waste of time because you know it's nothing they can do anything about. It's always someone else's fault whom you can't get hold of. So you're better off just sitting there and saying, "I'm ready to go when you are." If you got upset every time something went wrong on Tour, you'd be a nervous wreck.'

Golf is full of wasted time. You can't actually do anything with it because you're always waiting for something to happen: waiting to tee-off, waiting to catch a plane, sitting out delays. Christy O'Connor, Eamonn Darcy, Gordon Brand Jnr., and Roger Chapman carry telescopic rods everywhere they go, and spend their spare hours fishing. Chris Platts, David R. (Doctor) Jones and Jamie Spence, occasionally joined by Sam Torrance, have a poker school; Keith Waters plays the stock market; Phillip Parkin and David Whelan play chess. Gordon J. Brand sketches.

'I used to draw the view from the hotel room, but then we started staying in cheaper hotels and we'd back on to the bins. So now I pick up magazines which sometimes have decent pictures in, or I take pictures of people's houses and draw them. I've not sold a picture yet but I might have to if I keep shooting 74s.'

Brand is completely deadpan. He speaks in a slow, broad Yorkshire accent and his humour is so dry that you have to listen quite carefully to pick it up. But he is quite effortlessly and unintentionally the funniest player on the European Tour. His jokes are so involved and take such an age to tell that by the time you reach the punchline you've forgotten the beginning. And yet they are quite ridiculously hilarious.

'I suppose,' intones Brand when we discuss the problem of too much time and not enough to do with it, 'you're not too conscious of trying to kill time because it's the same every week. You're only on the course for just over four hours. It used to be five, but now they've started fining players for slow play so we've had to get a move on, which means we've got more time to kill. I liked it when it was slow.'

At the American Express Open in Los Brisas earlier this year, we were trapped in a cyclone for three days. We literally couldn't leave the hotel. The tournament was temporarily abandoned and eventually cut to 54 holes. Our only source of in-hotel entertainment – an indoor swimming-pool – was destroyed when a palm tree, bent double by the wind, snapped off at the roots and came crashing through the roof. If Denis Durnian hadn't saved the hour by producing a portable video and 30 video tapes, we might have all been taken away in strait-jackets.

It's at times like these when you need people like Wayne (Radar) Riley – who can lay claim to the feat of having been jailed three times by mistake – to entertain you with stories of past misdemeanours. Riley loves to shock. This he does rather brilliantly by doing such things as emptying his briefcase – which has 'National Sex Week' on the side and is filled with assorted trifles from sex shops and other dubious establishments round the globe – onto the table at inopportune moments.

In Montpelier, he woke up one morning at 8.27. Normally that wouldn't be a crime but his tee-off time happened to be 8.35 a.m. In any other profession he could have rolled over and gone back to sleep, then called in sick later. In golf, it meant leaping from the bed that instant, grabbing a handful of clothes and racing out of the hotel half naked. To the amazement of the courtesy car driver, Riley dressed on the way to the golf course and was just doing up his fly as he reached the first tee. He went out in three under par that day and holed-in-one to win a Volvo the next. By unfortunate coincidence, however, his licence had been endorsed when he was caught drunk driving a fortnight previously.

'What are you going to do with your car?' I asked when I saw him in Cannes the following week.

'I've given it away to charity,' said Radar brightly.

'What charity?' I said disbelievingly.

'Alcoholics Anonymous!'

Riley might be a prankster, and a very good one at that, but he is only a beginner when compared to the double act of Mark Roe and Robert Lee. Roe, the 1989 Catalan Open champion, is hyperactive with a lean, athletic build and overlong blond hair. Lee, by contrast, is tall and broad-shouldered with a close-crop of jet black hair. He appears (misleadingly) to be the steadier of the two. They are best friends and the best practical jokers on Tour. Their humour, however, is not to everyone's taste. It involves a certain amount of food throwing and a lot of antics with potentially disastrous consequences.

One of their best-known adventures began with a typical argument between the two of them. It was around midnight and Lee had just finished a lengthy phone call to his girlfriend. Roe was starting to drift off to sleep so he turned the television off. Lee, who was wide awake, mischievously turned it back on. Roe turned it off and Lee turned it on. When Roe took the batteries out of the remote control and threw them away, Lee got up and switched the television on at the set.

Tired and more than a little bit annoyed, Roe decided to put an end to the quarrel once and for all. He got out of bed stark naked, fetched a pair of scissors out of his hold-all and cut the live wire. 'Robert said I was just shrouded in a cloud of sparks,' grins Roe now. 'The room was illuminated.' The scissors melted in his hand. Half asleep at the time, Roe only realised afterwards what he had done. Lee lay on the bed laughing hysterically, the way people do when they have had a narrow brush with injury or death. Roe was completely unharmed, but he had fused the entire floor of the hotel.

'You know what life's like out here,' says Roe, 27, trying to explain the motive behind some of their madness. 'It can be very tedious. People don't really know what it's like. It's a hard way of life. You only have to look at the highs and lows. Robert, two or three years ago, was one of the best young players on the Tour and he was making plenty of money. And within a few years . . . well, he's made three cuts this year. There's a very fine line between success and failure. So if you have a little bit of fun – as long as it's not harmful – I think it's okay.'

The trouble is that many of their pranks come perilously close to ending in tears. A few years ago, for example, during the course of a daily ferry trip back and forth from an event held at Santander (Seve's course), Roe and a few other players began hitting balls off the tow rope on the deck at scattered fishing boats. They did it all week and never hit a boat. But on the last day there were a lot of spectators on board and it developed into a show.

'I teed it up,' says Roe, 'and I saw this boat; it must have been 200 yards away. I hit a huge slice. It was never anywhere near the boat. But the wind was bringing it in, bringing it in. The people in the ferry, they were off their seats watching this ball. It pitched straight in this fishing boat and hopped over the side. And this guy has gone. "What's happening?" And he's pulled his rod over the other side and he started fishing there.'

Now that story might have ended a little differently if the ball had actually hit the fisherman, and Roe was berated by the other players for that reason. But no harm was ever intended. What started out as fun just got out of hand. A lot of players get very annoyed by some of Roe and Lee's stunts, but really it is just their way of letting off steam.

'We don't drink and we don't smoke either,' says Roe in their defence, 'and one thing we do is we work very hard at our golf, because at the end of the day it's a job. If we want to have some fun afterwards, that's fine. You know Robert used to love discos? Well, I got associated with him for that although I never went to a club with him. I used to go to bed at ten and Robert would come in at one or two in the morning. But then his life changed because he met Liz [Lee's fiancee]. He never goes out anymore. He's in bed by ten.'

Roe is a mass of contradictions. On the one hand, you have this serious young man who married his childhood sweetheart and lives in a listed house, who loves books like *Watership Down*, and whose main hobby is collecting golf memorabilia. And on the other, you have this 'hell-raiser', to borrow Fox's phrase. I mean, this is someone who has owned and damaged nine cars 'very badly', starting with a blue Austin 1800 which he drove straight through a golf club wall while practising handbrake turns in an icy car park. He has emerged unscathed from every accident he has ever been in.

'That's the way we are,' explains Roe, who was a successful diver and gymnast in his teens, 'the way we seem to live life. All golf pros, when we get in a car we seem to think we're Emmerson Fittipaldi. We all love fast cars.'

A while ago now there was a tournament held at Albarella in Italy, where there were no cars at all, only bicycles and tricycles. The golfers cycled everywhere. Of course, the temptation to tamper with the bikes was irresistible to Roe and Lee, who were unscrewing saddles and hiding bike parts and bicycles in trees.

South African, John Bland, meanwhile, had soon tired of signing his tricycle in and out of the compound where they were kept and had taken to smuggling it into his apartment every night. After several days of watching Bland turn right out of the golf club and go racing down the street between two bollards and into his villa, Roe decided that he shouldn't be allowed to get away with it. So he moved the posts six inches closer together. Bland, of course, came down the hill at full pelt that evening, never expecting anything to have changed. His back wheels caught and buckled and he flew over the handlebars and landed in a heap in front of the bike. Bland sat up, dusted himself off, and, according to Fox, said, 'I'll get that Mark Roe, I know it was him.'

'These things happen,' says Roe, laughing at the memory. 'You need all these stories to keep you sane out here. You've got to remember it's not a normal lifestyle on Tour. It's unnatural. You're living out of a suitcase . . . you don't see your family. It's hard; it's very hard. You're lucky to be able to work six months of the year and make enough money not to work the rest, but then again you have to be very good. Nobody gives you anything, do they? You get what you deserve out here, you know. You're in control of your own destiny. If you make mistakes, there's only you to blame.

'You are not going to be able to do it forever,' says Roe. He knows that Lee, winner of the 1985 Cannes Open, the 1987 Portuguese Open and the 1984 and '85 Brazilian Opens, will have to go back to the School this year. 'You're going to be doing it four, five, ten years at most. If you're fortunate enough to do really well when you play, and you make enough money to live on, then that's great. Otherwise, you've got to look for different avenues when you're finished.

'One thing's for sure, it's great experience in life. It's a great learning process.'

Chapter Four

WINNERS

Photo: ASP, Stuart Franklin

Mark James: 'If I win a major, great, if I don't I'll take anything else that comes along'

'Winners are different. They're a different breed of cat.'

Byron Nelson

LEEDS, DECEMBER 1990. 'IF YOU'RE LOOKING FOR CONTROVERSY,' said Mark James on the telephone, 'it probably won't be worth your while coming down here. I'm saving it all for my book.'

Ah yes, a book. Half the Tour have ambitions of writing a book, it seems. But of course, Mark James intentionally or unintentionally is always controversial, so I go to Leeds anyway on a bitterly cold winter's day. James picks me up from the track by the roadside, which serves as a station in these parts (the stockbroker belt, nr. Ilkley). He is wearing a golf shirt and an anorak, and driving his wife's car; Jane is out shopping for furniture. His white cap, for once, is absent.

At the James's home, the last remaining members of a gang of 15 assorted workmen, including builders, curtainers, plumbers and carpenters, are making muffled hammering and drilling sounds on every level of the four-storey house. James busies himself making coffee in the natural wood and blue china kitchen – the only completed room – and then we clear a space for ourselves amongst the debris in the sitting-room next door. Brass pots, copper kettles and tweed coats are covered with a fine layer of dust.

'What I'll do,' I said, 'is ask you everything I want to ask you . . .'

'And I'll say: "I'm saving that for my book",' adds James with a grin.

Mark James has always been the calm eye at the centre of the storm of strife and dissension which has followed his progress since he came out on Tour in 1976. Whether by accident or design, the Mancunian who considered accountancy as a career and participated (or was accused of participating) in his early years as a pro golfer in numerous acts of devilment and roguery, leading to fights with the PGA Tour committee and running battles with the press. 'I was a little different in those days,' confesses James. But not all that much.

Ken Brown, the gentle 34-year-old from Harpenden Common, Hertfordshire, was a willing collaborator in all of these adventures, until they gradually moved further apart, got married and Brown went over to play on the US Tour.

'We used to go around an awful lot together,' says James, universally liked and admired in all circles except those official, 'because we both practised from dawn till dusk. For hours and hours we just did nothing else. And also, if we had a couple of hours spare, we'd walk around and watch other players – the successful ones.'

'It's rare to see players doing that now.'

'Well, it is for two reasons. Certainly because there are such big crowds it's difficult to see, and you can't get close to players like Seve. But it's also because, I don't know why, but it's sort of frowned upon these days to do something like that. You see it occasionally. It's the right idea, because if you don't play with them – and it's rare that rookies are drawn with top players – the only way to see them is to go out and watch.

'So that's all we did, Ken and I. We were very, very dedicated, just like someone like Faldo when he joined the Tour. He, probably more than anyone, has kept up a regime of hours of practice. I don't think anyone who's been on Tour as long as Faldo practises as much.'

'Faldo always seems to be working on his game. He doesn't really appear to go out.'

'Well, to be honest,' says James, 'I haven't found Nick like that. I've always enjoyed Nick's company. I think he's a nice guy.'

'But he doesn't go out much, does he?'

'He's unlikely to be seen at a disco at midnight, put it that way, and he's unlikely to have a hangover in the morning, but that's not a bad thing. I don't know how much he goes out and enjoys himself at home but he never does that on Tour.'

'You were telling me about you and Ken Brown,' I say in an attempt to lure him back to the original conversation. 'What did the two of you do to arouse all this controversy?'

'I can't go into details because I'm saving that for my book,' says James teasingly. So I approach the subject in a roundabout way.

'Were you a rebel at school?'

'I was, really. I mean, I was regularly getting thrown out of classes . . . I've always been a rebel in a way, but not completely.'

'Do you think that you and Ken seemed more rebellious than you would have if golf wasn't such a straight sport?'

'Probably,' says James. 'Plus, I happened to get into some unfortunate clashes at just the wrong moments. Those are all in the annals of the newspapers.'

'Tell me one.'

'Well, I'll give you the first example of what started off the problems between myself and the committee in 1977. I'm playing in the Portuguese Open. I've shot 75 in the first round at Penina, and the second round is at Palmares. I get to Palmares and I've got a dodgy knee – which I've had over the years. It doesn't stop me walking but it was a hilly course and there were no caddies and I would have had to pull a trolley. I just didn't fancy doing that . . . So I go to the starter. I say, "Look, I'm off in five minutes. I'm pulling out." And they fined me £50.'

'For a legitimate reason?'

'Oh yes, it was a legitimate reason. There was no other earthly reason for me to pull out. And that was the start of it. I tried to convince them it was ridiculous but they weren't having it, and really I was at loggerheads with some of the people on the committee for about four or five years after that.'

'But what did you and Ken do?'

'Ken and I never really did anything together – that I'm going to tell you about.'

'Randy Fox says you wore jeans at the Ryder Cup dinner.'

It is a minute or two before James can stop laughing long enough to reply. 'That's folklore,' he says. 'I mean, give me a break. Do I look that stupid? Wearing jeans at the Ryder Cup dinner? No . . . there's loads of those stories and that one is certainly not true.' That sets him off again. Dining out with young players on Tour, James hears these kind of tall tales on a regular basis. 'They'll say to me: "Is this one true?" And I say: "Tell me." They tell me the most wonderful stories, but unfortunately, they're not true. There'll be a tiny grain of truth in the bottom of the story somewhere, but most of it is total fabrication.'

'Doesn't that annoy you?'

'I quite enjoy those stories, like that one – jeans at the Ryder Cup dinner! It's amusing. It doesn't bother me in the slightest. But then I've never been too perturbed about what people have said, which may have been a failing of mine in the past. You need to be thick-skinned, 'specially when you've been regularly criticised through your career like Ken and I have. You have to become thick-skinned fairly quickly, else you let it get on top of you, simple as that.'

'Do you read the papers?'

'I read it and I think, well, I don't even know if they bother trying to rise above the level they've got themselves at. But it doesn't bother me. It bothers Jane a lot more than me. You know, even in the last couple of years, I've been at sort of – to use the word of the press – at "war" with them. And it's certainly not my fault. They're marvellous at twisting things.'

The thing is that it is a catch-22 situation. James has been hurt by the press so many times that he doesn't want to co-operate with them anymore. They, on the other hand, don't see why they should make an effort to portray him in a different light when he is so stubborn and unco-operative.

'I know what you mean,' says James when I explain this to him, 'but it goes deeper than that because I've been great for the press over the years. I've given them stories when there's been nothing else. They've had good mileage out of a player of my mediocre calibre over the years. They haven't been unfair this year, but last year they were ridiculous.'

James was attacked over a press conference in June 1989, where he listed off a number of complaints about the Irish Open which weren't considered valid, and which caused offence in Ireland. In particular, he moaned about the children who hang around the practice ground and putting green, demanding autographs and half the contents of the pros' golf bags in an aggressive manner which borders on rudeness.

'That was absurd,' says James crossly, 'absolutely absurd. Oh, it was crazy.

I was asked why I wasn't playing in the Irish Open and I reeled off about six valid reasons: the car park facilities, the children, the weather, practice facilities, no players' lounge. There's loads of things, and these days when we have 37 tournaments, you don't need to play tournaments like that. I went back to the Irish open this year and nothing had changed. And I knew what I was saying when I made those criticisms, and I knew that they would be seen as criticisms and not reasons why I wasn't playing. I thought maybe they'd have perked one ear up and said, 'This guy's right. Maybe he's gone about it the wrong way, but he's got some valid criticisms." But no, this year it was all just as bad as ever.'

Two weeks after the irish Open incident, James was again hauled over the coals; this time for withdrawing from the Monte Carlo Open after the second round, and after the cut had been made, thus costing another player the chance to play four rounds.

'I withdrew after two rounds,' argues James, 'which is perfectly within the rules of the game. You see, that was another thing. The press I got for that was just ridiculous. What annoyed me is that I was quoted as storming off the course. I came off the course [James enacts himself strolling languidly off the course] I said, "Has anyone seen the Traveleads guys? I can get home? Alright, I'm withdrawing." I don't exactly storm off courses.'

I change the subject, asking him how a golfer can tell whether his game will benefit from playing less or playing more. James only played 18 European tournaments this year, two of which he won, and eight of which he finished in the top ten. James says it is something which you learn by experience. Over the years he has had spells over three months where he has played ten tournaments and spells where he has played seven or eight, and he knows that he performs best when he plays a limited schedule. 'It depends on the individual, but I think an awful lot of players would benefit from playing a bit less.'

'Bernhard Langer says that it has to do with technique. I mean, look at Olazabal. He wins or finishes top ten virtually every time he tees up.'

'Yes,' says James, 'but he's a wonderful player. He'll be Number One in the world within a year or two, I would think. He's just a good driver, great iron player, great putter, wonderful chipper. Woosie was probably the best player in the world this year and Olazabal may be next.'

'Are majors very important to you?'

'Not really, no. If I win a major, great; if I don't, too bad. I'll take anything that comes along.'

'Most followers of the game would find it hard to understand that attitude because they place such importance on the majors.'

'But the pros don't, do they?' says James. 'The pros in Europe think of the British Open as a big thing and if you do well – even if you finish in the top twenty – it's nice to have had a reasonable Open and been up there. But certainly the American majors are not rated in Europe because hardly any of us get to them.'

'But there are players – like Faldo – whose whole lives revolve around the majors.'

'Sure, but Faldo's game is suited to majors. I mean, in the majors the emphasis is suddenly put on straight driving and putting, and those are Faldo's strong points. Happens at every major – except maybe the British Open. The fairways are narrowed down so you've got to drive the ball very, very straight; the greens are faster; the pins are put in funny positions, tucked away so you can't hit your second shot close. And if you can't hit your second shot close, you don't make birdies, so you have to hit it straight and you have to hole putts. Those are the two strongest parts of Faldo's game. He may not say that, but I think most pros would say that those are his two big weapons: straight driving and very, very solid – if not brilliant – putting.'

'Do you think that some people's games are just suited to majors then?'

'Oh, there's no question about that.'

'You don't think they are exceptional players?'

'Well, you have to see how they do in the majors and how they do in the other tournaments. I mean, someone like Faldo does better in majors than he should, relative to the other tournaments. You know, majors require a particular type of game.'

'What motivates you to win?'

'Making a living, simple as that. I mean, there's a million reaons I could spout off, but really all the guys on Tour are very competitive people. You put them round a table playing tiddly-winks and they're going to try their balls off to win. If you don't have that attitude, you don't succeed on Tour.'

'Why is it that players who might swing as well as you do on the range aren't winners?'

'Because,' explains James, 'on the range you're standing in one place, in one wind, with one shot, with one rhythm. You hit ball after ball. Anyone can hit good shots doing that. It's when you go out on the course and you get a change of wind, change of shot, change of lie, change of feel, then it's a different ball game. Then your technique has to stand up to the changes. If it doesn't, you don't do well.

'That's why I think a lot of the coaches these days make the mistake of not seeing their pupils play enough. I know [David] Leadbetter doesn't see enough of his players on the course, and Bob [Torrance] finds it very difficult. And I think, if they don't it's a mistake, because all the bad shots come on the course. I can be on the range and Gavin says: "That's perfect." Go out on to the course, play terrible, and we'll come in and there's two or three things wrong that he hasn't spotted before. He can only see them on the course.

Practice means nothing. I mean, I can stand on the putting greens and hole four-footers all day, but I can go out on to the course and miss them all day.'

Gavin Christie has been coaching James since long before he came out on Tour. A man of few words, he teaches a tiny handful of players, all of whom he threatens with excommunication if they talk to the press about him or his method. Two years ago he came out on Tour to work with James. 'It's a long process,' says James. He is talking of the learning process that is pro golf. 'I wish I knew then [in 1976] what I know now. You just learn so much every extra couple of years you're on Tour and, of course, the older you get, the less likely you are to make use of it. I mean, I knew nothing about the swing for years after I turned pro. I think very few guys who have just come on Tour do. The shame is that more of the younger players don't ask the older guys for advice, because it really takes an awful long time to learn about what's going on.'

'What do you think the key to a good swing is?'

'The key to a good swing, I think, is the body turn. I think, once you've done that, you've virtually cracked it.'

'Gavin says that he doesn't believe there's any such thing as an unorthodox swing, which is what everybody says you've got.'

'Well, it depends what you compare it with. I mean, they said that Trevino wouldn't last and he's playing as well now as he's ever played. They said Nicklaus wouldn't last. People don't know what a good swing is, that's the trouble. It was obvious to anyone that knew anything about the golf swing that Trevino had a good swing. I mean, even I could see that in those days.'

Christie teaches the Hogan/Trevino method. He sees the swing as simply being the impact position – that it is absolutely essential that a player is in the right position at impact. James agrees that that is vital, but he sees the rest of the swing as being slightly more important than Christie does in actually achieving that.

'Do you think you've got to be mentally strong to be a winner?'

'That's what people say,' replies James, 'but I think you really have to look at how you perform under pressure. You know, people never analyse themselves under pressure. I've spoken to people about the mental side and they either overanalyse and think things are happening which are just unbelievable, or they just have no idea that anything happens out there under pressure, so they just don't bother. It's one or the other.'

By analysing your own game, James means that a player should ask himself why he hit a bad shot. If the answer is, 'Well, I wasn't really sure what I wanted to do', then the next time he finds himself in that situation, he should take his time, concentrate, make sure he only has one thought in his head, and then hit the shot. In his early years on Tour, James kept statistics on his game: fairways missed left or right, greens missed left or right, putts missed left, right, short, long, wind direction.

'It takes the whole year to build up anything of note statistically, but you can do it eventually. You may find out that your weak shot is a mid-iron in a left to right wind. Then you can go to the range and work out why. You might think: "Well, I'm trying to move it against the wind all the time and it doesn't feel comfortable. I'll try moving it with the wind instead of against it." You write it down in a notebook, and when you come out the next season you haven't forgotten all those thoughts. You read it every few weeks to refresh your memory, and at the end of the year you have another statistical summary, and you find out if it's done any good . . .

'These things are obvious, aren't they?' says James, and he is absolutely right. 'If you don't care enough about your performance to think of these things, you're really not trying, are you? I mean, half the guys don't work hard enough, they don't go to a coach and they don't discuss technique, anyway.'

Talking to the players, I can never get over how different they are, both in their approach to the game, and as people. 'Really,' I observe to James, 'the only common bond between any of you is golf.'

'And a sense of humour,' says James, who has one of the best. He is very intelligent and his wit has been honed to razor sharpness. 'If you don't have that, you might as well go home.'

'Do you think golf is the hardest sport?'

'Well, it's difficult to say but I think an individual sport has to be harder. You can never ride on the back of anybody else. You can't have a bad day in golf and come out a winner. And every week you've got to beat 149 other people. In a tennis tournament you have to beat six other people. That's why the top golfers don't win as often as an Edberg, or a Becker, or a Lendl.'

'What do you love most about golf?'

'I think, being out in the open air. I like being out in the weather.'

'What attracted you to the game?'

'Well, I started just because my dad played and I picked it up. And then once you start as a kid, if you keep improving, you carry on. When people find their level at any career, they lose their edge. I just kept going and improving, and then even when you turn pro, you're always striving to improve. If you stop improving at golf, you're going backwards. The standard's so high now that you can't sit on your backside and say, "Well, I'll just do the same thing this year." You have to have a list of about 20 things you're going to try to make yourself better.'

'Can you tell when you're going to peak?'

'No, I haven't the slightest idea. I just work so that hopefully I get to a high level as soon as possible, and I try and maintain myself on a good physical and mental basis for the rest of the year and hope that I don't have any real problems with my technique or putting.'

James has found that keeping fit is tremendously advantageous to his concentration, and his golf game in general. He does strenuous work-outs with weights and aerobic exercises at the local gym two or three times a week in the winter. His other pastimes out of season include snooker and gardening, and visiting friends such as Howard Clark. Last week when blizzards caused a power failure, Clark went up to the attic looking for a torch, fell off the ladder and, according to James, cracked his head open and lay there with his eyes rolling.

'I said to Beverley [Clark's wife] that his eyes often do that on the course,' remarks James sardonically. Poor Clark had to have 16 stitches.

'What appeals to you about gardening?' I ask James.

'I love watching plants grow, simple as that. You know, I like putting them in and I like eating my own vegetables. I enjoy being out in the open and I quite like just pottering around the garden on my own. It's nice to be away from things. It's relaxing.'

He's looking at his watch. He has to go and fetch Jane from the furniture shop in a few moments, and I have to catch a train. I've been here an hour and I haven't even got halfway through my questions. James is so good-humoured and interesting to talk to that you tend to go off on tangents all the time. I have one question I am determined to ask. 'Tell me something unusual about yourself,' I say to James, 'that people would be surprised to know.'

James think about it for a moment.

'Well, I have dreams where I'm on the bridge of the Enterprise with Captain Kirk and Spock and sometimes we have to land on an alien planet. And if we get into a bit of trouble, I have to bail them out. That's a dream I have quite often.'

He is perfectly serious. I remembered then that he was heavily into science fiction.

'Absolutely,' affirms James. 'Oh God, it's *Star Trek*, the next generation, tonight. Mustn't forget. Oh yeh, I'm right into science fiction. I read a fair bit and I watch it whenever I can.'

'What are your goals?'

'I don't really have any. My immediate goal is to make the next Ryder Cup.'

'If you gave up golf, what would you do?'

'Well, I've tried my hand at a little bit of commentary this year,' says James, standing up and looking around for his jacket, 'and I think I could do that. I'd like to design golf courses; I feel I could be good at that. I could be a gardener but it's tough enough doing my own. Apart from that . . . It's too late to be a racing driver.'

'Why do all golf pros love fast cars?'

'Because they all drive like maniacs,' says James, laughing, 'simple as that. The extra insurance premiums for pro golfers are justified, I can assure you. Not that I've ever had to claim.'

'Mark Roe was giving me a run down of all the cars he's crashed and how he's crashed them.'

'They're crazy, those guys [golf pros who drive like maniacs]. They're not afraid of dying, that's the trouble.'

Mark James pulls on his overcoat and heads out the door. He grins over his shoulder. 'That's why I think I would have made a good racing car driver. I am afraid of dying.'

Chapter Five

JOURNEYMEN

Photo: Lauren St John

The face of Ian Mosey: 'I never had the talent to be great'

FEBRUARY 1990, DUBAI. THE FACE OF IAN MOSEY IS WORLD-weary, weathered and unshaven. Unruly strands of hair escape from under his white cap, which he lifts by the brim when he pauses in practice to wipe away the sweat below. He has been on this practice ground since sunrise, only stopping for a coffee, and though his swing bears the raggedness of exhaustion he won't leave before dark. That is his commitment. He realises that only by reverting, at 39, to his boyhood regimen of endless practice, is he going to survive on the Tour.

'It's like starting again,' says Mosey ruefully. 'I'm like a rookie who wasn't good enough to play in the early 70s, and now my game isn't good enough to play in the 90s. If I want to continue playing, I have to work very hard at it.'

No other sport demands as much or gives as little in return. Golf makes room for so few élite that a player only has to be lacking in one single ingredient required in a champion – whether it be confidence, talent or determination – to be lost in the anonymity of the pack.

Players like Mosey, self-confessed journeymen, are golf's survivors. They have to be. Between them they bear the brunt of the blows the game deals, with less of the rewards that compensate the best players for the mental and physical hardships golf forces them to endure.

'I wouldn't think there's anyone who doesn't start out imagining that they're going to be a big star,' says David Jones, Mosey's friend and fellow-journeyman. 'But as you grow into it, you realise that it's not everybody who does and you can't set yourself deadlines and say, "If I don't win a tournament by such and such a time I'm going to stop." Because basically it's the love of the game that gets you into it in the first place. I mean, once you've been on the Tour a certain length of time the last thing you want is an ordinary job, even within golf. So you sort of amend your goals as you go along.'

Ultimate satisfaction in golf depends on a player's goals at the outset, whether he plays for money, glory or for the love of the game. Ian Mosey has always played for playing's sake. As he observes, the way to become a champion is to set your sights as high as you dare. To this day, Mosey has never raised his above the level of tournament player. His only claim to fame in a career spanning 18 years is victory in the Monte Carlo Open – the time it was rained out and cut to 36 holes. That might bother someone to whom winning tournaments is the ultimate goal, but not Mosey.

'I never had a problem with that,' he says, 'because although I used to tell people what I thought they wanted to hear, which was very positive, very ambitious, I really wanted to be a Tour player . . . I was never a talented ball player. I never had the talent to be great.'

Not everybody's dream is as small.

'Last year a journalist asked me whether I'd feel I'd failed if I never won a tournament,' says Tony Charnley, a slender, unassuming man of Mosey's era. 'I said no at the time, but really I would.'

Charnley, whose career best since turning professional in 1974 was a share of second place in the German Open ten years ago, had ambitions of being a top player when he started out on Tour. 'I wanted to win tournaments,' says Charnley, whose Dutch wife, Lucienne, has caddied for him since they were married. 'But when I started I thought I was a good player. Then I saw everybody else and I realised I wasn't very good at all.'

It took him a long time to learn to accept that, to adjust his expectations. Even now, he can't understand why he hasn't done better; he feels he is as good a player as anyone else on Tour.

'I have thought about giving up,' Charnley confesses quietly, 'but then it's hard to know what to do. I don't really want to be a club pro. Four years ago I had a terrible year and my game was so awful I just got to the point where I didn't look forward to going away to play. I went to see Eddie Birchenough and I asked him – it's a difficult question to ask somebody – to tell me whether I should give up playing.'

Birchenough, who is pro at Royal Lytham, took Charnley for a coffee and asked him exactly what he wanted out of the game. Then they went out on the range and worked on Charnley's swing. Charnley has been going to Lytham for lessons ever since. In that time he has moved from 89th on the money list in 1985 (£11,857) to 47th place in 1989 (£62,953).

'I can remember Gary Player saying that you get out of the game what you put into it,' says Charnley, who has always worked hard in the belief that the more he practised, the better he would get. 'People say to me, "You've done well", but I don't feel I've done as well as I should have done. I'm my own worst enemy. Because if I felt I'd done well, perhaps I'd be more satisfied with what I've got to show for it.'

The 36-year-old from Derbyshire, who bought his first home last year, sighs. 'Deep down I really like golf and I want to do well. But then there's times when I think this is such hard work, there must be easier things I could do. But I know if I didn't play, I'd be unhappy.'

'Because you wouldn't have achieved your goal,' his wife puts in gently.

It's easy to look at players like Mosey and criticise. There is a consensus among people ignorant in the ways of the game that those players who appear to be playing the game merely to make a living are just taking up space. It is not their lack of ability that is objected to, it is their attitude. They are the players who often appear to be more concerned with enjoying life than striving for perfection, who are least often on the practice ground and most often out on the town, conspicuous by their lack of dedication and drive.

'They all say that they would like to win,' says American Ron Stelton, a journeyman by most people's standards, 'but their actions don't prove to me that they do. They don't work as hard as winners do, they don't take it as seriously . . . Some guys find it very important to also have a good time, and if their definition of a good time means going out to the pub or a disco, then they're going to pay a price for that.'

A similar attitude prevails among journalists and observers of the game. David Jones, quite rightly, is angered by it. 'The press tend to see it as a young pro would see it. What is the point of being out there if you don't think you can win *at the very least*? What is the point of being out there *simply* trying to make a living? If you don't feel you can win a tournament there's something wrong with you if you actually continue to do it. It doesn't basically seem to occur to most of the press and the spectator public that a professional sportsman may regard "success" as leading a life that he gets a great deal of pleasure and enjoyment out of, and making a pretty good living at it. Success is seen purely in terms of money amassed and titles amassed.'

In a way, journeymen are victims of the structure of the pro game. Because tournament golf is one of the few professions where monthly earnings are publicised, it is easy to point a finger at people who seem to be taking things easy. But to my way of thinking, if a golfer has been on the European Tour for any length of time, he must, by definition, be a good player and he must be working hard. He is, after all, one of the top 120 players in Europe. Nobody is capable of staying competitive on the Tour today unless they are putting in the hours on the practice ground, because they risk losing their playing card and having to return to the School. Believe me, professional golfers still make money the old-fashioned way – they earn it. No one in golf escapes without paying their dues. It's the nature of the game.

As Jones points out, 'There are people who have amassed vast fortunes and a great number of titles, and yet are very discontented human beings. In fact, there are people who have been a huge success at the game, who appear to have abdicated their responsibility as normal human beings to be courteous and friendly towards people and lead a sociable life.

'Now I could look at that and say they're very successful golfers but they're not successful people. You have to recognise if you're involved in the sport as a journalist or spectator that you don't have to be a big winner . . . to be out competing and playing on the Tour. All you need is the desire to be out there getting whatever you want to get out of it . . .'

Within the narrow confines of how followers of the game perceive that a pro golfer should conduct himself, Jones, 43, born in Newcastle, County Down, has frequently been judged and found wanting. It has been said that if he practised harder, if he played more tournaments, if he was more dedicated, he would have done much better in his career.

'I've heard it said about many, many people. I've heard it said about Peter Alliss because he made a decision at one stage in his life that he could no longer handle the torture of being out there trying to compete when he hadn't got a putting stroke anymore. He diversified and went into broadcasting. I've heard it said that that's a cop-out. Well, I think that is absolute bullshit. Why does he have a responsibility to the people who write about golf and observe golf, to continue to torture himself because *they* think he should?'

Jones took up golf in his late teens and turned professional in 1967. He is the calmest and most wise person I know. On Tour he is regarded as a kind of mystic. He plays with great feeling for the game and for the love of it.

Yet even Jones, who has a balanced approach to most things and rarely allows himself to be influenced by the opinions of others, found himself believing at the age of 40 that he had reached a turning point in his career. A watershed. Without thinking why this should necessarily be, he started to look for options. He agreed to take on the position as Irish National Coach and began to do more company days and clinics. Now, three years on, having lost and regained his playing card, he does neither.

'I did realise then that this notion that the press and some of my friends were looking at me and saying, "Jesus, what *is* he still doing out there?" was making me start thinking that way. I suddenly thought: "Why the hell shouldn't I be out here?"

'So once I'd started getting over the idea that because I no longer thought of myself as a potential winner every week, I had no right to be out here, I decided I was out here to enjoy myself. And the more I enjoy myself, the better I play and the more money I make. So that's obviously the way to look at it, not the other way round.'

Longevity is the thief of motivation.

'It's a question of how long you can remain competitive,' observed Mark James once. 'I think a lot of players lose the desire. Players like Brian Barnes, for example; he wasn't old when he left the Tour. Because you have to work hard, you have to keep fit and you have to practise. You have to keep moving with the times or you get left behind. And I think, more than anything, you have to retain an innate keenness for the game, otherwise it becomes too much hard work to actually play.'

No one understands that better than Mosey. Over the years, the endless grind and repetition of tournament golf has worn him down. Each season he has slid a little further down the rankings, a little nearer to losing his card. In 1989 he found himself clinging to the brink of the abyss. His marriage broke up after 13 years and he came within a whisker of going to the Qualifying School for the first time in his life, missing 19 cuts in 26 tournaments.

'It's sad that I did get down last year because I played so badly,' Mosey says in retrospect, 'because of all the players out here, I love the life most. I wanted to be a Tour player. I've been playing 11 months of the year for 15 years and I've been thinking about nothing else for 23 years. From the age of 15, this is all I've ever done. To the exclusion of everything. I've got no business interests, I've got no contracts, I just play. That's all I ever do. Unfortunately, that got the best of me. I got tired and just lost a bit of enthusiasm. I lost my game as well – I don't know which went first.'

Mosey is uncompromising. It is an integral part of his character. After talking to friends at the end of last year he resolved to change his attitude, his swing and his practice routine. He started by kicking the habit many players have of flying home on Friday when he missed the cut, staying on at the tournament instead to hit balls. It was counter-productive. The intractability of his nature meant that, having thrown himself whole-heartedly into this new discipline, he found it desperately difficult to accept that it was going to fail.

'Mose is probably going through the phase that I went through a couple of years ago,' says Jones understandingly, 'where maybe it's hard to accept that you're not going to play as well as you've done in the past, and you find it hard, as I certainly do, to keep the work-rate up.

'Once you've been on Tour a certain number of years you need to get away from it, and you can't. It's a treadmill. The very thing that you need, which is a good sabbatical spell away, is the very thing you can't have. Because with the rankings we have now, if you take six months off, you come back and you're nowhere. You can't get into playing anything. So you're on this constant seesaw where, if you don't play, you're going to lose your ranking, and if you do play, you don't play well.'

So Mosey modified his routine. A coach once told him that he would gain more from playing than from hitting hundreds of practice balls. This spate of manic practising has borne out the theory. Mosey intends to go back to his old ways – at least as far as practice goes. But it isn't this which is worrying Mosey; it is the realisation that he has lost the main source of his motivation for golf: his love of the game.

Years ago a player accused Mosey of loving the competition more than he loved the game itself. At the time Mosey flatly denied it. Now he realises that the man was probably right. 'I think I played so much, I got it out of my system.'

'Mose says that because he played for such a long stint, he just put too much into it; he can't love it anymore,' says Jones, who recognises his friend's dilemma. 'I don't know. Maybe that's the way it is for him. There are other people who love the game enough to play every single week of their life . . . But you know, after 20 years you don't feel like beating balls for eight hours anymore. Well, if you're not going to do that it's harder to be competitive, and if it's harder to be competitive then you fall into this negative way of thinking. It happens to everybody.

'It's like me going out today and doing 81,' says Jones drily. 'I mean, after four or five holes I'm thinking, "Jesus, what a shit-hole this place is." Basically, I'm saying it just as an excuse for not trying. But the bottom line is I know this is what I want to do.'

Most journeymen live on hope. As cruel as golf might be, it is also a game of miracles and anyone can win at any time. Andrew Murray, a talented player stricken by Spondylitus (a crippling disease), inspired a generation of players when he won the European Open at Walton Heath in 1989, having led the tournament from start to finish. So did Chris Moody, unlikely winner of the European Masters at Crans Montana in 1988.

Moody is something of a legend as journeymen go. He has a unique ability (or liability) to antagonise the most placid people on Tour ('You mean I've got a perverse sense of humour'), a talent for practical jokes and a weakness for beautiful women which will probably be his downfall. A student of the Henry Cotton approach to golf (have the best to play your best), Moody lives like a millionaire on a relatively meagre income. 'I play like a millionaire as well,' says Moody with a disarming grin, 'like I don't need the money.'

In mid-Tour he is taking a four-week break to go skiing in Crans Montana, to visit his coach David Leadbetter in Florida, and to get in a few extra flying hours before he takes his licence. When he returns, his new Mercedes 300CE will be ready for collection.

Suave and smoothly attired, blond hair closely cropped, gold chain winking at his throat, Moody looks as at home in the luxuriant space-age splendour of the Emirates Golf Club as Mosey looks out of place. He reclines in his chair, delighted, as always, to be the centre of attention.

'In a way I was just afraid of working,' says Moody, sipping a fruit cocktail through a twirled straw and trying to recall his aspirations on leaving school. 'Golf, as you know, is a lot of work, but it's different. I was never career-minded. I used to go for job interviews and it used to feel like I was volunteering to be admitted to prison. I used to feel claustrophobic.'

So Moody tried his luck on the Tour for 15 years with limited success. David Leadbetter, Faldo's coach, was the catalyst in Moody's uneventful career.

'Ambition made me go to him,' admits Moody sheepishly, having just spent ten minutes drawing an analogy between Sheik Mohammed's money and playing golf to prove that he wasn't envious of better players. 'I looked at my game at the end of '87 and I thought, "With the game I've got I'm actually going nowhere." The previous three years I'd gone 50th, 60th, 70th in the Order of Merit, and all I could see was carrying on in the same vein.

'I just felt that I had struggled along enough, seeing people fiddling with this and working on that, and never really known what I was doing, and I thought, if I'm going to get a solid game, someone else is going to have to show me how to do it. It might be the end of my career because, at 34 years old, how can you teach an old dog new tricks, but it doesn't matter because I'm not getting rich anyway.'

Eight months and as many missed cuts later, he became European Masters Champion, 'I like the NIKE slogan,' says the irrepressible Moody. '"Just do it."'

April 1990, Cannes. Nowhere in professional sport is the disparity between best and least greater than in golf. Each day, on the same golf course, millionaires and paupers play side by side. Mosey (whose career earnings at the end of 1990 were £291,344) and Ian Woosnam (whose earnings after 1990 were £2,061,738), practising next to one another in Cannes was a graphic illustration of the contradictions of the game.

Mosey's white shirt was crumpled and sweaty, his trousers baggy, his face unshaven. His mouth, shaded by the peak of his baseball cap, was set in grim determination. On the ground lay his slim green carry bag, clubs array and still grimy from practice. He had no caddie that week.

Beside him, Woosnam looked sleek and well-fed, immaculately turned out in a cream cashmere pullover and tailored trousers, every spare inch of clothing and equipment endorsed. His swing was smooth and effortless. He stared critically after each towering one-iron shot. Even Philip (Wobbly) Morbey, his caddie, polishing the club Woosnam had just used, appeared more prosperous than Mosey.

Mosey hit a shot fat. He bent down and gathered his clubs; the smile he gave me was weak. 'Well, if that's how it's going to be,' he said, 'I'm going to try putting.'

A hundred identical situations can be sketched. In any other walk of life such contrasts would create a breeding ground for resentment. On the Tour, nothing could be further from the truth. There is little jealousy or off-course rivalry between players. As desperately as each golfer wants to win for himself, he feels glad for anyone else who does.

But the endless toil and grind of golf without reward can have the effect of a water torture on the soul. Bitterness can creep up on a player before he realises it's there.

'What you've got to remember,' says David Jones, 'is that as journeymen pro golfers we've had ten or 15 years of being treated well, treated in many places that we go to like celebrities, following the sun, being able to do within reason exactly what we please, where and when we please, work hard when we want to, be lazy when we want to . . . Now there's not many people in that position and making money at it. So you've got to offset the dark sides that make you embittered against the positive sides.'

Mosey, born in Keighley, Yorkshire, hedges any questions on whether he harbours any resentment towards the top players by pointing out that the school he attended was concerned less with education than producing 'factory fodder'; that of all the children he grew up with, he made the most of the limited opportunities available to him. 'They knew they were going to do menial jobs and have dead-end lives. They knew that when they were 15. That was what the system did to them.'

In the manner of a boy who runs away to join the circus, Mosey escaped to follow his dream of playing the Tour.

More than most people, Mosey misses the good old days. It delights him to recollect how, for years, fish and chips were his staple diet, how everyone travelled by caravan or car, how little it was possible to spend at each tournament. 'My values are rooted in the wrong place for this lifestyle. I still think a pound is a lot of money.'

For him it was a great adventure.

'The job was to be out on Tour; to find a way of getting to the tournament. It wasn't getting on a plane and checking into a five-star hotel, then going out and winning £10,000.'

Even the bad old days seem pretty good to Mosey. He can recall playing the Madrid Open one year when the hotel was an hour's drive from the course and there was only one bus a day: at six a.m. The players used to arrive at the course in darkness, and there they would have to sit on their golf bags until the caretaker arrived to open the clubhouse. First tee-off times were ten minutes after sunrise. Dew-sweepers went off without breakfast or hitting a single warm-up shot.

One of the tournaments Mosey dreaded most was the Spanish Open, played at La Manga, which at that time was nothing more than a wind-tunnel of empty concrete blocks built on a strip by the sea. In early April it was still bitterly cold and there was nothing for the players to do. Most days Mosey got by on a couple of oranges and a piece of cheese because he couldn't afford the restaurant at the golf club.

He was quietly eating his snack in the locker room one morning when the attendant, an aggressive Spaniard who spoke no English, began to abuse him. 'I actually lost my mind,' recalls Mosey. 'I said, "Look, what do you want me to do? I can't afford the restaurant and you've shut the snack bar; I just want to have my orange." And in the end he fetched the manager who pacified him. But basically, it was like, "This club is not for people like you." I remember feeling really unhappy about that, because there was just no accommodation for the journeyman pro.'

Mosey's frank, unpretentious manner is his most endearing quality. He makes no excuses for being the way he is; offers no apologies for being careful or for dwelling on the past.

'What I'd like to know,' remarks one player, 'is how Ian Mosey can still be wearing Musingwear shirts when they haven't been dished out for eight years. And why they still look so good?'

The answer is in Mosey's garage.

Phil Harrison brought up the subject one evening in Montpelier. Mosey, it seems, cherishes possessions in the same way he cherishes memories. His garage at his home in Sunningdale is a miniature pro shop, an Aladdin's cave of golf equipment. The walls are lined with boxes of unused shoes, sweaters, shirts, balls and golf clubs. Even the Footjoys that he saved up to buy when he first came out on Tour are there. They cost £27 at a time when you could buy a pair of shoes for a fiver and he just couldn't bring himself to wear them. The shirts are still wrapped in their polythene covers. 'Well,' says Mosey, fielding our gentle ribbing shyly, 'as soon as you take a shirt out of the plastic it just becomes another rag that you put in the washing machine.'

For most of us, the Tour has an addictive quality as strong as that of any drug. David Jones admits he hadn't realised how hard it would be to relinquish it until he came face to face with the spectre of losing his card.

Mosey knows it already, but realises that he may have no choice in the matter unless his game improves. And because he has always relished the insularity of life on Tour and by choice has become reclusive, he now finds himself without contacts or contracts. These are things he could have taken advantage of when he played very well from 1980 to '86, but was so wrapped up in the game at the time he chose not to. As such, he has made no provision for the second half of his life.

He doesn't know the names of anyone on the periphery of golf: the reporters, the reps, the officials. When I approached him about an interview, he eyed me with deep suspicion and questioned me for a long time about what I was looking for. After ten minutes of assurances, he suddenly snapped: 'But who are you?'

'I don't think I'm that strange,' he says frankly, as though it's something he's given a great deal of thought to. 'It's just a life where people aren't necessary and I've got used to doing without people.'

On halcyon blue days like this, it is very easy to understand how a player can make a life out of pursuing an indeterminate goal.

Mosey's mood is buoyant, at once reflective and cautiously optimistic. In thinking of the past he is reminded of the reasons he chose to travel this long and winding road all those years ago. He tips himself back in the chair he dragged into the shade, so that the sunshine falls on his face, on the dark shadow around his jaw and the wry smile in his grey-green eyes.

'I think only time will tell whether I regret it. I do know for sure I only had one little self-doubt which must have been in about 1978. I had already been at it a long time and I was still pre-qualifying. I was on a long drive down from Newcastle, with no prospect of making any money and getting used to not making any money, and I thought: "Am I doing the right thing with my life?"

'I took about a day to think it through and in the end what I thought was, if I got to 40 and I was still a pro, if I knew that I'd tried very hard to get what I wanted, had a dream and followed a dream, well, I could live with that. Even if I'd made no money, I'd at least grow old knowing that I'd had a go at my one big ambition. A full-blooded go. I mean, everything brushed aside to be a Tour player. I had two bad years after that and then I started playing well, but I never thought about it again. I knew all along I could live with it either way.'

Chapter Six

LESSONS IN LIFE

Photo: ASP, Stuart Franklin

Perfection: Nick Faldo in full flight

VOLVO PGA CHAMPIONSHIP, WENTWORTH, MAY 1990. I LOVE the practice range. Given a choice between going out on the course in the early rounds of a tournament or playing golf myself, I'd choose the range every time. That's why my favourite days are practice days. In spring and summer they are the longest: hazy blue days given over to the exploration of the mysteries of the golf swing, to experimentation, to hours of idleness and talk.

The best time to get to the golf course is early, when the dew is still heavy on the ground and all the normal practice ground rituals are in progress: the scrubbing of grips and clubs; the emptying of golf bags, replacing old gloves and balls with new and packing rain suits, matching sweaters, Mars bars and fruit; the marking of golf balls with individual patterns; the cleaning of grooves with tee pegs; and the heavy clatter of range balls being washed and put into separate buckets.

All down the line, players will be loosening up. They might swing two clubs or put a club behind their back, loop their arms over it and twist. Most golfers start by hitting a few chip shots, work their way through alternate clubs to their drivers, and finally practise pitching and putting. Some players, such as Ballesteros, for example, like to warm up for an hour or more before going out on the course. Others, like Russell Claydon, the robust and easy-going rookie who ran second to Greg Norman in the 1989 Australian Masters, might only hit balls for ten or 20 minutes, just long enough to loosen their muscles before they play.

Walking slowly down the line, listening to comments passed and advice given, you can learn as much about the players as people as you can about their golf swings.

Today, like every day, Jose Maria Olazabal is locked into his own concentration zone, oblivious to the range malarky. Only Nick Faldo matches this level of practice ground absorption.

'How come you're hitting the ball so far now?' asks Mark McNulty, who was warming up beside him, as he pulls on his glove and prepares to go to the tee. He watches the Spaniard propel drive after perfect drive into the blue yonder.

'*Now?*' says Olazabal without looking up, and that one word speaks volumes.

Dave Musgrove, Sandy Lyle's caddie, has cleaned Lyle's clubs and is waiting for him to put in an appearance. He puts down his cloth and comes over. 'I've got a priceless exhibit here,' he says, and with the air of a conjurer produces a brown leather pouch from behind his back. Inside it is a used tee. 'Found it on the practice tee last week,' he says conspiringly. 'First one he's ever left.'

'Keeps them on strings,' someone commented wryly.

Musgrove put it carefully back in the pouch. 'Hey,' he said suddenly, as if a thought had just occurred to him. 'You don't suppose he left it there on purpose?'

Over a period of time, you get to know who hits the most practice balls (Vijay Singh) and who works hardest on their game (Bernhard Langer), which players have perfect practice ground swings but can't take their range game out on to the course, and which players can still return a reasonable score no matter how much they are struggling to hit the ball on the range. Every player out there is working on something, whether it be their equipment or swing. They might be trying to find the cause of a hook or a cut, wrestling with a putting problem, or just trying to recapture a feeling they had when they played their best golf.

For some the answer is a guru – mental or physical. Others have no need or want for either.

Vijay Singh, the Tour's only black golfer, has only ever been to one teacher and that's Vijay Singh. 'That's the way I started to play and I don't see why I should change. Why should I change my swing when it brought me all the way here?'

The tall Fijian, winner of the 1989 Volvo Open in Sardinia, the El Bosque Open early this year, and six titles on the Safari, Asian and Swedish circuits, is a believer in basics: to draw the ball, hit it right of the target; to fade the ball, hit it left.

'I think people get so confused with golf swings. A lot of people are out there right now doing a lot of things they don't even understand. Just because it's coming from a teacher, they're following it – even a lot of good players. That's why I haven't changed and why I'll never change. I think I have a pretty good swing and it's all mine, you know.'

Peter Mitchell agrees. 'People on Tour make the swing so complicated you need a science degree to understand it.'

'I think you've got to understand your golf swing,' says Australian Rodger Davis, unusual among the top players because he doesn't see a teacher at all. 'I don't think it's a good idea that you should be going to your coach every week, because all of a sudden you're not learning anything about your own golf swing. There are certain ways that you will play and there are certain ways that I will play, and in your mind it will be totally different even though it looks the same. I mean, I'm a firm believer that out there when you're under the heat, you can't go to your coach week in and week out. You've got to have enough confidence to know where your faults are, what they are, when they start to happen, and how to fix them.'

But often a player will go to a regular coach for reasons other than technical: to spot small swing flaws before they develop into major faults, for example, or boost his confidence. Grant Turner, the 1990 Zimbabwe Open Champion and Florida State marketing graduate, knows that he can ring Bob Torrance any time of the day or night and Torrance will reassure him and advise him on swing problems over the phone. Turner himself feels that the simple approach is the best approach in golf.

'The basic fundamentals are true for everybody. Plus keeping your head still. I think, that's the most basic fundamental. You can have everything else right and move your head and it's still not going to work.'

'Rhythm,' says Richard Boxall when asked for the key to a good golf swing. He clambers out of a practice bunker and knocks the clubhead against his golf shoe to remove the sand. 'I've only ever had three lessons,' explains the loquacious winner of this year's Italian Open, 'so I'm not really into the swing. I get tips every now and then, but I just try to keep it low (low to the ground on the takeaway) and slow. Just try to keep it as simple as possible. That's the best way.'

Irishman Eamonn Darcy is lunging energetically at the golf ball at the far end of the range. At first glance, his unorthodox method and flying right elbow appear to contradict every known swing theory, but his basic fundamentals and position at impact are almost identical to that of the best copybook swingers on Tour.

'The key to a good swing is rhythm and getting the club-face square when you hit the ball,' says Darcy, winner of 11 tournaments. There are few better ball strikers in golf. He thinks that people tend to concentrate too hard on the aesthetics of a golf swing and not hard enough on how they hit the ball. 'You have to be able to repeat it. You see so many guys who appear to have good-looking swings on the practice ground, but they can't repeat it on the course. I think that's probably because they lose their rhythm. It doesn't really matter how it looks as long as it works.'

His whole game is based on the rhythm principle.

'A lot of the good players,' explains Darcy, 'even if they don't swing the club textbook, they appear to have a lot of time to hit the ball. That's the secret of playing good golf. Timing.'

Wentworth, Wednesday, 22 May 1990. 'Generally speaking,' said Ben Hogan in *The Modern Fundamentals of Golf*, 'a teacher is no better than his pupil's ability to work and learn.'

In Nick Faldo, David Leadbetter found the perfect disciple. Rarely has there been a player with such infinite faith in his own and his teacher's ability, that he was prepared to put his future in the hands of that mentor and undergo the most exacting kind of physical and mental testing imaginable in order to achieve his goals. Leadbetter can recall Faldo's determination on arrival in Florida in May 1985, having made the irrevocable decision to rebuild his swing no matter how long it took. 'He said to me: "I don't want to win ordinary tournaments, I want to win major championships, and the first thing I want to win is the Open."'

At the age of 31, Faldo was, by most people's definition, a very successful golfer. A glowing amateur career had been followed by 11 victories in Europe, one in South Africa and, in 1984, his first win on the US Tour – the Heritage

Classic. But to Faldo all the accolades in the world were worthless if he failed to measure up in the ultimate examination of a golfer: the major championships. Three times in 1984 Faldo had come close to winning a major – in the US Masters, in the Open Championship and in the USA PGA – and three times his swing had collapsed under the pressure of the closing rounds.

A lesser player, reassessing his performance that year, might have been satisfied merely to have been in contention in three out of four major championships (the fourth being the US Open Championship). He might have seen these last-round misfortunes as part of a learning process. Not Faldo. He knew for certain – if no one else did – that the golf swing he had, as picture-perfect and rhythmic as it looked, would never make him the best player in the world. In Faldo's mind there was only one way to reach the top, and that was to find a teacher talented enough to strip his golf swing down and rebuild it from scratch. In December 1984 at Sun City in Southern Africa, he met the man he was looking for.

'I think he just realised where he could get to with my help,' says Leadbetter now, looking back at that time. 'We saw a glimpse in the early stages of his change and he just wanted it all. He wasn't satisfied with second best. He's very, very strong mentally. That's his good trait, obviously. There's a lot of people with good golf swings who really aren't able to apply themselves, because they don't have a strong enough mental attitude.'

'Is that what makes him the best?'

'Absolutely. He's very strong-willed and very determined and very single-minded in what he wants to do. He's a champion.'

But the world was aghast at Faldo's decision. They doubted the absolute sanity of any player who wanted to change what was ostensibly a sound technique – he had, after all, won five tournaments in one year with it – sacrificing whole seasons of his career in the short term, on the conjecture that a new swing would help him to win major championships in the long term. What if it failed? What if he wasted all those years when he could, conceivably, be winning a whole host of 'ordinary tournaments', and came back and major victories continued to elude him? What then?

Five years and four major championship victories down the road, Faldo has proved once again that when it comes to his career he almost always makes the right decision.

But could Faldo have become a great player with his other swing? That is the question still under debate. Leadbetter argues not. 'He was very limited in what he could do. He couldn't keep the ball down. He was quite a scoopy type of player. He used his hands a lot more than he should have done. You know, he's tall and a bit gangly, though he's very strong, and the problem was that he had a lot of wasted motion in his swing. As good as his rhythm looked and smooth as his swing looked, it was fairly inefficient with all the wasted movement. He would overuse his legs, overuse his hands and there was a lot of timing involved.'

These swing flaws caused Faldo to struggle in strong winds. The shots he hit were not penetrating ones, but high and floating shots that would be caught by the wind and pulled off line. 'That was the thing that was hurting him,' explains Leadbetter, who told Faldo that if he wanted to win the Open he was going to have to learn to flight the ball lower. 'So that really was the main purpose. That's what a good player can do with a good swing, control the golf ball, and as a result the winds aren't going to affect it so much.'

But in order to make that transition, it was necessary for Faldo to start again from scratch. He had to turn his back on the most barbed and spiteful criticism, as he slid from first to 12th to 42nd on the money list. He had to swallow his pride and enter voluntarily into the nightmare of playing badly, so that he might one day play well, hit 1,500 balls daily until his hands bled, and still maintain a full European playing schedule.

In 1987 Faldo reaped the ultimate reward for his efforts. When the mists came down and the wind and rain made a sorceress out of Muirfield, he made 18 straight pars to win the Open Championship.

It was as much a triumph for Leadbetter as it was for his pupil. The English-born golf professional, brought up in Zimbabwe, had turned to teaching after several unsuccessful years as a tournament player. When he agreed to take Faldo on, he knew that because of Faldo's extraordinary talent and the controversy which surrounded his swing change, the success of his own career would hang in the balance. They would stand or fall together.

In a way, teachers, like golf swings, come in and out of fashion. If a player, or a group of players, is doing well under a particular teacher, then everyone wants to go to him and everyone wants to swing like his players. Leadbetter, who at 37 is relatively young to be a world-class teacher, only really became famous when Faldo won the Open, although he had been teaching successful players like Nick Price, Mark McNulty, Dennis Watson and David Frost from very early on in their careers.

American Rick Hartmann first went to see Leadbetter in 1985 on the recommendation of Watson and South African Gavin Levenson (nicknamed 'Legs' because of his superb leg action). Leadbetter took one look at his swing and suggested a complete restructuring to achieve a simpler movement and put the swing back on plane. Five years later Hartmann's swing is only now beginning to approach Leadbetter's initial vision for it, and is repaying Hartmann's labours with consistency.

Two things have changed since the 32-year-old New Yorker began to see Leadbetter. The first is his coaching fee. Starting out as a golf teacher and trying to make a name for himself, Leadbetter made money coaching amateurs and taught professionals for free. Nearly a decade later, Leadbetter, who commands up to $6,000 for company days and clinics, still teaches his original pupils for nothing, but has established a fee structure for any new pupils he takes on.

'David, basically, is not a businessman whatsoever,' says Hartmann. Leadbetter has that in common with Bob Torrance, who once accepted a couple of boxes of golf balls from American, John Slaughter, in payment for lessons. 'I just set up a percentage of what I made, and that was just something I wanted to do because it's so hard to give money to him. Even when I tried to give money to him sometimes, he wouldn't take it.'

The other thing that has changed is the size of Leadbetter's teaching operation. At the time Hartmann started he still had a manageable number of professional pupils. His original clients excepted, the Leadbetter stable of winners today includes Scott Simpson, Howard Clark, Bob Tway, Sandy Lyle, Chris Moody and Anders Forsbrand, to name but a few.

'The problem now is the time factor,' admits Leadbetter, a health and fitness fanatic who runs and works out for 40 minutes every morning. 'So many players want to see me and I haven't got the time to devote to every player I'd like to.' As a consequence, he is in the business of training other coaches; two in America and one in Britain – Denis Pugh, based at Quietwaters golf club. Players who can't see Leadbetter will see them, and 'I will cast my eagle eye over them as and when I have the time.'

'It's a difficult situation, teaching,' says Hartmann, understanding Leadbetter's dilemma, but being more concerned about the detrimental effects it has periodically had on his game, as well as his confidence. 'Golfers in any form are demanding, whether it's Faldo, or Frank Nobilo or myself. Everyone wants to be treated as someone special, and obviously if you're not, then it's going to be cause for conflict.'

A week ago, Hartmann called Florida and spoke to Leadbetter's secretary. At his office, pandemonium reigned. 'This is supposed to be our quiet period,' the fraught woman told him, but between commercials, videos, books, interviews and lessons, Leadbetter didn't have a blank page in his diary.

'It's difficult for him to keep everything going smoothly,' says Hartmann, who has written several frustrated letters to Leadbetter, 'and to be honest, he can't. He's going to upset people with the amount of time he gives certain players, and this and that. I've had many discussions with him about it and been really pissed off with him about it. Sometimes he's not aware of the situation. You know, he doesn't do it on purpose. He's not that kind of a guy. But he's the kind of guy who can't say no if someone who doesn't even work with him comes up to him and says, "David, can you have a look at me?" He'll go and take a look and that's taking time away from someone else. Now that's his fault. He shouldn't do that.'

Training coaches to teach his swing principles might ease the situation but it won't eradicate it. Denis Pugh, for example, may be an excellent teacher in his own right, but he's not 'the best in the world', as Faldo has called Leadbetter.

'What makes him the best? I reckon it's his eye,' says Hartmann. 'I think his eye is incredible. It's a very special thing . . . he knows where he wants the club and he knows it quickly. And after he's worked with someone a long time he knows their swing so damn well; I mean, I could tell him something on the phone – where the divot's going or where the ball's going – and he knows what's wrong. David's very thorough in what he does. He keeps notes on everyone who goes to him. He's got a file on *everything*.'

Leadbetter's ideas are based on observation and experimentation on himself and other players, on the research which has been done on the kinesiological aspects of the swing, and on feedback from pupils.

'I don't like to say I have a method because I really try to work with individuals on an individual basis, case by case. But basically, I work a lot on balance in a golf swing and I work on setting up to the ball, which I think is pre-eminent for every golfer, never mind a Tour player. And from there really allowing the body to control what the hands are doing in the swing. I like to see as simple a swing as possible because I think the simpler the swing the more chance it has of repeating, and especially under pressure. So I like the hands and arms to pretty much react to what the body's doing, rather than the old thought of the hands and arms controlling the swing.'

One aspect of Leadbetter's teaching in particular highlights the differences between Faldo and other players. Drills. The miniature rehearsals of the golf swing, which Leadbetter believes create feel and muscle memory. 'A lot of players just take a drill and work on it and then go out and play, whereas Nick is constantly thinking about it and he'll work on it afterwards. He's always focusing on it and trying to fine tune it . . .

'You see, to play golf well,' explains Leadbetter, 'you have to have a feel for what you're doing. In other words, you can't think it. You have to have a sensation. So the drills really allow a player when he is practising to know that as long as he is working on them, he is probably doing the right thing as far as his golf swing is concerned. And hopefully, with a bit of practice, it will become instinctive.'

'That's what you want,' agrees Hartmann. 'Dave's the first one to say he doesn't want you thinking about six things when you swing, because it's impossible to think at that rate. I find it impossible to think about one. Faldo can get away with thinking about more, but Faldo's a very unusual case. I personally don't think he's a good example – that's my opinion – because of all the drills he goes through. For an average golfer to see him do that on the course and think they can do it is wrong. I don't think that's come across yet.'

It is also his opinion that this particular part of Leadbetter's teaching is going to be harmful to the game, for the simple reason that amateurs will learn by example. 'Faldo can do drills; not everyone can. I don't know anyone who can do them. David Frost is a very analytical guy so he can't get away with doing them. Faldo must not be analytical at all, or he must be able to shut it off somehow. But then he's got such a strong mind. That's his strongest point.'

He can remember playing with Faldo in the midst of his swing change. 'He couldn't get it near the course. There's no way he could go from one extreme to the other if he didn't have such a strong mind.'

'Really, to have a great golf swing you need to be fairly athletic,' says Leadbetter, responding to the criticism that a lot of amateurs and professionals are unable to imitate his method at all. 'Obviously, it's tough for everybody to swing in this way, and some people can only adopt part of my philosophy as far as what I think should take place. But there's many golfers out there who, if they understood what actually propelled the golf ball and how they could use their body in the most efficient manner, would be able to hit the ball better and have more fun.'

Few players understand their own golf swing as well as Leadbetter's best pupil does.

This morning in the press centre Faldo told us that his leg action is still a recurring problem. 'My hip action gets too excessive on the backswing. It doesn't resist enough to create torque.' He informs us of this with relish. There's nothing Faldo likes more than expending his energy on ironing out swing flaws.

I watched them working on the range later. The tall, gaunt figure of Leadbetter in familiar pose – legs astride, arms folded and eyes shaded by his baseball cap – watching over Faldo.

'What we're really working on now,' says Leadbetter, 'is trying to keep him solid and firm, keep his legs secure, and really get his body working efficiently. You know, it's not the easiest game when you're tall. It's much better when you're Ian Woosnam's height and your sense of gravity is low; there's a lot less to go wrong. People say it's nice to be tall, you've got a nice wide swing arc. But it also causes problems with inconsistency.'

On the practice ground the differences in his approach to each player and his awareness of the importance of psychology in teaching are immediately apparent. With Faldo, he has an almost telepathic communication. Neither says much. Leadbetter might squat down and hold Faldo's legs, or touch a knee occasionally, but for the most part, there is only that silent assessment of each shot until a tacit verdict is reached.

With Sandy Lyle – who has finally decided to put his fate in one teacher's hands – Leadbetter is reassuring, sensitive to the Scotsman's distress. He repeatedly demonstrates movements through the swing. After 18 months of struggling Lyle is frustrated and his frustration is renewed with each shot. At one point he rams the wood he is using back into the golf bag. Leadbetter's tone is calm and soothing. He allows Lyle to pick out a club he feels comfortable with.

How difficult it must be to teach the hardest game in the world to the world's best players.

'It's an extremely difficult game to teach sometimes, because you're dealing with players' moods and the way they feel. I guess,' says Leadbetter, 'a sign of a good teacher is knowing what to say and when to say it.'

But as Hogan said, a teacher is only as good as his pupil's ability to apply himself, and even that is not enough if he doesn't inspire confidence in the player. 'There has to be a certain chemistry between a teacher and a player for it to work,' explains Leadbetter. With Faldo and Leadbetter, all of these elements combined to produce a major champion.

'Do you think it is possible for you to win the Grand Slam?' Faldo was asked this morning.

'Sure it's possible. It's just very difficult.'

'But it's not a realistic probability, is it?' probed the reporter.

An unfamiliar look of hurt crossed Faldo's face.

'I feel it is,' he said. 'I feel it's possible.'

So does Leadbetter.

Without any shadow of doubt, the biggest single contributing factor in their joint success is Faldo's unshakable conviction that with Leadbetter's help he will get to where he wants to go.

'Because he believes in him,' says Rodger Davis, 'mentally he's now a different person on the golf course. And once you've got a strong mind, I wanna tell you, it's pretty hard for anyone to beat you.'

Even at his absolute lowest ebb, Faldo remained tunnel-visioned. He never ever lost sight of his goal, and he never lost faith in his teacher. 'It takes a lot of discipline and fortitude to do that,' says Leadbetter in admiration. The respect is mutual. Faldo might be the greatest advertisement on earth for Leadbetter's credentials as a golf teacher, but he is also Leadbetter's greatest personal reward.

'He's come such a long way,' says Leadbetter with pride. 'I mean, he was always a good player, but he's turned into a great player. Arguably, the world's best. He's got so much good golf left in him – so far to go. A lot more majors on the cards.'

Thursday, 24 May 1990. Smoke curls between the brown, tobacco-stained fingers of Bob Torrance and leaves trails in the air as he gesticulates.

'I think weight transference is very important,' he is saying in the gravel voice of a lifelong addict. 'I would possibly say that that's the most important part of it. A lot of people talk about tempo in the golf swing. Tempo is nothing to do with the speed you swing the club at. If tempo is the speed you swing the club at, then Hogan had none because he swung the club so fast, and Snead had everything because he swung the club so slow. Tempo is the backswing flowing into the downswing and that is the crossroads of golf. If you can get that move correct then I reckon you're 90 per cent there.'

Once an alcoholic, Torrance is now a workaholic, preaching to a growing number of converted on the European Tour. Where Leadbetter might only see his pupils three or four times a year, Torrance follows the Tour throughout the season; but between them they teach more players than all the other coaches combined. The list of players now beating a path to the Torrance school of instruction is long and distinguished – David Feherty, Anders Sorenson, Phillip Walton, Tony Johnstone, Peter Baker, and so on – but like David Leadbetter, the Scotsman's reputation as a teacher was founded on just a couple of players: his son, Sam Torrance, and Welshman Ian Woosnam.

What are the swing principles of the best golf coach in Europe?

'Well, the most important thing to start with is the set-up and posture,' explains Torrance, who does a lot of preliminary work before taking on a player. He has to establish what a player wants from him and where he wants to go, and whether or not they agree on swing method. 'There's a lot talked about the grip, which I think is very important, but not as important as some people say it is. If it works, that's all that matters. The backswing is the most important, because if you don't load the gun then you can't pull the trigger. You can play good golf all your life with backswing thoughts only. You can't win with downswing thoughts.'

In Torrance's classroom one maxim prevails: 'Never weaken the strong to strengthen the weak.' One of Torrance's theories is that a coach should always work on the strongest points in a golfer's swing instead of concentrating on eliminating the flaws. This is where he comes into his own, in his approach to unconventional methods. He doesn't, for example, believe that crossing the line at the top with the club is a fault if it works.

'Why is it a fault? You can do five wrongs and one right and be a great player. And you can do five rights and one wrong and you couldn't play. Trevino did five wrongs and one right.'

Another Torrance precept is that the method must fit the golfer and not the golfer the method. 'You really can't teach two people the same thing. I mean, Ian Woosnam's five-foot five and Nick Faldo's six-foot five. How can you teach those two people the same thing? The two greatest golfers that ever lived were Ben Hogan and Jack Nicklaus and their swings were poles apart. So who's right and who's wrong? You've got to work along these lines.'

In this game Woosnam's height has been as big an advantage as it would have been a disadvantage in most others. It's because he is so small and so strong that he has a swing which is unique in golf for its compact simplicity and the power which it generates.

'The thing about Ian's swing is there's no bits and pieces to it,' says Torrance.

'I always feel that a good golf swing looks free and that it flows. There's no bits and pieces here, it just flows.'

If Woosnam has one recurring fault then it is pushing the ball out right. 'The effort I'm putting in to try and hook it is unbelievable,' he said when I questioned him about it. 'Whereas before I used to draw it when I was trying to fade it, now I'm trying to hook it just to make it draw slightly. I've had it for two and half years now. I can't figure out what it is.'

'What does Bob think might be causing it?'

'He doesn't seem to know what it is either. It's something very minor. I'll get it one of these days.'

But overall his game is good. Starting out, Woosnam was a streak player, shooting a string of low scores and then struggling for a fortnight. 'Now I might go through a day or two when I'm playing badly, then I'll get it back quickly. I know what to do with my swing pretty well to get it back. Some other lads, they haven't got a clue. That's the trouble with having teachers; you've got to have them around you all the time to sort you out. But when you can do it yourself, you can put yourself right very quickly.'

'Don't you rely on Bob, then?'

'I don't really listen to Bob,' said Woosnam. 'Not a lot. I have him there now and then to see what he thinks. He's more like a video camera to me – to tell me how I've got my left wrist, and everything. Because everything he says to me, really, I know. Some of the things he says to me I disagree with, so I don't listen to it. But he might just say something. He's mainly a good confidence booster, you know. He'll say, "You're playing well", and that sort of thing.'

One thing that all Torrance's pupils agree on is his ability to make a player feel good about himself.

'You must give time to building a person's confidence,' says Torrance firmly, 'especially if he's not playing so well. If he's playing well you don't need to build his confidence because he's got that anyway.'

'Bob knows what he's talking about and he communicates it well,' says Grant Turner, who has worked with Torrance for the last two and a half years. 'And he's very keen as well. He's not like some coaches where you're just a way of making money and they don't really care. I mean, he does care a lot.'

On the table in the crowded golf club bar, the black Guinness is almost gone. Torrance flicks his ash in the general direction of the ashtray. He considers the role of the golf coach as a psychologist.

'Well,' he says, 'I just say to most of my players if they're in contention for the tournament, I say, "Look, these are the happiest days of your life. Why don't you go out and enjoy it."'

Dusseldorf, August 1990. At the far end of the practice ground is the Mizuno caravan. Most days clubmaker Barry Willett will be standing in his customary position at the top of the stairs, cigar in hand, still smiling about the previous evening, doubtlessly spent in the company of the Japanese technicians – none of whom speak more than a few words of English – in the best local bar or restaurant. Willett likes to keep one eye on his workshop and the other on the range. That way he knows exactly what changes a player has made to his clubs and he can see how he hits the ball with them afterwards.

On the face of it, golf as a game has changed little since Old Tom Morris won the Open at Prestwick in 1861. The only real differences lie in the amount of time modern players spend on the practice range, the advancements made in our understanding and knowledge of the golf swing, and the research which has led to a technical revolution in golf equipment. Golf has become an exacting science.

Recognising the importance of these three things, and realising that they were the main reasons for the rapid development of golf on the other side of the Atlantic, Neil Coles made the assertion some years ago that there would never be any depth on the European Tour until the players worked harder on their games. And as far as he could see, they would never work harder on their games until practice ground facilities were improved. It was Coles' idea that good range balls should be supplied and collected so that players no longer had to bring their own or send their caddie – who might have already spent four or five hours out on the golf course – out to fetch them. It was his idea that there should be a purpose-built practice range at every tournament, and his idea that there should be an equipment van on Tour full-time, with professional clubmakers on board, capable of making every conceivable adjustment, repair, shaft change and grip change possible to the players' clubs.

In 1985, after years of searching for a financial backer, the first equipment van, custom-built and sponsored by Mizuno, came out on the circuit. The response surpassed all expectations. In the first week Willett, and three highly trained Japanese assistants, worked over 14 hours a day. Now, five years later, Taylor-made and Wilson have followed suit with their own equipment vans.

'I think players were aware of equipment before that,' says Willett, unanimously known as Europe's best clubmaker by the players, 'but they didn't really know what type of shaft was good for them. And where a player would be conscious of his glove size, he wasn't very conscious of his grip size. Now he'll come in and say, "I'm a 58 with two wraps in the right hand." They're all conscious of the shafts they use, as well. They've picked it up just over the last few years.'

As Mizuno's club designer, Willett finds that it is the Tour players who create developments and changes in technology. Every single golf club produced by Mizuno is introduced to the professionals before it goes out to the public. Like everything else in golf, from swings to course architecture, Willett says there are trends in equipment. At the moment on Tour it is metal woods with graphite shafts, and classic blade clubs. Peripheral-weighted and toe-heel weighted clubs are gradually going out of fashion.

Is it a good thing that equipment is becoming so advanced?

'I don't think you can stop that,' says Willett. 'It's impossible to say: "That's the best set of golf clubs that have ever been made, let's stop." We've got to go forward. And it's a funny thing. You look at equipment you thought was very good five years ago and now you don't like it. The next golf club is going to be the best golf club ever made, and that's the thing we're looking for.'

Every single player has his own idiosyncracies where equipment is concerned. Woosnam likes S400 Dynamic shafts in his irons and X2s in his woods. Manuel Pinero is very particular about his sand-iron. He will have a quarter of an inch off it and then a quarter of an inch put on, have it flattened half a degree and then made half a degree upright, have half a degree loft added to it and then want it a degree stronger. Olazabal is always changing the loft on his putter. Some players like the hosel and the leading edge of a club to be in line, others like it slightly offset. Some like the club-face of their irons open, some like it shut. Others like to see a hook on their drivers, because even the best players have a tendency to push or pull the ball slightly.

According to Steve Mata, Taylor-made's popular Mexican clubmaker, Eamonn Darcy, is by far the most pernickety player he deals with. Darcy has been known to change his grips four times in one week. And this year alone, Mata has made him up more than 50 different drivers. Why? 'Because he's getting older and he can't hit it as far as he used to, and he wants to . . . He's very fussy. He knows the look of a golf club the way he wants it. He has a very good eye for clubs.'

'Seve's very particular about the way the faces are on his drivers,' says Willett. 'He likes his long irons fairly upright, and he likes the top cocking up off the ground more than most players do. It's very personal. It's like swing-weights. Two guys might have the same build, the same sort of shaft and the same type of club, and you'd think they'd have the same swing-weight, but they don't. One might like D1 and the other might like D4.

'Shafts are also quite difficult to match in with players. I know when I first did some work with Olazabal, going by the size and build of him, I thought S300s would be perfect. But in Switzerland he came in and said that he had just hit some shots with Seve's irons – which have X100 shafts in – and he hit them better than he did his own. Now Sandy Lyle, Ballesteros and Nick Faldo all use X100 shafts. Because of his size, you wouldn't think Olazabal would need the same.'

The most drastic change a player has made to his equipment this year is that of Nick Faldo to his grips. David Leadbetter is trying to stop him from breaking his wrists too quickly on the takeaway and Faldo has gone from using grips with three layers of tape on a 58 cord to ten layers under the left hand and six layers under the right.

'I'd say Nick knows what he wants more than anybody else,' says Willett, who used to do a lot of work with Faldo at St Georges Hill where he has his own workshop. 'He spends a lot of time making sure it's right. He is as particular with his equipment as he is about everything.' At the French Open this year Faldo, who was using a persimmon wood driver with a steel shaft at that time, came into the workshop and saw a Mizuno Turbo Metal driver with an X Gold Graphite shaft in it. He hit ten shots down the range with it and went straight out and played, finishing fourth in the tournament.

The combination of the Tour players all trying to get everything done at the same time, and at once, and the Japanese technicians – whose English only Willett is really competent at deciphering – leads to some hilarious situations in the workshop. John Bland, who is one of the funniest players on Tour anyway, came into the workshop one day and as usual began to give the Japanese a hard time. The workshop was busy and Bland was impatient.

'Come on, Sho-ji,' he hassled the man working on his clubs. 'You Japanese are the slowest workers I've ever seen.'

Sho-ji, of course, was unable to respond to this because he could hardly understand the language. He ignored Bland's heckling and carried on at his own pace. After about ten minutes, Jose Maria Olazabal arrived. Sho-ji, who was very proud of Olazabal because he was a Mizuno player, greeted him delightedly. 'How you doing, Jose?' he asked the Spaniard.

'Don't you talk to that Spanish guy,' cried Bland. 'I'm a South African. You look after me first.'

Sho-ji stopped what he was doing. 'Score, Jose?' he said to Olazabal.

'Seventy,' replied the Spaniard.

'Oh, very good,' praised Sho-ji. 'Well done. Very, very difficult golf course.'

'Don't listen to him,' instructed Bland. 'Get on with my job.'

Sho-ji stopped again. 'John-san,' he said, 'Score?'

'Sixty-eight,' said Bland smugly.

'Oh,' said Sho-ji, 'very, very lucky.'

Out on the range it goes on, the constant working, changing, refining, searching. Maybe Leadbetter is right after all. Maybe there is no secret. Maybe, as he says, 'The only secret, really, is patience, perseverance and practice. They'll help to get where you want to go – as long as you're working along the right lines.'

Chapter Seven

TRIUMPH AND ADVERSITY

Photo: Phil Sheldon

In front of the Royal and Ancient Clubhouse,
Nick Faldo reaps the ultimate reward for his efforts

OPEN CHAMPIONSHIP, ST ANDREWS, MONDAY, 16 JULY 1990. There is a buzz in the air, a curious hum, an electricity which sends a shiver down my spine and makes me laugh out loud. The sky is blue, the wind is fresh and there is a pervading smell of sea salt, suntan lotion and history.

Nothing prepares you for your first visit to St Andrews. No photograph or oil painting, no television picture or film could make your body tingle the way the atmosphere does here. Standing on the Swilcan Bridge with the clubhouse before me and the most infamous hole in golf – the Road Hole, 17th – behind me, emotion rises up and threatens to overwhelm me. The greatest golfers who ever lived have crossed this burn, their shoes have rung on these stones. Before this week is out one of the men here now will become one of them, if he isn't already. I watch players putt out on the 18th green beneath the empty leader-board and I wonder what they are thinking. What are their expectations? Their aspirations?

In 1978, Tommy Nakajima came to the penultimate hole of the Open Championship in contention for the tournament. On the green for two, Nakajima's first putt was a fraction too strong and his ball caught the slope and slid over the brim of the Road Bunker. Fearing the terrors of the Road more than that of the trap, Nakajima swung too cautiously and left his ball in the bunker – twice. Nakajima, who had taken 13 on the par five 13th hole at Augusta only three months previously, grew desperate. He put everything he had into his third attempt and blasted free. One chip and two putts later and Nakajima walked off the green with a nine.

The mysteries and ambiguities of the Old Course have not abated with the passage of time; technical advancements have not tamed her. In a world where golf course architects are striving to create by artifice what St Andrews is by nature, she remains the blueprint; a hand-made analogy for the capriciousness of the game of golf itself.

Tony Jacklin went out in 29 in the first round of the 1970 Championship, before a thunderstorm flooded the course and stopped play until the following day. When morning came, the spell had been broken. Instead, destiny decreed that it should be Doug Sanders who arrived at the 18th green needing a three-foot putt to win the Open, Sanders who should miss it, and he who should lose the ensuing play-off to Jack Nicklaus.

'I get asked if I ever think about that putt,' says Sanders, who has made a kind of emotional pilgrimage with his wife to St Andrews this year. 'I say I don't think about it too much. Sometimes I go five minutes without it crossing my mind.'

Six years after winning the last Open Championship held at St Andrews, Seve Ballesteros sits behind several microphones and a miniature flag of Spain and watches the world's press file into the interview room. He is a happy man. His black eyes crinkle at familiar faces, his mouth stretches into a helpless grin. These last two weeks spent fishing, practising, cycling and watching the Tour de France on television have relaxed him. He looks more contented than he has at any other time during this troubled year.

'It's always nice to be back to the place where I have such good memories,' smiles Ballesteros. 'I must say, to win the Open is something special, but to win at St Andrews, that's something very few people have the chance to do and I'm fortunate to be one of them.'

Can he recall every shot he played when he won here in 1984?

'Of course,' replies Ballesteros. Playing a practice round yesterday with his brother Vicente, he remembered every one of them.

'How did you play the 13th?' asks an American reporter, testing him.

'Why?' asks Seve, knowing it but rising to the challenge anyway. His teeth flash in his brown face. 'The 13th? Four-iron to the right, nine-iron to 15 feet, two putts.'

The 17th hole was more significant, being the hole where the Championship was won. 'Vicente,' Ballesteros tells us, 'says it's the toughest par four he ever saw.' He himself agrees. 'I think the 17th, if there's a little bit of wind against, you must play it as a par five. But on a day like today, definitely you must make par.'

In 1984 Ballesteros came to the Road Hole tied with Tom Watson on 11 under par. Watson made bogey from the fairway. The Spaniard hit a driver up the left-hand side of the fairway, and then with an area no bigger than a postage stamp to work with, he hit a six-iron to 25 feet and two-putted. That approach shot, combined with the fact that he was only in one bunker the entire week – an achievement of some note at St Andrews – won him the tournament. 'The more I look at that shot,' says Ballesteros laughing, 'the more impressed I get myself. Because if you look where I was, to put the ball where I did on the green, I guess, was very lucky.'

'You are a lucky player,' a journalist points out.

'Yes,' says Ballesteros, acknowledging it matter-of-factly. 'Always have been.'

Some good fortune would not go amiss now. For most of this season Ballesteros has not played well, particularly in the majors. At the US Masters he was unhappy with his game. He found a lot of trouble and, unusually, had trouble extricating himself from it. He fell away without ever really presenting a threat.

At the US Open, the only news he made was when he sacked his caddie, Ian Wright. Wright was distraught. He is a very proud person and it wounded him deeply. Nevertheless, it had been building up for some time. Wright had angered Ballesteros earlier in the year by getting a contract with a vehicle manufacturer to drive a car which had something to the effect of: Ian Wright

(Two Bags – as he is nicknamed) who caddies for Seve Ballesteros, drives . . . written on one side. Ballesteros was enraged and demanded that Wright give back the car immediately. No sooner had that row died down when Wright went out and got himself a lucrative contract with Boss clothing, which Ballesteros is paid to wear, and which Wright was in immediate danger of losing if he no longer worked for the Spaniard.

To this day Wright denies being fired, but according to caddie-talk (which is almost certainly true in this instance), he turned to Vincente (Chino) Fernandez – the Argentinian who got him the job with Ballesteros in the first place – for help. Fernandez persuaded Ballesteros to take him back until the end of the year but couldn't convince him to let Wright caddie at the Open. So, despite the fact that Ballesteros's record in the majors whenever his brothers have worked for him is distinctly uninspiring, Vicente will caddie for him here.

Questioned on his poor form in the run-up to the Open, Ballesteros says he is playing much the same as he was going into the Championship in 1984, and not a lot worse than he was prior to winning at Royal Lytham two years ago. 'There's nothing wrong with my game,' he insists. 'There's nothing wrong with my swing. It's just a matter of confidence.'

The subject of his so-called swing change, aided and abetted by Vicente, is broached. For months the reporters have written of little else. Nobody can believe that a player of Ballesteros's calibre should want to remodel a swing which has won him nearly 70 tournaments world-wide. Ballesteros's good humour begins to evaporate. Apparently, the reports have been exaggerated. 'People keep saying I am changing my swing,' he says brusquely. 'Why should I change my swing when I've been the best player in the world for ten years? It's just small details. I think my swing has been good to me so far. It's just a matter of confidence.'

As Ballesteros says, his self-assurance will return with one great round. Out on the range this morning, he looked as though he was feeling shots again, not just hitting the ball. He should do well this week. He loves St Andrews with a passion and a golfer always plays well on a course that he has a good feeling for.

Tuesday, 17 July. Colourful streams of people flow through the streets of St Andrews on to the sea of green. From my vantage point at the top of the stand beside the first tee, I can see for miles in any direction. To my left is the silver curve of the bay; in front of me is the grey outline of St Andrews, perched on its rocky promontory – an entire town given over to the golfing obsession; the course with all its famous landmarks – the Valley of Sin, Hell bunker, Walkingshaw's Grave and The Elysian Fields – stretches away to the right. Below me, miniaturised in real life, is the Royal and Ancient clubhouse.

To this day women are not allowed through its portals. However enough progress has been made in the outside world to force the octogenerian members of the R&A – who run the home of golf like a masonic sect – to allow women journalists into the clubhouse during the week of the Open Championship. We are now allowed into the hallway, but no further. Once, when I summoned the nerve to ask if there was a ladies toilet in existence, I was grudgingly escorted to the Royal and Ancient Powder Room: a standing-room-only facility located in the kitchens.

I am very reticent when it comes to matters of sexual discrimination. I like to go where I please and be accepted and judged on my merits as a writer and a human being, and the fact that I can be barred from a clubhouse, of all places, on the grounds that I am a woman, infuriates me so much that I deem it safer to stay away. Sexual discrimination, in my opinion, has about as much place in today's world as apartheid does. Liz Kahn (another woman golf writer), on the other hand, believes in fighting for equal rights. She asked the R&A whether they made a policy in the past of not allowing women reporters into the men's locker-room and, having been informed that they hadn't, was in the process of asking the attendant at St Andrews whether he had seen Gary Player, when she was bodily evicted from the clubhouse. Michael Bonallack, Secretary of the R&A, told her that she had made a mistake. She wasn't, he assured her, then or ever, likely to be allowed in the men's locker-room.

'When I die,' wrote Kahn, in her article on the incident (*Mail on Sunday*, 22 July), 'I have asked Mickey Walker, woman golf professional, to take my ashes to St Andrews and scatter them in the North room of the Royal and Ancient golf club. It may not be the Kingdom of Heaven, but it is probably the only way I will ever enter that hallowed ground. How Mickey will get in, I do not know.'

Down on the putting green, an Aussie three-ball posed obligingly for a photograph. 'You want to take a picture of me eating my rabbit food?' asks Ian (Hollywood) Baker-Finch, with a grin. He is eating prawn and salad sandwiches for brunch. His form is good and he is feeling optimistic about the week ahead, determined to make amends for 1984 when, having entered the last round joint leader with Tom Watson, he shot 79 and finished ninth. He has rented a house alone this week, giving himself space to breathe, to concentrate. 'That's the way I like it. That's perfect.'

The starter is working himself into a frenzy. He can't understand that the pros are pretty relaxed about practice rounds. He's having a fit because they're turning up late, swapping partners, or not turning up at all. Red-faced, he rushes up to Greg Norman who is idly practising his putting while he waits to tee off. 'Mr Jones is not ready,' he worries.

'Right,' shouts Norman to his playing partners, 'We're out of here.'

He putts out his remaining balls. 'Hey pooftah,' shouts a voice from the first tee. The Shark draws himself up to his full height. 'Barnsey,' he booms. He strides over to embrace Brian Barnes. They make an incongruous couple: Barnes, with what in all probability is a Vodka and orange in his hand, his golf shirt fighting a losing battle with the waistband of his shorts; and Norman, every inch an athlete, the ultimate sporting success story.

In his press conference, Norman brimmed with confidence. Yes, he was playing wonderfully well. He had played consistently good golf all season. He had only had two bad rounds – the first at the US Masters, where he shot 78, and the third round at the Anheuser-Busch Classic, two weeks previously, where he shot 75. What department of his game was particularly good? Well, all of them. He only had to string four good rounds together and he'd be in with a chance on Sunday afternoon.

'I have good memories of last year, though I was disappointed,' says the Shark. 'I watched it last night on TV and I really felt that I did not play badly at all.'

Norman arrived at the 18th hole in the sudden-death play-off for the 1989 Open at Troon needing a birdie to win the Championship and a par to stay alive. Incredibly, his drive found a fairway bunker, his second shot found another, and his third was out-of-bounds. 'Unfortunately, my drive landed on a hard patch,' says Norman in retrospect. 'I had 318 yards to the bunker. To this day, I would not have hit any other shot.'

But that was just one shot and one major. If you had said at the start of Norman's illustrious career that by the age of 35 he would have won only one major championship, you would have been laughed out of town. If you had said he would have snatched defeat from the jaws of victory in at least four others, you would have been taken away in a strait-jacket. Yet he has.

In the 1984 US Open, he shot a final round 69 to draw level with Fuzzy Zoeller and force a play-off, causing the amiable Zoeller to wave a white towel in surrender. The following day, after shooting a 75 to the American's 67, it was Norman's turn to wave the white towel. Two years later, shortly after bogeying the 72nd hole of the Masters to lose to Jack Nicklaus, he was beaten by Bob Tway in the US PGA Championship when Tway holed his bunker shot at the last. In 1987 Larry Mize holed his fluke wedge shot in the play-off to steal the Masters green jacket right from under the Shark's nose. And then Mark Calcavecchia got the better of him at Troon.

There have been others. It's got to the stage now where you don't wonder how Norman is going to win the tournament, you wonder how he's going to lose it.

Norman, to his credit, seems to have turned it around and made it into something positive rather than negative. 'If other guys hole their shots and pip me, I can't help that. I have no control over what they do. If they do it to me, it is a sign I am in contention more than anyone else. Maybe it makes me a better person, a better player, more resilient. I've had a lot of good out of it.'

The Great White Shark bares a row of white teeth. 'I'm holding fairly high hopes for myself this week,' he says.

Wednesday, 18 July. Nick Faldo went to his first Open Championship in 1973. Then aged 16, he drove up with his dad and stayed in a tent. 'I remember it was so cold, I walked around with my pyjamas on under my clothes. I watched Weiskopf practise in his street shoes. There was just something about the way he was swinging. I said to my dad: "He'll win."'

Strange that Tom Weiskopf might be looking at Faldo now and thinking the same thing.

Faldo *looks* like a champion – strong, fit and dominant. He removes his dark glasses and regards the press through deep-set blue eyes. He listens to the first question put to him, flicks irritably at an imaginary speck on the table in front of him, then he fixes the reporter with a concentrated frown.

'What score's going to win it? What did Seve win it with? Twelve under? Who knows? If I knew that I'd be a stockbroker.

'What lessons have I learnt from other majors? I take them all one at a time. After winning the Masters and missing by a stroke in the US Open, I just go at the majors as hard as I can. I think they're the most important thing in my career at the moment. That's what I channel all my thoughts into.'

Faldo's Open record is astounding. Besides his win at Muirfield in 1987, he has at various times finished third, fourth, fifth, sixth, seventh and eighth.

'I thrive on the majors,' he says. 'When you get into a position to win it's nerve-racking, but that's what it's all about. Nicklaus used to look into the crowd on Sunday afternoon and say, "Isn't this great. This is what I've been working for." You've got to take a step back and look at yourself. You want to get into that position so there's no point in being scared of it.'

Under cloudless skies, with only the mildest of sea breezes, the Old Course is as benign as a pussycat. If the weather doesn't change, somebody is likely to match Curtis Strange's course record 62, shot here in the Dunhill Cup a couple of years ago. 'There's not too many records you think too much about,' says the US Open champion, 'but having a course record at St Andrews, that's something special.'

When he first came to St Andrews as a Walker Cup player in 1975, Strange's immediate reaction was one of bewilderment – that of most uninitiated. 'I guess the first time you play here you come away feeling like everyone does, "What the hell was that?" But the more you play St Andrews, the more you appreciate it.'

'You have to defend yourself against the course off the tee,' said Ballesteros on strategy, 'avoid the bunkers, then attack the course from there . . . You've got to put the ball in the right place, which is left, I think. This is the problem. It's the only golf course in the world where you have to play left.'

'Yes, you can bale out left all day long,' replies Strange, 'but the further left you go, the tougher your second shot is going to be . . . I think strength is very advantageous on this golf course. Strength being that you have to hit the ball a long way.'

'I found the Old Course disappointing in my early years,' recalled Tom Watson, 'because I thought the luck of the bounce was too prominent in scoring. Now I realise that this is the essence of the game and it's how it should be played. You have to take the bounces as they come and get to know them the best you can. I think it is the most difficult to know and understand of all Open courses because of the blindness and misdirection inherent in the course. At first I didn't understand it; I didn't like it. Now I love it.'

Thursday, 19 July. The worst of the Open Championship is that it is full of reporters from all around the globe – many of whom don't usually cover golf and don't know the first thing about it – in search of a bit of sensation. Scott Hoch and Nick Faldo, paired together in the opening rounds, were their first victims. The tabloids reported Hoch – who missed a two-foot putt to lose the 1989 Masters to Faldo – as having said that he hated Faldo, that Faldo was universally disliked by other professionals and that the people in Faldo's home town would rather see Hoch win than Faldo.

'What was all that in the papers?' Trevino, who was talking to Canadian Danny Mejovik in the locker room, asked Hoch.

'I said some things,' said Hoch miserably, 'but I never said all the bad stuff.'

He said as much to Faldo on the first tee. 'Don't worry about it,' said the Englishman, 'I don't read it, but I know exactly what's going on this week.' Years ago, an incident like that would have really got to Faldo. Today he just accepted it, reassured Hoch, and went out and shot 67.

Though the wind was blowing in the opposite direction to that in the practice rounds, the scoring was good. Norman and Michael Allen, winner of last year's Bell's Scottish Open, both shot 66 to take the first round lead. Behind them came Nick Faldo and Peter Jacobsen on five under par, and Christy O'Connor Jnr, Ian Woosnam, Ian Baker-Finch, Martin Poxon and Craig Parry on four under.

'This course is tough,' observed Norman, 'and you've got to take advantage of any situation you get given and accept that you're going to get into trouble.'

'The elements are what make this golf course so difficult,' said Trevino who shot a first round 69. Diet Coke in one hand, cigarette in the other, he gesticulates to the press corps. 'In my opinion, the pin placements were very difficult today, and rightly so because the R&A knew it wouldn't blow.'

Trevino maintains he hit his best shot of the day at the 17th, a three-iron which rolled off the green and on to the road. He managed to get up and down for par. 'It's just a very difficult green to land the ball on,' says Trevino. 'That green is a seven-iron green. It's not built to take a five-iron or a four-iron.'

'It doesn't reward intelligent golf,' said Arnold Palmer of the Road Hole. 'It rewards poor shots and penalises good shots.'

'Do you think it should be changed?' someone asked Trevino.

'Don't ever change anything at the Old Course,' shouts the Mexican, horrified. 'Please don't touch it.'

'Are you pleased to be on the leaderboard at this stage of the tournament?'

'Always, always. You always want to start fast. You always want a good first round in a major.'

Friday, 20 July. One of the reasons why golf is the greatest game ever invented is that anyone can win at any time. Even in a field such as this, where 156 of the best players in the world are competing for a total purse of £825,000, unfamiliar names from the lower rungs of tournament golf keep appearing with delightful incongruity at the top of the leaderboard. Jamie Spence, an unknown Englishman from Tonbridge, Kent, playing in his first Open, went out this morning and shot 65. His round of eight birdies included one at the Road Hole – the equivalent of an eagle on any other. Walking down the 18th, he looked up to find himself at the summit of the leaderboard with Payne Stewart.

At 27, Spence has visited the Tour School five times. His best finish ever in a tournament was ninth in the Belgian Open earlier this year. He has missed the last four cuts.

'First and foremost, I just want to say that this round is for my father,' says Spence, a slender young man with a boyish face and a shy smile.

Last Christmas, his father had a heart attack. 'That was a bad time,' says Spence quietly, 'and it stuck in my mind. It changed my attitude to the game. You get so wrapped up in your own little world. Golf was so important. It still is, but it made me realise that golf is not everything, and making a bogey or three-putting doesn't matter in the long run. I just go out and enjoy it now.'

'Do you think you can win the Open?' he is asked.

Spence gives a short laugh. He's more of a realist than that. 'Well,' he says, 'it's a dream, isn't it?'

Meanwhile, the Great White Shark was on the warpath. The candy-striped figure of Payne Stewart was an early casualty; Norman ate his lead for lunch. He reached the turn in 33, with birdies at the fourth, seventh, eighth and ninth. Behind him came Faldo, and behind them both came the diminutive figures of Australian Craig Parry and Welshman Ian Woosnam, each chasing his first major victory.

For several holes, the four matched each other birdie for birdie, then Norman and Faldo began to draw away, ending the day joint leaders on 12 under par for the tournament. Parry slipped slowly down the leaderboard, eventually coming to rest on eight under par. Woosnam, who came to grief at the 17th where he took a double-bogey six, was a stroke behind.

After his round, Norman looked invincible. 'I'm playing well and putting well right now,' he says. 'When I get to the green I feel I am going to make the putt.'

'He can overpower a course like this,' says Nick Price, who is lying seven under par for the tournament. 'There are bunkers that come into play for the rest of us that he doesn't even see. He's going to be a hard man to beat. We're all going to be chasing him.'

'I definitely feel I can win this week,' says Norman. 'That will be my approach, to go for it tomorrow. I am enjoying the game, I'm not really charged up or excited. Right now I'm in a good position. If I don't come out and do something spectacular tomorrow, I'll still be in a good position come Sunday.'

Nicklaus, it was put to Norman, believes that in order to dominate golf a player has to be dominant.

'What is dominant?' asks the Shark, considering the point. 'Is dominant going out every week believing you can win? Well, I do that anyway. That's just the way I am. I'm a very confident, positive person.'

One thing is for certain, the outcome of tomorrow's battle between the giants of world golf will prove – at least in the collective mind of observers of the game – who really is the number one player in the world.

The cut fell at 143 – one under par, three shots lower than that of the 1989 Open at Troon which was the lowest cut on record at the time. The list of the guillotined read like the Who's Who of golf: Seve Ballesteros; defending champion Mark Calcavecchia; Tom Watson, winner of five Open Championships; Craig Stadler, 1983 US Masters champion; Curtis Strange, US Open champion; Gary Player and Arnold Palmer, who have won 16 major championships between them.

Saturday, 21 July. Two years ago Greg Norman went up in an F14 jet over St Andrews. 'Have you ever been in a dog fight?' asked the pilot during the course of the flight. When Norman replied in the negative, the pilot called up another on the radio and a mock dog fight ensued. They hunted one another through the skies. 'Keep a lookout for him,' requested the pilot, 'and tell me when you see him.' Norman gazed out into the blue. 'There he is,' he cried suddenly, spotting the other jet. Without warning, the pilot dived; the ground came up and the G-force hit Norman like a brick wall. He was copiously sick.

Sometimes golf's maxim is wrong. Sometimes it's not how many, it's how. In years to come, the annals of golf will only record one outcome that third day.

Faldo and Norman's respective scores of 67 and 76 will be nothing more than numbers on a page. Historians who may never have walked the course that day will write that Faldo struck a psychological blow at the first when he birdied from 11 feet, while Norman, who had hit his approach shot inside Faldo's, made par. They will note that Faldo turned in 33, leaving Norman three shots adrift; that the Englishman salvaged par from a near unplayable lie in the gorse at the 12th, but that the Australian could do no better than bogey from the fairway; that Norman missed from short range at the 13th, 14th and 15th holes; and that the two players, level at the start of play, were separated at the end by nine strokes.

Golf is not a fair game. It does not reward proportionately that which is put into it. To some people, it will give more, others less. It has no favourites and makes no concession to greatness. Today, it was Faldo who got the breaks, another, it might have been Norman on whose head those blessings were heaped.

Only Norman knows what really happened that day. Only he knows where the magic went. But in the absence of any such explanation there was nothing left to do but listen to the opinions of other players.

'Greg didn't have the run of the ball,' commented Faldo. 'His putting hurt him. Every time he didn't get a break or didn't get the ball close, three-putting killed him.' Norman had five three-putts during the course of the round. That's *five*.

'He was cruising along very nicely,' said ex-European Tour player, Simon Hobday. 'He should have just kept cruising. I think he tried to either beat Faldo, or to beat the golf course. You cannot push golf courses like that. He tried to overpower the golf course and the old bitch bit him. And, of course, the more it bit him, the more he tried to push. He tried to carry the bunker here and take a chance there.'

The comments written on the bottom of Norman's score sheet were terse: 'Just putted terrible . . . Had a couple of bad breaks on the 12th and 13th and that was the end of my day.'

While Faldo and Norman locked horns at the top of the leaderboard, a 24-year-old Midlander by the name of Paul Broadhurst went out and shot a record-breaking 63. His outward half of 29 was matched in the afternoon by Baker-Finch, who, having begun the day a distant eight shots behind the leaders, collected five birdies and an eagle for a 64. He ended the day tied with Stewart in second place.

Sunday, 22 July. Only two players on the course today were applauded as loudly as the winner was: Sandy Lyle and Greg Norman. Lyle was so proud to be standing on the first tee on the final day with a chance at a top ten finish, anyone would have thought he'd won the tournament.

The Shark, too, walking down the first, was given a rousing reception. His face split into an ear-to-ear grin. But to his more cynical followers, his final round of 66 to finish fifth proved nothing. Sure he was going to do alright in the last round – there was no pressure on him. As far as they were concerned, Norman had choked once too often.

In the weeks before the 119th Open Championship, Nick Faldo had two dreams. In the first, he dreamt that on the fourth day of play he would lead the tournament by five shots after three rounds, and in the second he dreamt that he would play the final hole of the Championship leading by four shots.

Call it a premonition, call it what you will, Faldo had no intention of leaving anything to chance. Most of his life has been spent in preparation for days such as these. Early this morning he was out with David Leadbetter working on his putting in jeans and a tee-shirt. When he felt the nerves begin to take hold of him, he went back to his hotel and slept until it was time to warm up for his round.

I went out with Faldo and Baker-Finch in the cool of the afternoon, walking alongside bright banks of spectators. Stewart was just ahead of us, bizarrely resplendent in stars and stripes – the colours of the National Football League – and gold-tipped shoes. You couldn't imagine someone dressed like that holding up the claret jug.

Faldo entered the final round with a five-stroke lead, and no one since McDonald Smith in 1925 at Prestwick had failed to defend so great an advantage. It was Faldo's hour of glory and he enjoyed it. All his work had been done in the first three days: his 54-hole total of 199 beat Tom Watson's Muirfield record by three strokes. He played steadily, cautiously even, but always poised for flight.

On a day when the wind blew strongly from the east and the pins were placed in the toughest positions of the week, Zimbabwean Mark McNulty shot a flawless 65. Earlier in the week he had echoed Strange's comment that strength was an advantage at St Andrews. 'I disagree,' said Paul Stephens, his caddie, at the time. 'I think it is a straight-hitter's golf course.' Stephens' theory would seem to have been borne out. Birdies have been scarce today but McNulty had seven and never dropped a single shot.

I left Faldo and the forlorn Baker-Finch at the 14th and went ahead to the Road Hole, where I sat on the cold stone wall and watched the final act in the drama unfold. Ian Woosnam disappeared into the depths of the Road bunker. When he re-emerged, his late charge for his third successive tournament victory and his first Open title had ended. He finished tied third with American, Jodie Mudd.

Next came Stewart, who had drawn within two shots of Faldo with six holes to play. He sent his approach sailing over the road on to the grassy verge beside the wall and came distraught to weigh up the consequences, chewing gum furiously all the while. A shot dropped there and a five from the Valley of Sin, and the American was left to share second place with McNulty.

In winning the Open Championship Nick Faldo became the first British golfer since Henry Cotton before the Second World War to win the title twice, and the first man since Watson in 1977 to win both the Masters and the Open in the same year. His last-round score of 71 for an aggregate of 270 surpassed Ballesteros's record by six strokes.

Some moments in golf are so precious that they stand apart from all others. Framed in our memories is a picture of the Golden Bear, putter raised heavenwards, as he claimed the US Masters title, aged 46; so, too, is that of Ballesteros striding gloriously to victory here at St Andrews; and Sandy Lyle's ecstatic dance across the 18th green at the US Masters.

Nick Faldo has earned his place among them. Breaking through the crowds in the brilliant light of evening, arms raised in a victory salute, he was hailed as the best golfer in the world.

As a child, Faldo had another dream. In generations to come, he wanted people to say: 'Did you see Nick Faldo play? I did and he was quite something.'

I did, and he was. Quite something.

Chapter Eight

RUNNING TO STAND STILL

Photo: ASP, Stuart Franklin

Sandy Lyle walks the long road to recovery

MURPHY'S CUP, YORK, AUGUST 1990. THIS MORNING SANDY Lyle went out and shot a 67 on Fulford Golf Course to finish fourth in the tournament. Nothing unusual in that. Nothing you wouldn't expect from a man who has won two major championships and 21 tournaments world-wide; but worth a mention because it is the first time Lyle has shot four consecutive rounds under 70 (five if you count the pro-am) since the European Open in September 1988, and only the third time he has shot a score below 68 in a European four round event since the Bell's Scottish Open in June 1989.

His score wasn't the only thing worth remarking on this week. Ambling down 15 on the first day with that long, loping stride of his, Lyle noticed something almost as distant a memory as rounds in the low 60s. He nudged his caddie, Dave Musgrove. For the second time in nearly two seasons, Lyle's name was at the top of the leaderboard. Something inside him stirred. 'I saw his eyes light up,' said Musgrove. 'He started to get interested.'

In the press centre afterwards, Lyle, who kept his name on the scoreboards for the rest of the week, was doing a pretty poor job of trying to appear nonchalant. He looked as though he was doing mental cartwheels as he went through his birdies and bogeys for reporters.

'You had ten single putts,' a scribe says, working it out.

'Ten single putts?' echoes Lyle who hadn't, taking a sudden interest in his coke can to hide his delight.

Yes, he said, he was feeling cautiously optimistic, particularly after his successful week at the Open. No, he hadn't seen David Leadbetter since then, but he had been working hard on his game and it seemed to be having a positive effect on the swing flaws he was trying to iron out.

'Otherwise,' says Lyle casually, 'I'm playing well, putting well, and I played with a bunch of nice guys today.'

'What will you take if you hole in one,' someone asks, 'the money or the stout?' The sponsors, you see, are offering 13,750 pints of Murphy's Irish Stout or the cash equivalent of £12,650 to any player holing in one at the 175-yard 14th hole.

'Oh, definitely the stout,' says Lyle, who has vested interests, being a pub owner himself.

'Careful, you might be quoted literally,' said the reporter, who wouldn't be so bold if he was talking to any other top player. Lyle takes the comment in the light-hearted vein it was intended.

'Well,' he says, 'it would be very hard for McCormack International Management Company to take their 20 per cent.'

And as he watches the press have a laugh at the expense of IMG, Lyle allows himself the luxury of smiling that big smile.

Sandy Lyle possesses in large measure all the nicest attributes a man can have: honesty, generosity, good-humour, and heart – the first requirement of a champion. All of those characteristics have been tested to the utmost over the last 18 months and none have been found wanting. For that reason, as Lyle emerges from a slump which is, arguably, without parallel among the great players, the prevailing attitude towards him is one of admiration rather than pity.

Once more, and for all the right reasons, Lyle has got the reporters reaching for their notebooks and pens. Now that stories about Lyle's slump are old hat, the time is ripe for a few column inches to be devoted to the Lyle comeback.

Strange how, in newspaper language, a subject which has innumerable facets, like golf or the lives of the people who play it, tends to take on a stark black and white simplicity. The facts are skeletal: a certain player shot 78, 77 in the final rounds of a given tournament to finish last, for example. The third dimension – factors affecting the player which might not be immediately apparent, such as his private life, equipment problems, pressure, loss of confidence – is considered, but due to space and deadline interdictions can rarely be subjected to prolonged or detailed examination. Thus, when the game of Sandy Lyle began to take its downward spiral in the early months of 1989 the ostensible facts as they presented themselves were recorded along the following lines:

Nestlé Invitational, Orlando, Florida: Scotsman, Sandy Lyle, was yesterday disqualified when he chose to walk off the golf course rather than complete his round, knowing he would miss the cut.

That's where it all began, at the 1989 Nestlé Invitational. Lyle had not had a good day. He had visited every bush and bunker on the exacting Bay Hill course, found every bad lie, and had watched innumerable putts lip out for bogey. Finally, on reaching the 36th hole of the tournament, he had continued the trend of that miserable round by hitting his tee shot into the lake. There was no question that he would miss the cut. So Lyle did a most uncharacteristic thing. He handed his driver to Musgrove, and instead of walking back to the tee to play another ball, he marched straight off the course and went home.

In the seven weeks preceding the event, Lyle had won over $279,000. At varying times he had been placed tenth, second, third and second, and on arrival at Bay Hill he was lying fourth on the US Tour money list. When looked at in relation to this record, the Nestlé Invitational incident seemed the obvious trigger of the ensuing series of misadventures. Five consecutive missed cuts – including one at the US Masters where Lyle was defending champion – had followed it, and they had been superseded by a row of shabby finishes on both sides of the Atlantic and a further four missed cuts.

But the warning signs had already manifested themselves more than five weeks before. At the Los Angeles Open, Lyle began to feel the first stirrings of alarm.

'Even though I finished second to Calcavecchia, I was starting to lose it. I wasn't happy. I came back home for a couple of weeks afterwards, didn't practise very well, went back out [for the Nestlé Invitational] and it just went sour. The whole thing just fell to pieces. I lost it there and then on the spot.'

But a player of Lyle's ability doesn't just lose his game overnight. Not unless something precipitates it. Not unless something hurts him so badly that he no longer feels he can play the game. In Lyle's case, could that something have been the devastation which followed the marriage of his ex-wife to another man? Or even the tensions and anxieties which accompanied his own second marriage?

'No,' says Lyle frankly. Shaded from the sunshine by the white table umbrella, his blue eyes are as guileless as a child's. 'My home situation was pretty much on a level. All the problems with the break-up of my marriage were settled.'

He pauses, framing his sentences carefully to avoid misinterpretation. 'The lifestyle I have at home is very normal. You've been to my parents' house and we have a very happy family. No worries in that department.'

I went to Hawkstone Park in the autumn of 1989. While a thunderstorm tore at the rugged Shropshire landscape, I sat in an armchair and talked to Lyle's parents. The lounge of their tiny cottage is strewn with fragments of his past: a stuffed cobra, grey with age, doing battle with a sharp-eyed mongoose, which Lyle brought back from the Nigerian Open one year; photographs of him and his sisters; silverware won; books and magazines and press cuttings.

'It'll all be like a bad dream to him,' said Alec Lyle, a gentle Scotsman who has taught Sandy since childhood, 'and he'll be grateful and a better player when it's all over. I know he will; I'm not just saying that, because he's always worked very hard ever since he was a little boy.' And he remembered Sandy as a child, driven inside by the snow, hitting balls by lamplight against a suspended rug in a disused locker room; Sandy aged 13, doing 30 press-ups daily on his fingertips; and Sandy practising his swing endlessly with his back to the wall – a drill devised by his teaching professional father to make his swing more upright.

In the cosy domesticity of the family lounge, while Mrs Lyle poured tea and handed round biscuits and Sandy and his dad discussed motor-racing, the nightmare that Lyle's slump had become faded into nothingness the way dreams do with the coming of day.

'It's hard to pinpoint a certain thing,' says Lyle now, nearly a year later, still searching for a logical explanation for something that defies logic, 'but I've always been troubled by a flattish backswing and sometimes it gets worse, especially on the takeaway. The mental thoughts I was working on a year ago were the wrong thoughts. I was trying to make my swing more upright but I was going about it the wrong way on the takeaway.'

Golf, you see, is a game of opposites. Lyle reasoned that by getting his left shoulder more under his chin through the swing, his arms would automatically lift and his swing plane would become more upright. 'It doesn't work that way in the golf swing, because if I tilt my shoulders, my left arm stays close to my side and my swing gets shorter. And if I turn my shoulders, the arms go up. That's really what started it. I was playing for six months to a year thinking, "I must get my shoulders more under to make my swing more upright", and I wasn't doing that at all. I was just making my swing even shorter and I can't afford to do that, I have a short enough swing as it is.'

Lyle came to the end of 1989 drained and dispirited. His final position of 53rd on the money list was a career worst by four places. Since turning professional in 1978, Lyle had only twice finished outside the top 12 on the Order of Merit, and he had won it three times.

The season had taken its toll on him far more than it might have if it hadn't been a Ryder Cup year. From the first moment he began to struggle, the pressure was on for him to recover his form in time to make the team. The Ryder Cup question hung over his head like a guillotine.

'How could Tony Jacklin pick Sandy?' people said.

How could he not?

A fortnight before the team was chosen, Lyle gave himself an ultimatum. 'I said to myself that if I didn't start playing half-decent golf and scoring during those two weeks [the Benson and Hedges in York and the World Series in Firestone, Ohio], I couldn't expect to sort of turn it on the week of the Ryder Cup. And I played lousy. I couldn't face the thought of being picked for the Ryder Cup team and playing badly.'

Immediately after finishing 37th in the World Series, Lyle dropped the first bombshell: he wouldn't be playing. Then Jacklin dropped the second: Christy O'Connor would.

'I did what I felt was the best thing,' says Lyle, 'and it took a lot of courage to make that decision. You're obviously going to get some sort of flack from the press but I was doing what I thought was best for the team. At the time I wasn't playing well. Maybe if I could have been there in spirit it would have helped, I don't know, but I think there were other players who were playing well at the time and they could take my place.'

'Did the media put a lot of pressure on you?'

'It didn't help an awful lot. But, you know, if you're a world-class player renowned for your consistency and tournament victories, and all of a sudden you're not playing consistently, there's going to be pressure. I try to avoid it as much as possible but it's still there.'

'Do you read any of it?'

'Not a lot, no,' says Lyle with a slightly apologetic glance at me. 'I get feedback from other players or my wife, saying they've written this or that. I take it with a pinch of salt. You know, you've got to have the press because you're a golfer on the European Tour. The two things go together.'

So Lyle took a long winter lay-off. In some ways he felt that tiredness had played its part in his persistent failure to resurrect his game (the previous winter he had played virtually continually in Australia and the Far East, beginning the next season with no respite), and he hoped that a rest would go a long way towards solving the problem and healing the wounds. It didn't. Lyle began the 1990 season in America with a missed cut at the Tuscon Open in America, and followed it with six more, interspersed with five mediocre to poor finishes.

The Lyle who came home to England early was a man at his wits' end. He decided then and there that the time had come to put himself into the hands of the one man he was convinced could help him. He called on David Leadbetter.

Nick Faldo was lured into a discussion on Lyle during a press conference at the PGA Championship at Wentworth in May. His mood, as is his wont these days, was amiable. After dealing with his own affairs he indulged himself in a plateful of salmon sandwiches and sat on behind a small forest of microphones, seemingly content to engage in small talk.

Did he, we asked, think it was a good thing that Lyle had finally committed himself to David Leadbetter?

'Sandy and Lead.?' mused Faldo. 'Yes, of course. Last year he was really faffing around. He was going to about five coaches and that's not really fair on the five coaches. It's all down to him now, how he takes it in, how hard he works.'

At the end of last year, after Lyle had seen Leadbetter for a short spell of time, Faldo says that he tried to help Lyle with some of the things he was working on. 'He was trying to get the pre-set drill right so I told him that you've got to have the club on the ground to get the parallels right. The pre-set drill is one of the simplest. For me, really, the hardest thing has always been getting the leg action right.'

Inevitably, that old bone – the much-publicised rivalry between the Scotsman and the Englishman – was dragged out from under the rug. Faldo's eyes, as masked as Lyle's are revealing, look guardedly out from under their lids at the press. Yes, he says, with scarcely a pause, he misses the competitive rivalry that Lyle once offered.

Lyle, when I had asked him whether the antagonism between him and Faldo was merely a product of the media's active imagination, said: 'It has been exaggerated over the years, yes,' without much conviction. 'I mean, we're not the sort of buddies who would go to each other's houses. We keep ourselves to ourselves . . . we don't have much in common. But Gill [Faldo's wife]is very nice,' said Lyle, unconsciously betraying himself. 'She gets on well with Jolande, so one half has done alright, anyway.'

In the interview room at Wentworth, Faldo says without a shade of superciliousness: 'Sandy's lost at the moment. He needs to get it going and get back into it. He's got to go through the whole process of getting it going in a tournament under pressure to test the swing. He's got a hard slog ahead of him.'

The unfortunate thing about losing your game is that you begin to receive advice from all quarters. Last year, Lyle, clutching at straws, listened to everyone.

'I went to a lot of teachers,' he admits. 'I had a lot of people writing to me, I had a lot of players saying things. They'd say one thing then someone else would say: "Well, you don't do that, you do that." The complete opposite. So you'd sort of go one step forward and two steps backwards.

'But the reason that I was looking around at different coaches is that my father's nearly 70 now and he's not going to be around that much more. I mean, it could be another 20 years, but he doesn't travel with me an awful lot and I was really looking for somebody I could see in America and see in Britain that I could trust . . . You know, I was having a bit of a bad time and if someone could get me going well, then it was worth while.'

Jimmy Ballard, a top American coach, had the most success with Lyle in that particular period. He at least got Lyle hitting the ball with some sort of conviction, which no one else had really managed to do. But Ballard doesn't travel to tournaments at all, not even those within the United States. Lyle would have had to make frequent pilgrimages to Florida at a time when he desperately needed regular attention. So, he put the idea of working with Ballard aside. At that stage of his career it simply wasn't practicable.

'I think, nowadays, with the scoring getting so low and the intense competition, you almost need somebody there every two weeks to make sure your rhythm is good,' explains Lyle. 'Feel can be very misleading in a golf swing, so if you've got someone looking from the outside saying your rhythm's a bit quick but your swing's alright, that makes you feel a little bit better. You just work on your rhythm and it all comes back again.'

In May, Lyle began working with Leadbetter. They started by addressing the biggest problem first: Lyle's loss of confidence. As Leadbetter says, golf is such a mental game that when a golfer is playing well he never thinks he will play badly again, and when he is playing badly he never thinks he'll play well again. 'It's just magnified when you're in a situation like Sandy, who has been right at the top. It's a struggle internally more than anything else. He'll be back. It's just a matter of being patient.'

Physically, Lyle's problem is the lack of balance in his swing. Leadbetter's aim has always been to improve his weight distribution so that his body is in a better position through impact, and he doesn't have to use his hands as much to hit the ball.

'Funny thing is, better mechanics lead to better mental thoughts,' says Leadbetter. 'A lot of people think, "Well, it's just mental. He's a great player; he doesn't need to change his swing.'' Well, he doesn't need to change his swing that much, but there's a couple of things he needs to do, and if he does them, he'll find his confidence will come through in his game.'

'Was it not necessary for him to rebuild his swing, like Faldo?'

'No. Different kettle of fish. Nick is such a perfectionist and he really likes to understand what's going on in the golf swing, to the point where he's very intense about getting his golf swing the best it can be. Obviously, everybody is to a certain extent, but Nick is a fairly mechanical player and as a result can play with mechanics. Sandy is a little more of a feel-type player so he'd have to try to blend the two.'

Lyle is convinced that Leadbetter's way is the right way forward. 'I've always been a very natural player but I'm working on a system now where if things do go wrong I can correct them within weeks or days rather than years. I'm not trying to make myself into a machine like Faldo; I'm just trying to build a swing that will be a little safer and more consistent so that I'm knocking at the door most weeks trying to win tournaments. At the moment I'm just going through the transitional [period]. It takes time – mental changes, physical changes. It can take years . . . to get it right.'

Open Championship, St Andrews, July 1990. Had you asked all those people to show hands at the start of the week who thought that Lyle would still be here at the weekend, you'd have been lucky to count to five. Lyle certainly wouldn't have raised his. Yet his opening rounds of 72, 70, ensured he made the cut, the lowest in Open Championship history, with a shot to spare.

'I feel like I've won the tournament,' said Lyle on Friday evening, beaming round at the world's press.

A reporter, rather cruelly, told him that someone in the press tent had been offering odds of 1,000-1 against him making the cut.

'Someone should have taken him up on them,' was Lyle's wry comment.

On the third day, Lyle's approach to the tournament had changed. The first two rounds he had played the Old Course conservatively. 'Knowing that the cut was going to be low because the wind wasn't severe added pressure straight away, knowing that I've been struggling to shoot under par. And disaster lurks round the corner all the time on that course.' With the biggest hurdle safely negotiated, Lyle could afford to play St Andrews the way he likes to play it, with calculated aggression.

Walking behind Lyle on the third day of play, I witnessed the most extraordinary display of emotion and goodwill towards the Scotsman by the gallery. One couldn't imagine Faldo at the height of his powers engendering quite the same affection. It began on the first hole with a standing ovation and had a ripple effect. Wave after wave, like wind through a field of corn, the galleries took up the applause as he walked down the front nine, round the loop and back again.

'The crowd support was tremendous,' said Lyle, who came in with a 67, afterwards. He was slightly overwhelmed by it all. 'I nearly walked into a few bunkers watching them.'

It says something about the man that so many people want so badly for him to recover. Throughout the last two seasons Lyle has received cartloads of encouraging mail from fans and well-wishers, and enough advice on his game to last him a lifetime. One man suggested that he watch videos of the Battle of Britain in order to boost his morale. Personally, I would have thought that, if it is inspiration Lyle is in need of, he need look no further than the footage of himself winning the Masters at Augusta.

Has he devoted much time to watching it? Has he slowed down that perfect seven-iron shot and studied it frame by frame?

'I haven't looked at it very much, no,' says Lyle with typical ingenuity. 'I've got it all firmly fixed in my memory banks. It's history now . . . but nice history. You can look back at it and say, well, I did it. A lot of people wish they had been in the same situation. But to me that's water under the bridge now. You've got to look ahead.'

On the last day of play at St Andrews, Lyle's intention was to try for a top six finish. That was his ideal, really, his week had already been made. He was just pleased to have survived 'a very nerve-wracking week', to have lived on past the halfway mark where the best players in the world in far better form had crumbled, and to be going in the last round with a chance to do well.

'Dave,' I said to Musgrove on the range that final morning, while Lyle was warming up for his round. 'Do you think that Sandy is close to playing as well as he used to?'

'No,' said Musgrove.

'No?'

'Well, we're seven shots behind the leaders.' His grin is sardonic. 'Course he is. Yesterday he played exactly like he used to play. Exactly.'

Ironically, Lyle's level par score for an aggregate of 281 and a share of 16th place was one shot better than his total at Royal St Georges in 1985, the year he won the Open Championship.

Was the Open a turning point? 'Well,' says Lyle, who has learnt the value of being a realist rather than an optimist, 'it was a good starting point.'

Murphy's Cup, August 1990. Lyle's fine performance in the Open Championship owed as much to the help of a second protagonist as it did to the teachings of David Leadbetter; namely, that of Australian sports psychologist, Dr Noel Blundell.

Lyle was introduced to Blundell, who also works with Rodger Davis, two weeks before the tournament. Mark McCormack, head of IMG, felt that Blundell might be able to help Lyle as much as he had McCormack's tennis-player wife, Betsy King. With Lyle, Blundell works a great deal on concentrational techniques which prevent a player's mind wandering to possible dangers ahead, or poor shots just played. One of the exercises he advises players to do is focus on the smallest possible target, for example, the left-hand side of a tree or a stone in a bunker.

'It's really all about concentrating well over every shot,' says Lyle, 'being totally immersed in it, which is easier said than done. But if you approach a shot in the right way and you've got your brain working the right way, it makes an awful lot of difference.'

Golf is a game where the boundary between success and failure is infinitesimal. As Lyle himself once said: 'There is a very fine line between playing well and playing badly. People who run or swim have the same problem. They'll lose a race by a thirteenth of a second. That makes all the difference.' If Blundell can help Lyle increase the rift between the two extremes, then working with him, like working with Leadbetter, can only be a good thing.

'Well, it's got me thinking about every shot and picturing the shot and clearing the static away,' says Lyle. 'Because a lot of the time you've got static in the brain, where there's confusion about ifs and don'ts . . . We're going back to instincts and things. Trusting yourself. Because, you know, I wasn't so much struggling with my game out there, I was fighting a battle with myself most of the time on the golf course. With frustration and "Oh, here we go again, it's a bad lie." Now when I get a bad lie, I'm so busy working out what I'm going to do that I feel a lot calmer.'

With the renovation of his swing and the restoration of his peace of mind in hand, Lyle can now afford to attend to the chaos in his own home. For the last 18 months, his life off the golf course has been disrupted by a herd of builders, intent, in the way such people often are, in drawing out the agony of extending the Lyle house for as long as humanly possible. Sandy and Jolande, his wife, meanwhile, have been reduced to cooking, entertaining and sleeping in two rooms. The rest are submerged under a morass of dust and brickwork, the floorboards lifted and electrical works stripped.

Jolande cast herself in the role of supervisor. Her husband has left her to it. 'I just say, "Yes",' says Lyle. 'Easy way out.'

When the builders finally quit the house each evening, Lyle likes to relax by watching videos – mainly comedies and dramas of the *Lethal Weapon*, *Mad Max* and Arnold Schwarzenegger genre – and eating out with close friends, like neighbour Russ Abbott.

'What else do you do that's interesting?' I ask, in the unlikely event that Lyle has a range of exciting hobbies which he has left hitherto undisclosed.

'There's nothing that interesting. I live like a normal human being, really. I don't have gold-plated bath taps and things like that, just normal chrome – and I wash the dishes.'

'Woosnam's got gold taps.'

Lyle bursts out laughing. 'Diamond studded as well, I wouldn't be surprised.'

Out of the corner of my eye, tapping their fingers on the white table and poised for an impromptu interview, I can see a BBC film crew. They, like everyone else, want to play their part in Lyle's recovery. Lyle, of course, doesn't mind in the least. He is so overjoyed to have given them all something positive to write about and talk about that he's prepared to sit here all day.

For the first time in a long time Lyle is looking forward to tomorrow, to going out on the golf course and to competing. In this frame of mind and playing this well, it is easier to believe that come next season or the one after that, he'll win another major. Too many people have doubted it. Sandy Lyle among them.

'There's times when I've thought that, yes. But what Noel Blundell said to me was: "You're a very special person. You've got a lot of talent, and you never lose talent. If it's there, it's there to be brought out again."'

Chapter Nine

ROUGH TRADE

Photo: Lauren St John

Veteran caddie Pete Coleman, who has worked for Bernhard Langer since 1980

MADRID, SPAIN, APRIL 1990. THE HOSTEL WHERE THE CADDIES stay is on the sixth floor and smells of wax floor polish and the cooking of the Italian family who run it, but it's clean and comfortable and, at £10 a night with bathroom en suite, you can't ask for more.

I stayed with the caddies the week of the Madrid Open.

They come here every year and know it well. Our *pension* is situated in a grim concrete block and faces the Palace Hotel, an elegant chandeliered and marbled affair policed by uniformed doormen. The players used to stay there in days gone by so it was handy for getting courtesy cars and buses to the course each morning. Their new hotel is a good half hour's walk away. It costs each player close to £1,000 a week bed and breakfast but it has at least got satellite television, great views over the city and the latest line in luxuriously appointed lifts, complete with stereophonic sound.

Our own humble abode was reached by way of an eerily lit spiral staircase, or a lift which dangled precariously from slim steel ropes like a crate on the end of a crane. Faced with these options, Lindsey Anderson – a Scottish girl caddie with whom I roomed – and I always chose to sprint up.

I don't ever remember being so shocked by a city as I was by Madrid. Beneath the crumbling monuments and palaces, amidst the welter of construction and destruction and the interminable roar of traffic, there is a kind of wholesale decay. Prostitutes with hard, embittered faces blow kisses from darkened doorways, neon signs illuminate the merchandise of sex shops and strip joints; outside McDonalds a drug addict spits curses at passers-by.

The caddies found their own particular haven in Viva Madrid, a bar of doubtful repute, not far from the Prado Museum in the city. A rough band gathered there nightly and pursued their various inclinations. The rest of the caddies spread out through the city, enjoying, in most cases, comparatively quiet evenings out.

Times have changed and caddies with them. In Germany I stood and watched two caddies cleaning clubs in an old stone trough. It was a scene from another age: the scrubbing brushes, the cloths striped black with dirt from the grips, the clubs sparkling silver in the sunlight, the foam spilling over the edges and forming pools around their feet.

'This is where you find the real workers,' says Stephen McAllister's caddie, a Scottish lad of 25, with a sly glance at me. They all think that anyone who spends as much time hanging around the range and talking as I do can't possibly be doing any work.

'Hard work,' I scoffed. I enlisted the support of Jimmy Heggarty's Irish caddie, who is twice Frank's age. 'These young caddies don't know the meaning of hard work, do they?'

'Aye, you're right enough there,' was his sour rejoinder. He has a wonderful face – the kind of face a character actor would die for – nut brown and etched like a road map of life. Hunched under the weight of the golf bag, cigarette suspended from his lip, he nodded toward a leafy tangle of bushes. 'We used to sleep under them things there.'

I had a sudden vision of caddies, ill-shaven and smelling faintly of drink, trussed like fowls in blankets beneath hedgerows.

'And you used to wash in them things there?' I said, goading him slightly. But he shook his head at the stone trough. He described caddies showering under streams of rain water running from roofs, sharpening old razor blades on rough stone walls and shaving by their window reflections.

The reality of caddie life in those days wasn't quite so romantic. Caddies were regarded as little more than winos who slept under hedges. There was a term for the way they lived – 'skippering'. It came out of a story about three drunk caddies at the Benson and Hedges in York one year, who, having no place to stay and no particular desire to look for one, climbed into a skip and fell asleep. They were woken the next morning when the refuse collectors arrived to take it away.

Another caddie, similarly intoxicated, was sound asleep in a barn when it caught fire. He only woke up when his shoes began to curl up at the toes. That was how he appeared on the tee the next morning, boots still smouldering, charred and smelling of smoke.

'That's the kind of image that went with the past,' says Tour caddie-master, Willie Aitchison, firmly.

'Now, today's caddie, there's a lot that maybe drink and maybe don't, but there's a fringe element which even dabble in other things which I don't like, like drugs. But they've got a lot better and they've got a lot to look forward to. The whole scene's changed. There's a lot of money involved, there's a lot more places to go. When I started, there was only about eight or ten tournaments a year.'

Now there are 30 or 40 tournaments and a caddie can work from January to January if he chooses. The boom of golf as a sport and the subsequent inrush of money to the game brought with it a sharp rise of overall standards on the Tour. It revolutionised caddying as a profession and altered the lifestyles of the people who made a career of it out of all recognition. More caddies can make a living out of bag-carrying and a handful can make a great deal of money at it. Many of the top caddies now travel and stay with the players as a matter of course, and their relationship has improved as a result. There is, however, a definite distinction between the two. A kind of invisible barrier. A caddie, however wealthy or well-educated he may be in his own right, still belongs to a different and perceptibly lower class than a player.

For those who dream of caddying, of walking up the last at St Andrews carrying the Open Champion's bag, the Tour has the appeal that circuses once had: a gritty, hands-on, sawdust glamour, the prospect of a gloriously footloose existence and the freedom of working for oneself. It attracts a bizarre cross-section of people. Like a gay band of gypsies they proceed in a caravan from tournament to tournament. Some travel with all their worldly possessions in rucksacks slung over their shoulders; others are richer than a few players will ever be. Their pasts are often shady, their futures uncertain, their reasons for being on Tour questionable.

In Dusseldorf I struck up a conversation with a caddie, in deference to whose wishes I shall call Peter, lest 'they' get to hear of his whereabouts. The route by which he had come into caddying was not atypical. He had started by helping out a player at one event, and enjoyed it so much that he had decided to come out on Tour. His background was, he said, 'the casino business', and he refused to be pressed for details. As he continued, his tale grew, by degrees, more arcane. He gave the impression that 'they' were Britain's answer to the mafia, and that his knee caps' chances of survival would be considerably reduced should he reveal what he knew. He spoke of villas in Portugal, flats among the gentry in London, shopping sprees at Harrods and Lotuses bought for cash.

I was intrigued. What on earth had he been up to? Why on earth was he caddying when he had all that money? Why the secrecy?

But the mystique was dispelled in an instant by a player who Peter had been employed by. It transpired that he had been a croupier with the franchise for several cruise ships in the Bahamas. When the bottom had fallen out of the business he had returned to England, and now lived with the heiress to one of the oldest and largest firms in the United Kingdom. He caddied, it appeared, because he loved to caddie.

There are others. There's the Baroness, for example, a wealthy middle-aged Dutchwoman, who pops up from time to time on the Continent and acquires herself a bag for the week. Whether or not her title is genuine is unclear, but she sports a pink cap of the Ben Hogan variety and spends a good deal of time taking photographs of players on and off the golf course (which has not endeared her to them). Her intentions, one suspects, are not entirely honourable.

Another intriguing story is that of Irish, a roving caddie of indeterminate age. According to caddie lore, Irish, who is allegedly the nephew of a former Irish Prime Minister, has forfeited his inheritance and been branded the black sheep of the family by behaving in a dissolute fashion and following the Tour. Now he is an opal dealer of some note, buying the stones in Australia and selling them for small fortunes in places like Switzerland.

They are a strange mix, the caddies, impossible to categorise. There are people like Alastair, Denis Durnian's caddie, who has an honours degree in history; Simon Jenkins (Psychological Simon), who is doing a Doctorate in Sports Science, and has written a tome entitled *The Sports Science Handbook*;

ex-businessmen, like Martin Rowley and John (Hortie) Hort; ex-professional golfers, like Andy Prodger and Max, who used to carry Rodger Davis's bag; and odd-ball characters like Dominique, a crazy old Portuguese with a head full of jumbled English phrases and not too many links for them.

Caddies have a caricaturist's knack for illuminating a person's salient features and every one of them has a nickname. There's The Padre, The Brain, Fishfinger, Sponge, Squirrel and Jaws. Caddies of the same name are often distinguished by the player they work for, i.e. Olazabal Dave, or by the town they come from, i.e. Turnberry George.

So caddies have changed professionally, but in all other respects they are the same. They might not sleep under bushes but they have in common their hopes and their struggles with the vagabonds of the past. Theirs is a life which shares all the bad aspects of a golfer's – the pressures, the long hours of waiting and boredom, the struggle for survival, financially and competitively, and the loneliness – for far less personal gain, though not necessarily less satisfaction. And it is a life conducive to drinking, gambling and cruising the seamier sides of foreign towns; escaping from whatever they are running from, or searching for whatever it was that they came looking for.

Dubai, February 1990. Willie Aitchison and I sit high on an empty grandstand, talking golf, caddies and players from another era.

'Caddies are a different breed of men to what they were when I caddied,' says Aitchison reflectively. He is one of the old school, the kind the sentimental image of a caddie as a player's friend, adviser and conspirator was founded on. He views most young caddies with suspicion and a certain amount of condescension.

'A lot of them think they're caddies because they carry a bag and give yardages, but that's not where caddying starts and ends. That's only one part of it. You've got to take into consideration the elements, the person you're with, the type of course. Yardage is just a percentage thing. You've still got a club to select.'

In Aitchison's day there was no such thing as yardage books. All caddies could eye-ball (judge distances by sight) and choose clubs accordingly. The first time he went out with Lee Trevino, whose bag he carried for 23 years, they were walking down the fairway and the Mexican said: 'What is it?'

'A seven-iron,' said Aitchison confidently. Eye-balling, as he says, at least gave a caddie the courage of his own convictions.

'I didn't ask you the club,' said Trevino, 'I asked you how far it was.' Aitchison, of course, didn't know. 'Then how the hell do you know it's a seven-iron?' asked Trevino, annoyed.

'Because that's what I've been trained to do,' replied Aitchison.

'Well then,' said Trevino. 'How do you want me to hit it? Do you want me to hook it or do you want me to cut it?'

But when Aitchison – who has in his career won five amateur titles with Michael Bonallack, and six majors, and worked with players of the calibre of Sam Snead, Raymond Floyd, Gary Player and Tom Watson – won the Open in 1967 with Roberto de Vicenzo, he eye-balled the entire tournament.

The latter was one of his favourite and most emotional victories. De Vicenzo, the popular Argentinian, had begun the final round two shots ahead of Jack Nicklaus and three in front of Gary Player. Of the three, he knew he was the least fancied to win the tournament, and Aitchison remembers him saying on the first tee: 'If the people want me to win, I win for them. But they must come and watch me, not go watch Jack.'

'It took nine holes for the public to realise that it might be Roberto's year because Nicklaus couldn't get past him,' remembers Aitchison. 'We came onto the 16th tee and we knew we had to finish birdie, par, par. But as Roberto started his backswing, the spectators leaned against the chestnut fencing [the old method of cordoning off fairways] and there was a screech. He sort of half topped it and it was heading for out-of-bounds. I just shut my eyes . . . Fortunately for us, there's a practice range in the middle of Hoylake [and it landed there]. I was up to the ball first . . . Roberto came up to me, visibly shaking with excitement . . . He said, "What is it?" and I never hesitated. I never thought it was possible for him to miss that shot. He took the three-wood out and knocked it on – a par five – and two-putted for birdie.'

Aitchison's voice comes from a thousand miles away. His eyes are blurred with the vividness of recall, his mind filled with the bright colour of that day: the sweet smell of trampled grass, the sharper smell of sea salt on the wind, the dull roar of the crowd.

'Eighteen was a three wood over the bunkers downwind. The feeling I've never experienced again. The kids, they were jumping up and down and the tears were running down the man's face. Couldn't see the green. Could not see the green. He said: "Willie, just give me a club. Any club for the middle of the green." And I always remember it was an eight-iron and he put it behind the pin.'

Such times are the ultimate test of the bond between player and caddie, a partnership, which like that of a coach and his pupil can only really be successful if the chemistry is right.

Max Faulkner, the 1951 Open Champion, and his caddie, Mad Max, had a marvellous rapport. Mad Max was an absolute eccentric, walking the fairways in outlandish attire, feathers protruding at rakish angles from his hair. He had a pair of opera glasses without lenses which he would put on when he approached the green, before making a great play of inspecting the line for clues like Sherlock Holmes. 'It's slightly straight, Mr Faulkner, sir,' he would pronounce at last, or words to that effect.

Aitchison and Trevino had a similar relationship. They bounced one-liners off one another with dead-pan delivery and comic timing, delighting the galleries. 'Everybody thinks he's a clown.' Aitchison remembers Trevino differently. 'He's an entertainer and that was how he thought of himself. The public are his audience; the golf course is his stage. And he never forgets that the people behind the ropes are the people that allow him to play golf.

'He's a true golf professional in every sense of the word,' says Aitchison. 'I've seen him work seven hours on the practice ground and maybe play two rounds of golf into the bargain. I've done that with him. And he was so meticulous. When we started to play the small ball he had to find out how far he could hit each club down wind, into the wind, in cross winds. Consequently, I used to go and stake the practice ground off and we would do it over and over again. That was how thorough he was.'

The opening shot of the 1970 Piccadilly World Match Play is a close-up of Aitchison, tears streaming down his face, in the aftermath of the final between Trevino and Nicklaus. Trevino had been five down with eight holes to play and had clawed his way back to be one down with two holes to play. He stood up on the 17th tee, pumped up to the point of near explosion – because, as Aitchison says, 'Five down to Nicklaus, you think you've got no chance' – and hit his drive out of bounds to lose the match two and one.

'When we played the second ball off the tee, I went down to the ball. I was standing there thinking of what might have been and the tears just started rolling down my face. And he was standing there with tears in his eyes because he was so hell-bent trying to beat Jack head on.'

Such are the agonies and ecstasies of golf and of caddying, and nowhere are the contrasts so sharp as in majors and in match play.

In 1972, Trevino and Tony Jacklin – who was at that time the hero of the British public after his victories in the Open Championship in 1969 and the US Open in 1970 – played together in the final round of the Open at Muirfield. Jacklin would never be the same again after that day. But Aitchison, who was caddying for Trevino at the time, claims that the dramatic outcome of that round was not so much the result of what took place on the 17th green, as is generally believed, but rather of what happened on the 17th tee.

Trevino was first off. He addressed the ball, took one last look down the fairway and was just about to start his backswing when a cameraman shot out of the gallery and scampered across the fairway. The Mexican backed off and set up again. A split second before he began his backswing, a second man emerged from the crowd, this time carrying a tripod. His concentration broken, Trevino rushed his drive and hit a poor shot into the bunker.

Trevino was furious, but he reasoned that no matter how good his drive,

Jacklin was unlikely to reach the green in two playing into the wind. His own ball, however, was buried deep in a pot bunker and his escape finished short of Jacklin's drive. He hooked his next shot into the rough. Jacklin, meanwhile, had hit his second shot some 60 yards short of the green. Trevino's fourth was over the back.

'So it really looked as though Jacklin was in command,' recalls Aitchison. 'It was just a matter of chipping and putting. But when I got up to the ball, I swear to God, it looked like there was only one place for the ball to go, and that was in the hole. I could actually see it. And that was what happened.'

According to Aitchison, Jacklin had made the classic mistake of watching where Trevino's ball pitched, and in doing so, believed that the green was running faster than it was. He forgot that Trevino had been hitting out of the rough. His chip shot came up short and he took two putts to get down. Jacklin himself says that he believes Trevino's fluke chip-in brought about the premature demise of his career.

The only gamesmanship Aitchison ever saw Trevino use was in that match. After the Mexican holed out, Aitchison, high on emotion, went running to the 18th tee. Trevino stopped him and told him to let Jacklin go on to the next hole alone. 'He said: "When I get on the tee, give me my driver. I'm going to hit it while he's still dreaming." And he did. He hit it so fast and so far he actually sickened Jacklin. Jacklin put it in the bunker then. He didn't even finish second. I think the will to win had completely gone out of him.'

Nowadays Aitchison works for the phenomenally talented Mark Davis. 'You can chalk him up as your next superstar,' said Aitchison confidently, earlier in the year. Just lately, though, he's begun to have second thoughts about the 23-year-old from Essex. Davis, who is a diabetic, is too aggressive in some ways on the golf course, too negative in others, too rich [his father has a private plane and several houses dotted round the globe] and perhaps a little spoilt.

'Whether he has the desire to do well, I don't know sometimes,' says Mark Roe. 'It's easy for him to walk away and say, "Sod it, I don't need it." Whereas other people have to do it. It's their only chance. They're hungry to do well.'

Roe is friends with the hyperactive Davis, who is alternately nicknamed Vidal (because of his stylish haircut) or Mad Dog, depending on who you are speaking to. 'Most of us,' comments Roe on Davis's off-course activities, 'seem to have limits. There's a certain point you'll go to and you won't overstep the line. With Mad Dog there are no limits.'

In terms of his own character, snatches of Aitchison's conversation are more revealing than he might like to think.

He tells, for instance, a story about a time he and Trevino were invited to a ball in Paris. They were both staying at the King George Hotel because for the most part Aitchison went everywhere Trevino did, stayed in the same hotels, flew in the same private planes. At first Aitchison declined the invitation on the grounds that he had nothing to wear, but then at Trevino's insistence, went with him to an evening wear hire shop. 'He dressed me up like an oil-baron from Texas. If you'd seen me, you'd a thought I was John Wayne.'

So Aitchison went to the ball clad in all his finery. But halfway through the evening he slipped out through a side door and wandered around in the darkness, up the Champs-Elysées and under the L'Arc de Triomphe, until it was over. Aitchison smiles at the memory. 'I didn't feel that it was my cup of tea,' he explains.

And so to this image which persists of caddies as ruffians and reprobates. They are still there among the new, clean-cut young caddies who are filling the ranks.

'Caddies are still the same as they always were,' affirms Damien Moore, who works Canadian Jim Rutledge's bag, 'but they've cleaned themselves up in a way. They just dress smarter and they've got some sort of code. They're still bad.'

He can remember finding John Graham, who now works for Mark James, unconscious on the floor of a disco in Switzerland one year. It was 5 a.m. and Graham, who was carrying David Frost's bag that week, had to be on the tee at eight. Somehow he made it. Frost shot 63 that day and won the Rolex watch for the lowest round of the tournament.

The subject of this sordid allegation is unrepentent.

'I've just had my week's wages, right,' says John Graham (Scotchy), digging deep into the pocket of his trousers and pulling out a handful of change. His laugh reveals a chipped front tooth. 'Five pounds. I can't believe that's all I've got left from £250.'

I can. A paltry sum has gone on accommodation and food and the rest has been taken care of by Viva Madrid and gambling. Graham, with occasional assistance from Tony (Chubby) Chandler, an ex-Tour player who now owns his own management company, and Paul Carrigall's father (a bookmaker), is the Tour bookie. It's been a bad week for the horses.

Beneath his brown leather stock hat, Graham's face is the colour and texture of leather, his hair bleached, his eyes a faded blue. Every movement he makes is slow and deliberate. Cool. He drags long and hard on his cigarette and doesn't visibly exhale. Not a single wisp of smoke appears.

At 30, Graham has caddied for some of the best players in Europe: Sandy Lyle, Jose-Maria Olazabal, Howard Clark, and Brian Barnes and Michael King at the height of their careers. He started with Lyle in 1978, Lyle's rookie year on Tour, when the Scotsman was still relatively unknown. Two seasons later they had won four tournaments and the Order of Merit twice together. According to Graham, when they eventually parted company, it was because Lyle was under pressure from IMG to take a 'name' caddie. Graham was not surprised.

At the World Matchplay in 1979, Lyle had dropped him for a week in favour of famous caddie Alfie Files and then taken him back at the next tournament, the Lancome Trophy in Paris.

Thinking about the Lancome, Graham is reminded of one of his favourite stories. He chuckles to himself. 'This is a classic,' he says, in case there's any doubt.

'One night six of us caddies went into Maxims. What a meal we had! King Crab for starters, prime beef steaks and all the trimmings, eight bottles of wine. We had coffee, big cigars. Then the bill came. It must have been £3,000. The caddie who was going to pay for it told the waiter to add another ten percent for a tip. Then he signed for it under a different name and we just got up and walked straight out.

'I've always been sort of . . . bad,' he observes calmly when he has stopped laughing. Graham's record bears him out on this. To date, he has been jailed three times in Spain, 'for nothing', and once in Paris for fraud. In Majorca earlier this year, he was one of three caddies locked up and fined £200 for being drunk and disorderly – 'For nothing at all, man . . . *Singing! And they lock you up for it!* It's shocking.'

Two of the caddies were robbed by a hooker that week (a regular occurrence). They paid her to spend the night with them, and in the morning, handed her the key to the apartment and naïvely told her to let herself out. Half an hour later a van drew up and removed all their belongings and everything that wasn't bolted down in the apartment.

As an example of past sins, Graham cites a time when he was caddying for Dillard Pruitt in Switzerland. Pruitt missed the cut and Graham proceeded into the nearest bar to drink away the weekend. He bought everyone who entered the room – locals and players alike – a drink. When the barman presented him with the tab, Graham told him to put it on room 105. Unfortunately for him, Richard Boxall, whose room number it happened to be, walked in at that moment and naturally enough went up the wall.

Boxall would be the last person in the world to hold a grudge against anybody, but every now and then as a reminder to Graham, he'll shout cheerfully across a crowded bar, 'Room 409 this week, John, if you're interested.'

Graham's fondness for drinking and gambling has cost him a few choice bags but he has an excellent working relationship with Jesse – as Mark James is popularly known. James is such a good-natured, easy going player, he is the perfect foil for Graham's tendency to go off the rails. 'He's good,' drawls Graham. 'Nae bother. Reads his own yardages. He just brings me in sometimes to read putts. He'll sort of say, "Read the greens, John." And then when I get one wrong he'll say, "Oh, just forget it, John."'

One year at Crans-sur-Sierre, venue of the Ebel European Masters, Mark James's caddie for the week (not Scotchy) failed to turn up for their round.

'You're fired,' said James when the caddie came to him with excuses.

Caddie, in tears: 'You can't fire me. I need the money.'

'I can and I will,' declared James.

Caddie: 'I'm going to go up to the top of that glacier and throw myself off.'

James: 'Do you know the way?'

Needless to say, the caddie didn't do anything of the kind. He stayed on in Switzerland for the summer and made a fortune.

In contrast to James, Howard Clark, his best friend, has such a bad reputation among caddies that most of them won't carry his bag. The fact that Fanny Sunnesson managed to last an entire year with him is one of the main reasons why the other caddies don't resent her working for Faldo. They think that anybody who can cope with Clark for that length of time has definitely served their apprenticeship.

'Clarky?' Graham says, one eyebrow raised. 'Hard man. Really, really hard.'

He tells a story about Clark at the 1980 Open Championship at Muirfield where, in true caddie fashion, Graham emerges as the innocent party. It's the royal 'We'. *We* made a birdie on 17 and then *he* drove it out of bounds.

'He's got it going pretty well,' says Graham, recalling part of the round, 'and we get to the eighth hole and he says, "What do you think it is here, John?" I said it was a two-iron, short of the cross-bunkers. He said: "It's not. It's a one-iron." So he hits a one-iron and he just turns it over into the left-hand rough. His head's off. Wrong club and all that. So he chips it out, knocks it on to the green for three. His first putt goes four feet past the hole. And he's staring right at me and his eyes, they're sort of hanging out. You know what I mean? He's giving me a death stare. I thought: "Jesus Christ!"

'We get to the tenth and it's blowing a gale, *hurricane*, into our faces. What does he do? Tops it . . . On 12, he's got a three-foot putt for par and he misses it. He turns to me and he says, "John, what have I told you about walking around when I'm putting?"

'I said: "Clarky, there's a million people out there!" and after that everything I said was just totally wrong.

'He gave me murder on the course that day,' says Graham finally. 'I never worked for him after that . . . You see, Clarky off the golf course, right, is brilliant. He's a great guy. But on the course he's hard. He's the hardest guy to work for.'

Australian Vaughan Summers was another player whose temper on the golf course was legendary. On one particular occasion Tim Lane, an ABC commentator and reputedly a gentle, philosophical man, caddied for him. While they waited on the first tee of the tournament, Lane decided to share the wisdom of Rudyard Kipling with the volatile Summers. 'If you can keep your head when all about you are losing theirs . . .' he recited.

Summers agreed that it was a maxim worthy of consideration. On the first hole he hit a fine drive and an excellent second shot to 20 feet. Then he three-putted. In a flash, he lost his temper and kicked the golf bag. 'Any more fucking quotes from Rudyard Kipling,' he fumed at the unfortunate Lane.

The contrast between most players' personalities on and off course is stark. 'Jeckyll and Hyde,' says Andy Prodger, Faldo's ex-caddie, who should know. 'The thing is,' comments Prodger, 'the more money there is involved, the less these players seem to enjoy their golf . . . They know they can't make a mistake and if they make a mistake, they can't seem to get it out of their minds.'

That's why Willie Aitchison maintains that to be a good caddie, you have to be part psychologist. 'You have to take an interest in the guy and learn what his idiosyncracies are. Know what his good habits are and what his bad habits are.'

'You have to be their best friend and their butler,' adds Damien Moore. 'You have to take all the shit, because it's always your fault. They've got to blame it on someone. You've got to always be behind your guy, even if his head's off. You've got to calm him down.'

Madrid Golf Club is a sanctuary in comparison to the city. The stately mansion which serves as a clubhouse overlooks a course built among forests and valleys. The practice ground is one of the best this year and the weather is fine, so every player not on the course is out hitting balls.

'In the States we have a saying about people like you,' Steve Bowman is telling his Australian caddie. Two Shots, teasingly. 'You're an accident looking for somewhere to happen.'

'He's already happened,' shouts another Aussie caddie delightedly.

Two Shots – so named because he reputedly cost Terry Gale a two-shot penalty in the Australian Masters – just grins from ear to ear. He knows he is a walking disaster area. This is the caddie who, stuck for accommodation at an English tournament, took himself off to the local police station and asked for a bed. Amazingly enough, they lent him their sofa for the night. Two Shots, however, didn't get much sleep. Alone and frightened in the station, he spent most of the night on the phone to the Samaritans.

'He's only just started and he thinks he knows everything,' says Damien Moore mockingly one evening in Madrid. Two Shots (whose real name is David McHugh), at whom this remark is directed, looks indignant. At 19, Moore, a tousle-haired, sleepy-eyed young man with red cheeks and big brown eyes, might be the same age as Two Shots, but he is already the more experienced of the two by four or five seasons. Both of them are part of a new generation of caddies: better-dressed, cleaner living, more ambitious.

Moore has been working since the age of 14. The caddie-master at Wentworth, his local club, was the sort who encouraged young boys to carry bags in favour of going to school, at an age when money took precedence in their minds over arithmetic (which is why there are eight ex-Wentworth caddies on Tour). By the time he was 16, Moore was caddying full-time.

He carried Gerry Taylor's bag the first year the PGA Championship was held at Wentworth and was surprised to find that a lot of the Tour caddies weren't much older than he was. When the tournament ended, Moore packed all his belongings into three carry bags and came out on Tour. He's been travelling ever since.

Moore slept rough at first because his tent was stolen at the next tournament. 'That's what it's like when you first come out here and you don't have no money. I'd go to sleep about 12, wake up at five and go into the clubhouse and have a shower for about two hours to warm up. It was pissing it down with rain and the wind was blowing and I was on a bench in the starter's tent . . . but I loved it because I was out on the Tour.'

For six months Moore free-lanced. 'I couldn't keep a regular job 'cause obviously they didn't believe that I was any good at that age, didn't think I was responsible. Because, remember, you're making decisions out there that could cost them thousands of pounds.' But he considers all the ensuing hardship between coming out on Tour, working for Neil Hansen, and getting a full-time job with Rutledge, a top 50 player, well worth enduring. He knows how much money it is possible for a good caddie to make. 'I'll be in place for a good job next year – top 20 hopefully. I'm being lined up for it. It's taken me a while but I should be moving up in a couple of years to a top job.'

The caste system among caddies is one of extraordinary complexity. It begins with nationality: Irish caddies work for Irish players, Australian caddies for Australians, and so on. But it goes deeper than that. A caddie's status within the system of hierarchy is dependent on his player's ranking in the Order of Merit, on how long an apprenticeship he has served and on how good a caddie he is considered to be by the powers that be in the caddie ranks.

Luck does play its part in the bags that a caddie gets but there is also a strict code of ethics which has to be adhered to when getting jobs. It is inadvisable for anyone to jump the queue for the best bags before they've served their time and paid their dues. Only one or two caddies have beaten the system, most notably Ian Wright and Fanny Sunnesson, both of whom were in the trade for a comparatively short time before getting top bags.

The money that can be made in caddying is potentially enormous, but only for those who work for the best players. The supposed average wage is £250 per week but not every player will pay that, particularly if their caddie is just a casual. Now £250 might sound like a reasonable sum of money but it just barely covers a week's expenses on the Continent. The only way for a caddie to actually make money is on his percentage, which varies from player to player. Most golfers will pay the basic wage, as well as seven per cent for a win and five per cent for a place.

It's difficult to work out exactly what the top caddies do earn since a tendency to exaggeration in all matters fiscal goes with the job. John Graham claims to have made £30,000 last year with Mark James. Paul Stephens, Mark McNulty's caddie, drives a Mercedes 300CE and is supposed to send his children to private schools if that is any indication of wealth. Caddies like Wobbly, Sunnesson and Pete Coleman are believed to earn upwards of £80,000 a year.

Talk to caddies long enough and you'll find that most of them are planning to quit the Tour, if not this year then certainly at the end of next, and lead a 'normal life'. They never do. Come the start of the new season, they'll all be there, waiting for that lucky break – for a good bag or a tournament victory. The caddies themselves have a name for people who do this. They call them 'lifers'.

'It's certainly a very difficult thing, to actually stop caddying,' admits Prodger. 'It's a gypsy life and it's a challenge. It gets in your blood. Each week you're working for nothing unless your player is doing well. So the pressure is on you to help him do well.'

'I'm free,' says Sullie, a grizzled old veteran of both the US and European Tours. 'I'm a free bird. I fly wherever I wanna fly, nest wherever I wanna nest.'

On the matter of the nomadic life they lead, caddies and players are strangely divided. Most players loathe Tour travel, or at best can just about tolerate it. Caddies, on the other hand, are addicted to life on the road. It's why they came on Tour in the first place.

Lorne Duncan, a tall Canadian with an open face and the healthy skin that comes with spending most of life outdoors, became a caddie so that he could see the world. 'This is the best, you know. I get to make money and see places at the same time, and then I'm flexible enough that I can take three months off every year to do some real serious travelling.' This year he will be working on five different continents, before taking time off to do some serious travelling. He plans to journey overland from Delhi to Calcutta, fly to Rangoon, and then in January take the Trans-Siberian Express from Beijing to Helsinki.

'The appeal of caddying has changed over the last few years,' says Duncan, son of a golf professional whose own father was caddie-master at St Andrews. 'It used to be that it was an alternative lifestyle in which you did what you wanted to do; where you were your own boss to a certain extent . . . But as the money has crept in people have begun making more decisions for you . . . People now tell you what you have to wear and how to behave and whether you can go into a clubhouse or not.'

The urge to settle down has never come over him. Stability, he says, doesn't hold anything for him. When he eventually gives up caddying, it will be to go off to Africa and obtain a pilot's licence which will make it easier for him to travel.

Quitting the Tour is a hazy notion for John Graham and not one that he plans to give any thought to in the immediate future. 'I couldn't do another job,' Graham says laconically. 'Caddying's the best job in the world.'

Perched on a bench in the dark mahogany clubhouse, Graham drags deeply on his cigarette. Its tip glows orange in the dim light.

'What's so good about it?' he muses. 'What's so good about caddying? You're just there. In the frame, out the frame. And when you're in the frame, it's a great job.'

Chapter Ten

MASTER CRAFTSMEN

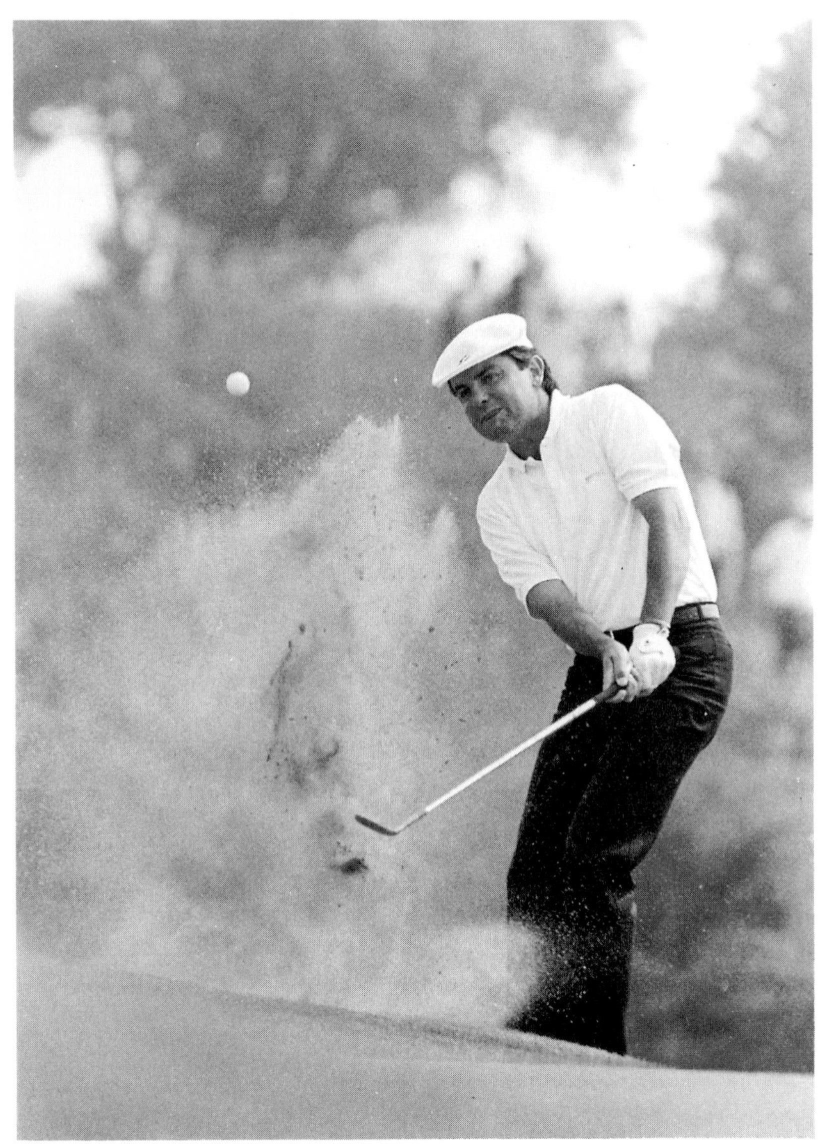

Photo: Jan Traylen

Master craftsman: Mark McNulty swings out

TAKEN OVER THE YEARS, A PLAYER'S GAME CAN BE A MIRROR that reflects his personality, his lifestyle, his state of mind. Everything he puts into it shows. So does everything he doesn't. Thus, the hardest workers, those players who are most single-minded, who live their lives carefully with their golf game in mind, are the best.

Except in this one instance, golf can seem to be an unjust game. In other sports and other vocations a man can hide much behind an amiable façade, a show of dedication. But not in golf. In this game you only get out that which you put in. That's why a player's success on the golf course is inextricably tied to his lifestyle off it. And what Doug Sanders meant when he said: 'To win a championship does not mean that you are a champion. To be a champion you have to conduct yourself in a certain way.'

French Open, Chantilly, 1990. The air was heavy with the sullen stillness which precedes Paris storms when Mark McNulty walked on to the 18th tee with a measured pace. His practice swing was smooth and unhurried, his tee shot no different. 'He's still got that same old swing,' said a friend who has known McNulty since junior golf days. 'Still looks as though he's had an air shot,' he says, meaning that there's no hit in McNulty's golf swing. Backswing, downswing and follow-through blend fluidly into one.

McNulty's ball found its customary position on the fairway – dead centre. Beneath his white cap, his expression was engrossed. Thus immersed in his golf game, his only concession to anyone or anything is a brief consultation held with Paul Stephens, his equally taciturn caddie. Is he aware of entering the cocoon of concentration other players say he does? 'Most of the time, yes. And particularly when I'm in the position to do well, I find I'm more tunnel-visioned and into that concentration. It's not easy for me to be swayed out of it but I can usually tell when I am . . . It's not that I'll hit a bad shot but over the next ten or 15 minutes something will happen which will tell me: "Your lapse in concentration caused an error here." It happens. But that's part of golf.'

McNulty rarely loses concentration when he is in the position to do well, however, and he was in no danger of losing it now. His approach to the long 18th finished 15 feet from the pin. As the first dark spots of rain began to fall, he holed a birdie putt for 63. Strokes that is. A two-shot penalty on the first made it a 65. Not bad around a course which is recognised as one of the toughest in Europe.

All week McNulty has been doing what pros do most, experimenting with different putters to find the one that is going to give him the best feel on the day. This week, unusually for McNulty, he has been so uncertain about which putter he feels more comfortable with that he has been leaving the choice between his old bullseye putter and his new La Femme bullseye putter (ladies' model) until he gets to the first tee, then handing the one he doesn't want to

Stephens to give to the starter. Today – the second day of play – Stephens forgot to take the putter out of the bag, which meant that McNulty was in breach of the 14-club rule. A double bogey on the first hole and a bogey on the second, and McNulty was standing on the third tee looking a dead cert for the afternoon plane to Heathrow. Nine birdies later and he is in contention for the tournament.

Was he angry with Stephens for effectively costing him the course record, the Rolex for the lowest round, and a share of the halfway lead? The press wanted to know.

'It's just as much my fault as Paul's,' McNulty instantly assured them. 'And more importantly, it was because of that I realised that if I didn't do something quickly, I'd be on the plane home. If that hadn't happened I might have shot 73 instead of 63. Who knows?'

It is this kind of graciousness, combined with a winning attitude and a superb golf game, which has made McNulty one of the most respected players in Europe on and off the golf course.

'This course [Chantilly] is so suited to McNulty's game that it might have been designed for him,' a player commented to Paul Carrigill on the range this morning. 'If that's the case,' retorted Carrigill drily, 'every course in Europe must have been designed for him.'

I relayed this to McNulty later, and though he smiled at the compliment, he took it perfectly seriously. 'It's true,' he says. 'I've finished in the top ten on every course in Europe.'

Since turning professional in 1977, the Zimbabwean short game maestro has had 31 tournament victories world-wide (32 by the end of 1990). Out of 19 European tournaments played in 1987, 13 were in the top 20, 12 were in the top 20 in 1988, and 12 were in the top 20 in 1989. His final positions in the Order of Merit since 1986 have been sixth, second, sixth and ninth, respectively.

The media are slow to recognise such achievements, particularly when the player is not British or not considered 'good press'. After watching McNulty play superlative golf at the Benson and Hedges earlier this year, a reporter turned to me and said that it was a shame the Zimbabwean was such a nondescript player. This was not an attack on McNulty as a person. What he meant was that McNulty's game is not impressive in the areas that make the most impression. He is not a long driver although he is adequate; he is not overly aggressive; his iron play is faultless but not special. But his consistency and short game are second to none. Those, however, are quiet talents. A 50-foot pitch from a difficult lie to within a foot of the pin, rarely looks as dramatic to the spectator as does the 320-yard drive.

McNulty is not unduly concerned about the lack of recognition he gets, preferring to let his victories speak for themselves. He, like the other players whom the spotlight passes by, knows that everything comes through playing good golf.

Epson Grand Prix, September 1990. Mark McNulty, more than most players, lives his life in a way that's conducive to becoming a champion. It's there in his manners, in his appearance, in the way that he conducts himself. It's not something he considers essential to playing good golf. It's just the way he is.

'I think most guys who become brilliant at their particular sport or business are, nine times out of ten, born that way and are going to be that way because of the power of their minds. Obviously it helps, particularly in sport, to look after yourself. It's very important in golf because golf is a sport where you can play at top level from 22 to 60 – Nicklaus and Player have certainly proved that.

'I would say,' says McNulty in his quiet, considered way, 'that Gary Player is the best example of looking after yourself as far as eating and exercising goes, and Bob Charles comes close. Then there are exceptions to the rule as well. Walter Hagen used to drink a lot. A lot of guys do drink a lot and abuse their bodies and still are great. So really, the common denominator between them is the power of the brain. It's what you want in life – what you want to achieve. Self-confidence and self-belief.'

Physical efficacy may not have been McNulty's strong suit through his career, but mental toughness has. Never has that been more apparent than in the 12 month span between October 1986 and October 1987 when he won an incredible 13 tournaments, and in this season, which has been remarkable not only for its consistency but also for the level at which it has been maintained. In 21 European starts, McNulty has finished in the top ten 15 times, including two victories – one in the German Open, the richest tournament on the circuit – and was losing finalist to Ian Woosnam in the World Match Play last week. At this point in time, he leads Ian Woosnam, Jose Maria Olazabal and Ronan Rafferty on the Volvo Order of Merit, with earnings in excess of £380,000.

'I'm playing the most consistent golf of my life,' said McNulty in a press conference this afternoon. 'I might not be playing my best golf ever. It's difficult to draw comparisons between '87 when I played well and now.'

'How do you explain your consistency?'

'Well, I think it's hard work, motivation and will, basically.' McNulty laid the groundwork for the season by taking a long break over December, January and February, and then, thoroughly refreshed, spent a month practising and preparing himself.

'I think my strong point is my mind,' admits McNulty frankly when asked for his strengths and weaknesses, 'and my weak point is possibly the physical state of my body . . . If I had a bigger and stronger body I might do better, but if I had a bigger and stronger body I might have a pea brain. So you've got to take what you get. And I think I'm fortunate enough to say that when I do well in the game, it's normally due to the fact that my brain is active in the right direction.'

'Do you ever read books like *The Power of Positive Thinking?*'

'No, I've only read a few just for the sake of reading them but I don't have to read them. There might only be a small percentage of my year when I have no confidence. A lot of it is willing yourself and making yourself do things the way your brain wants to do them. I like to strive for perfection, even though I never attain it. Perfection, I suppose, is playing a par four in two, a par five in three and a short hole in one, for eighteen holes.'

Ben Hogan said as much.

It is McNulty's firm belief that setting standards and setting goals are the keys to success. 'It's important to set yourself goals that you're always looking up to. If you start at the beginning of the season and you say, "I want to earn X amount of money", and you get it very quickly, then you've gone past your goal and you're going to sit back on your laurels for the rest of the season. I think you've got to set yourself a target that is almost unattainable and strive to reach it.'

Ian Woosnam has similar ideals. 'You've got to set your goals as high as you possibly can,' says the Welshman, 'then even if you do well you don't get excited about it. You know what I mean? A lot of players get excited about winning a tournament. It's only one tournament. To be the best player, you have to win 30 or 40.'

McNulty is the perfect illustration of that philosophy. Last month he won the German Open for the third time, yet he doesn't look any more excited about it than he would about going to the supermarket. For him it was a tiny landmark on the road of achievement he has set himself.

He studies each victory objectively, separating luck from performance. 'Nine times out of ten when you win a tournament, you've got luck and you've got everything going your way anyway. So you take that luck and you say to yourself: "How did I play?" "Well, I played nicely." "Can I play better?" "Yes." "When do I expect to play as well as I did then?" "I expect to play better in three or four weeks time."'

If McNulty decides that he couldn't have played better golf than he did, he looks at his performance in relation to the best tournament victory of his career. At this point in time it is still the German Open in 1987, where he finished with a record 72-hole score of 259, 27 under par. The day he thinks he performs as well as he did then the German Open will be wiped from the top of his table of triumphs, 'and a new level of play – in as far as winning play is concerned – comes to the fore.'

'What I'm trying to say,' explains McNulty, 'is that after each tournament victory I want to do better. How much better can you do than winning? You can win again and win by more and play better. It just depends on how you figure you can do better.'

Despite McNulty's long break over the winter, the strain of continually being in contention is beginning to tell. 'I expect a lot of myself,' he says, 'and with me expecting a lot of myself, I think at times I'm putting a lot of unnecessary pressure on myself . . . It's a fine balance at the end of the season, making sure you have the energy to keep on competing at a high level. And if you overdo it you just go stale.'

The delicate balance between playing too much and playing too little applies as much to the start of the season as it does to the end. 'There are times,' says McNulty, 'when you'll be going along nicely and a lapse in concentration causes a disaster. Why was there a lapse in concentration? Maybe because you've played too much over the last six weeks and your break in concentration had to eventually come. So it's obviously important then, in the same context, to pace yourself correctly. Every time a good player plays, he wants to win.'

Almost all the top players – Ballesteros, Langer, Lyle and Faldo – gear their playing schedules around the major championships. Mark James concentrated on four main tournaments when planning his year: the Memorial Tournament at Muirfield Village in May, the US Open in June, the Open Championship in July and the US PGA Championship in August. By the end of 1990 he will have played a total of 18 European events – almost half that of some of the lower-ranked players on the Tour. 'I want to give myself a chance of performing a hundred per cent everywhere I go,' James said at the beginning of the season.

Like athletes and tennis players, the best golfers are capable of preparing themselves mentally and physically to peak at a given time. But does a player get the maximum from his game by playing less or playing more? Will his game retain a sharp competitive edge if he isn't facing tough competition regularly?

'I think only the person himself is able to judge that,' replies McNulty. 'I think Mark is the kind of player who can afford to do that anyway. Whereas, you might get a young player who's not exempt for three or four years who can't afford it . . . It's the affordable position you get into which is created by being a good player. And a good player is a person with a good mind, who can take the ups and downs of life as well as golf.'

'What separates good players from great players?'

'It's definitely the brain.'

'But it's also desire, surely?'

'Sure, but that's your brain. Your head is in control of everything . . . your confidence, your capacity to do well, your motivation – that's the same as desire, but you can have desire without motivation and you can have motivation and no desire . . . I mean, Seve will be 90 before he realises that he won't be able to win another major. And Nicklaus . . . he's an incredible man. His motivation levels are unbelievable.'

'What motivates you?'

'To be as good as I can be,' says McNulty with quiet determination. 'I always feel I can get better and if I get better I'll win more tournaments. Winning as many tournaments as I possibly can in my short little lifespan is a big motivation. I don't think money is necessarily a motivator, but there comes a time in a tournament when you're playing the last holes – you're five shots back and you can't win – and it's a question of doing the best that you can because there's money at the end of the line, although I don't think people necessarily think of that.

'The most important thing really is that we all play this game to win, and if you become a winner, there's a great sense of achievement and satisfaction that you've achieved a certain aspect of your goal or goals . . . I don't necessarily want to walk down the street and have everybody say, "There goes Mark McNulty." I don't want that at all. I want a private life. You just want within yourself to win.'

Irish Open, Portmarnock, June 1990. It takes a certain amount of audacity and innate self-confidence to place a bet on oneself, particularly when the bet is to win the Order of Merit. Australian Rodger Davis has never been short of either. That's why he walked into Ladbrokes, the bookmakers, at the start of the season and laid £1,000 at 33-1 on the counter. 'It was done for confidence,' explains Davis. 'Believing I could do it and just backing it up.'

Davis, you see, believes that goal-setting and, more importantly, realistic goal-setting, is an integral part of success. He doesn't see the bet as a contradiction in terms. The theory behind it has been thought out very carefully. Davis reasoned that because the top players in Europe – namely Ballesteros, Langer, Lyle, Faldo, Woosnam, Rafferty and Olazabal – have made rods for their own backs this season by demanding appearance money at every event and refusing to play if they aren't paid, they could cut the number of events they compete in to as few as 12. Davis intends to play in 25. In previous years, playing in half that number, he has finished eighth, ninth and seventh on the money list. Besides which, if Davis does end 1990 as the European number one, he stands to win £40,000.

All of this fits in nicely with another one of his theories.

'I think you should give yourself rewards for your hard work and the way you play,' says Davis. 'If you don't, really you're not getting anything out of the game. Set yourself down a nice holiday, or nice car or a beautiful house, or whatever, and give yourself a reward for playing well. Why just stash it away?'

In 1985, Rodger Davis, winner of ten European and Australian tournaments at that time, threw up everything and went home to Australia to try his hand at motel ownership. He was tired of never seeing his family and frustrated because he wasn't holing the putts that win tournaments. Bankruptcy forced him back again, Davis, who had invested all his winnings in the motel and in houses which he rented out, lost every single penny. And as he says, 'Being broke is a big motivator.'

'I've always been a fighter,' says Davis now, 'and I suppose the fight started with: (1) Making the decision I was coming back on Tour, because I thought that was my only way out of the "normal job" situation. (2) To get back on Tour I had to get fit and I had to practise, and in accepting that you've got to do those things, all of a sudden you can set yourself a routine and you can set yourself goals, and that, I think, is when you can start climbing the ladder.'

According to Davis, there are two ways to a goal set in golf. One is to do it with statistics – fairways hit, bunker shots, putts – and to practise the areas that you are falling down in. 'I mean, people who don't take statistics would say they're putting poorly: "I had 32 putts today." Except that it's not actually their putting because they've hit all their second shots 30 feet from the hole and they can't one-putt. But if you actually go into your statistics then it leads you to set your goals, because you're actually working in the correct areas.'

The other way is to set specific monetary targets. Davis has the same philosophy towards this as Greg Norman does towards majors.

'When you set your goals,' I asked the Shark, 'do you say to yourself, "I want to win three majors," or whatever the case may be?'

'No, because you can't,' said Norman firmly. 'It's like going out on the golf course and saying, "I want to make eight birdies." You can't tell yourself you're going to do that. You can say, "My goal today is to go out there and shoot the lowest possible score."

'But it's hard to say: "I'm going to make eight birdies today, no problem." I defy anybody to go out there and do that. You can't see a number in your mind and chase that number. You can go and play one shot at a time. And that one shot is going to lead you to the next shot. But if you're trying to play the next hole before you've hit this shot, it's not going to work.'

Davis applies that logic to a 72-hole tournament: 'I don't plan to birdie certain holes. I purely and simply play each shot at a time and I've found that by doing that, you can shoot 63. Whereas, if you think, "Right, I'll par the first two and birdie the third," and then you start off par, par, par, you'll think, "Now I've got to pick one up." You know, you're putting stupid pressures on yourself. If you play one shot at a time then if you have a bogey, okay, you have a bogey. You might birdie the next hole.'

At 39, Davis, while being less of a convert to the fit-for-life way of thinking than McNulty, firmly believes that the way a player lives his life is directly related to his success on the golf course.

'Well, the way I look at the Tour is like I'm at home,' says Davis, explaining his approach to diet and fitness. 'Now, for instance, if you're having a meal at home you don't have entrées, main course, dessert, coffees or liqueurs. You just have a main course. So when I'm on Tour I try to do the same thing. There's no need to do all that. There's no need to go partying. One thing I do is set myself a programme. I have two alcohol-free days a week and during tournaments I might have a glass of wine during dinner. And it lets your system catch up. If you can just flush yourself out with water twice a week, you give yourself a chance.'

For fitness and stamina, Davis does flexibility exercises and sand-dune running to strengthen his legs, because he is convinced that if a player's legs get tired on the golf course, then he is not going to be able to hit the shots under pressure that he needs to hit. Over the last few years, however, Davis has begun to concentrate harder on mental training than physical training. Like Sandy Lyle, he goes to Australian sports psychologist, Dr Noel Blundell.

'The one good thing about those sort of guys,' says Davis, 'is that for them to help you, you've got to be very truthful. It is hard but at the end of the day you want to be successful and half the battle is owning up.'

Blundell regards each player as a completely unique individual and adapts his methods accordingly. With Lyle, he mainly works on concentrational techniques; with Davis he works on routine, the importance of which he places a great deal of emphasis on. It is Blundell's belief that a player is capable of acquiring mind memory as well as muscle memory. Say, for example, he usually hits a shot within eight seconds of walking up to it. The closer he can keep to that routine, the more familiar the body is with the situation, and the less likely the mind is to fall prey to negative thoughts. And, like a grooved swing, the easier he will find it to repeat the same pattern under pressure.

What Blundell tries to establish is exactly how much a player's routine changes under pressure. He found that in the final round of a tournament, Davis took approximately seven seconds to hit the ball whereas, in the opening rounds – where Davis tends to struggle – he took anywhere between five and 12 seconds.

In other words, Davis is an excellent pressure player, but like Mark James, he finds it difficult to get motivated in the early rounds of an event when he isn't under the heat.

Davis applies the principles of routine to everything he does on and off the course. If, when he is on the putting green, he usually hits two practice putts, puts the putter-blade in front of the ball and then behind, and then makes his stroke, he will try to repeat that exact pattern every hole he plays. When he arrives at the golf course in the morning, he goes out to the practice range exactly 55 minutes before his tee-off time and hits balls for half an hour. Putting takes another 15 minutes, and then precisely seven minutes before he hits off he walks to the first tee. He likes to arrive there five minutes before he plays his shot.

'You should never really change your routine if it is a good one,' says Davis. 'Bob Charles believed in a 12-hour routine. If he was off at 8.30 a.m., he went to bed 12 hours beforehand, because he wanted to wake up four hours before he hit off. And it doesn't matter if it is 4.30 a.m., he'll set his alarm. They've proved in the States – I don't know whether it is right or wrong – that the body doesn't really wake up properly for four hours.'

Davis has had no physical coaching for the last ten years. He keeps a check on his swing with the aid of a video camera. He knows the one major swing fault that he has, and he can pick it up straight away. 'I've got a lateral weight shift where my left knee straightens on the backswing and I start getting a certain type of shot. I think every player has one major fault and it keeps creeping back at some stage. It doesn't matter what swing changes you make, that fault will be natural to you. Now, I think, it gets to the stage where – "Do you know what yours is?" If you do, then you can get out of it pretty quickly. If you don't, then you can be stuck in the doldrums for ages trying to figure it out.'

'Do you think that's what is wrong with Lyle?'

'Could be,' says Davis, non-commitally. 'But the worst part of it is that it's not that your swing is changing so much, but all of a sudden, mentally, you think it is . . . so we're back to the mental side again. Mentally tough. You've got to be mentally tough. I mean, you look at guys like Ballesteros, Woosie, myself, Langer and Faldo, who are winning tournaments. You know, there are other guys on the Tour who hit it as good as us. Maybe their course preparation isn't quite as good . . . but at the end of the day they hit it as well as we do. So I think it comes down to mental toughness in the end.'

'Is that the common denominator between the best players?'

'I think so. I mean, look at Tom Watson. What a great mind and a great architect for a round of golf. And Peter Thomson – he virtually looked at it like a game of chess. You had to hit it there to get to that green. He was the one that started it off, specially on the links-type courses, and now everybody's doing it.'

Davis's own game preparation and career plans had to be put on hold for most of last season after a physiotherapist attending to a trapped nerve injured his neck very badly. The man didn't bother taking X-rays beforehand which would have revealed an old injury caused by a head-on collision in 1971. Instead, he set to work with gay abandon on Davis, who has restricted movement of his neck, and snapped the capsule off a facet joint (feeds blood naturally into the vertebrae). Davis subsequently had acupuncture and various other treatments, all to no avail. It wasn't until he saw a specialist midway through the season that the problem – an inflamed root nerve – was located and cured within three weeks.

By the time Davis had built up the wasted muscles, however, it was too late for him to attempt to achieve the goal he had set at the beginning of the 1989 season, which was to win the money list. But to Davis, who immediately made the Order of Merit his goal this year, it was only a temporary set-back.

'I have,' Davis informs me, 'had to change a few of my long-term goals over the last couple of years, because I've already achieved them. You know, that's the other thing. You shouldn't set ridiculous goals but you shouldn't make them too easy. That can affect you, too. If all of a sudden you start achieving goals that you thought were realistic, then you've got to set tougher ones for yourself. While you think you're competitive and you can win, I think you've got to keep making it harder for yourself, and then there's always something round the corner. You stop when you stop playing.'

Whether or not Davis wins the money list, he has already planned a few rewards for himself ('If you're working hard at the game and putting everything you have into it, you should really give yourself a reward for doing that, whether it be financial or material'), and for his family, who 'have to put up with the way of life that we lead'.

'If you've set realistic goals all the way along,' says Davis, who spends his winters deep-sea fishing, shooting and playing cards, 'and you've achieved those goals, then at the end of your career if they turn around and say, "Well, you only ever got ranked 20th in the world," you can say, "Well who cares? I've been a great success." Because at some point in time you've got to say, I was never going to be number one. And because you've set yourself goals and you've obtained them, you can't knock yourself.'

Chapter Eleven

LEGENDS

Photo: Phil Sheldon

Symbol of a bygone era: South African Simon Hobday

YORK, ENGLAND, 7 AUGUST 1990. INTO YORK'S TRENDIEST restaurant walks Simon Hobday clad in red pants and a stiff-collared golf shirt (from the previous day). In a room made up almost entirely of Levi 501 wearers, Hobday looks about as fashionable as a dinner jacket at an acid party. But he is in his element. He is as comfortable in this environment as he has been holding court on the putting green for the best part of the day; as equal to the occasion as he is on the range, swinging as beautifully as Ben Hogan under the admiring gazes of a dozen players. On the European Tour, Simon Hobday is a legend.

In a sport full of drudges, of conformists, of players whose lives have been devoted to the strict adherence of rules and regimens, Hobday is that rare jewel: a rebel. Tales of his exploits are quintessential Tour lore; ten years after he quit the European circuit, they are still as fresh as this morning's news. Nothing you hear these days is in quite the same league. There's no comparison, for instance, between a story about Mark Roe taking an air rifle from the boot of his car and using the sign behind the 14th tee at Moor Park for target practice, and one about the events preceding Hobday's night in a Mexican jail.

Hobday is one of the last remaining symbols of a bygone era when players took neither themselves nor the game too seriously. All of that has changed. It's becoming increasingly obvious that unless a new generation of personalities are introduced into the game without further delay, all humour will be lost from professional golf. As it is, characters on Tour are becoming as rare as albatrosses.

Having said that, I am a fierce critic of articles which state categorically that there are no longer any amusing or entertaining players in the game. But after giving the matter some thought, I have decided that, although any person closely involved with the Tour could name you at least 30 pro golfers who are renowned pranksters and practical jokers – Mark Roe, Robert Lee, Roger Chapman and Gordon Brand Jnr, etc. – or have wonderful senses of humour – Mark James, Gordon J. Brand, David Feherty, Tony Johnstone and some of the Australians, for example – not one of them would appear so to the spectator public.

And as for real characters, well, you'd be hard pressed to think of more than one or two. There'll never be another Max Faulkner, or a Trevino, a Doug Sanders, a Gary Player, or a Brian Barnes. But then that, of course, depends on whether your definition of a character is someone whose escapades tend to be drunken ones; or a wise-cracking showman like Trevino.

'I think, when they say the characters have gone out of the game, they mean there's none of this staying out till three in the morning and getting drunk like there used to be,' said Mark Roe when I asked him about it. 'You're just playing for too much money. It's too serious a business . . . They *were* great characters, but they used to drink like fish those boys. You shouldn't have to become a character by going out drinking all hours, or womanising, or whatever.'

Mark James came by while we were talking.

'Do you think there are no characters left on the Tour?' Roe asked him.
'There are more characters now than there ever have been,' said James.
'But there's no one like Trevino, is there?'
'Trevino?' said James, with a snort of disgust. 'You call that a character? He doesn't say a word for 15 holes, and then he sees the cameras and he comes out with all these one-liners.'

Right now I'm watching one of the former category of characters pour himself a Carlsberg Special, and idly wondering whether the Seniors Tour is ready for him. Hobday confesses to being nervous and looks horrified when I produce a tape recorder. 'What kind of stories do you want to know?' he keeps asking. We embark on several safe subjects, beginning with a discussion on the merits of tournament professionals as people.

'This is a gentlemen's game played by gentlemen,' shouts Hobday, since the din is rapidly approaching a crescendo. 'And if they aren't gentlemen, they bloody soon will be.'

Several people look up, startled. Hobday takes not one iota of notice. He has been attracting attention for most of his 50 years. Born in Mafeking to veterinarian parents – one of whom was awarded an MBE and the other an OBE, he can't remember which – he moved to Zambia at the age of two when his father was called in to deal with an outbreak of foot-and-mouth disease. He played golf from an early age and continued a successful amateur career long after he became a farmer.

In 1970 disaster struck. The Zambian government deported him for playing golf in South Africa and took away his farm. He was given two options by the British High Commission when he appealed to them: he could move to Britain and live on the dole, or he could move to Rhodesia. He chose the latter. With no alternative means of making a living, he turned professional and came to Europe. He was 28 years old at the time.

Nine years ago he took a year off the Tour to move his family to South Africa and never returned. The Tour became all-exempt and Hobday refused categorically to go to the Qualifying School. Instead, he amassed a small fortune in the car alarm business and continued to play the Sunshine circuit. But now, prompted by the creeping advance of old age. Hobday has decided to 'take up the cudgel' and try his luck on the Seniors Tour. 'They had two Seniors events in South Africa. I went to watch and I thought, "Shit, I can beat those guys." So I got keen again. It's not often in life you get an over.'

I bring up a recent conversation I had with John Bland, who said that he doesn't think that the European Tour Qualifying School breeds winners in the way that the old system of pre-qualifying did.

'I agree with that,' says Hobday immediately. 'Because you might have a player that's exceptional like Olazabal, but before he gets on Tour he has to go to the School. So he goes to the School and he has one bad week and he's gone for the rest of the season. Now what does he do? He goes back to selling cars or training shoes or whatever. Then he goes back to the School the following year and has another bad week. His heart's broken. He doesn't come out again.

'Whereas, in the old days when they pre-qualified, they would have about 30 spots and the guys that could play got in. If he played four rounds he'd play the next week . . . and eventually he worked his way up to winning tournaments. I don't know how many people are out there that could win tournaments that aren't actually playing . . .

'So I agree with John,' says Hobday finally. He has to go to the Seniors Qualifying School in America later on in the year. 'I didn't know he had that much brains to actually work a thing like that out!' he says with a grin, knowing perfectly well that Bland is anything but unintelligent. Swirling the amber liquid in his glass, he turns his attention to Bland.

'Do you know the difference between Bland and a coconut? You can get a drink out of a coconut.'

Hobday laughs delightedly at his joke, but not maliciously. He's the kind of person who can insult people's babies without causing offence.

'He's actually got quite a capacity for practical jokes, John. We've a fellow in South Africa called Phil Simmons who's a big strong bloke – one of the longest hitters in the world – and Blandy started this thing going quietly around the Tour where everybody called him Phyllis. You'd get the guys on the scoreboard putting up Phyllis instead of P. Simmons. And John would send him [flowers and] telegrams from overseas saying things like: "We had a wonderful night together, Love Bruce." The man went crazy.'

Last year Bland started everyone on Tour calling Hugh Baiocchi Cliff (Richard) since Baiocchi has the same kind of ageless face as the singer. Baiocchi got his own back. At the 1989 Murphy's Cup he and one or two other players organised a first-aid buggy and a nurse to fetch Bland from the practice ground and carry him to the first tee. A dozen players had formed a reception committee and were all falling about when he arrived. Bland was livid.

'Right, Baiocchi,' he said to the South African, who was laughing loudest. 'When customs hold you up for four hours at Jan Smuts [Johannesburg airport], don't come crying to me.' Bland, you see, has friends in high places.

Hobday listens. 'Thank God there's just a little bit of fun left. Those things used to happen all the time when I was out here. Nowadays the boys are very serious . . . They can't release themselves, they're playing for so much money. I mean, they've got to have a few beers and they've got to relax. The boys aren't relaxed at all. Take a guy like Martin Poxon, for example. I mean, hell, he doesn't know anything other than the golf club. There's nothing else in the world other than hitting golf balls. Sam Torrance and Noel Ratcliffe – they used to go out and have a pint. Now they're all dedicated, the lot of them. In the old days, if we missed the cut that was the signal to blow the brains out! That was it. Take the town apart! Now they miss the cut, they go to the next tournament, they practise.

'The money's done that but it's also improved the standard of golf unbelievably, particularly from the bottom. The winning scores aren't that much different, but if you think you can make the cut by shooting level par or one over out there today, you are living in a dream world.'

The other big change in tournament golf since Hobday played is the way the golfers are looked after. The Tour sponsors, Volvo, provide courtesy cars, players' lounges, catering facilities, superb practice ground facilities, and so on ad infinitum. At the start of every tournament players are given four dozen balls and a handful of gloves, and are kept regularly supplied with shoes, sweaters, shirts and visors. In Hobday's day, players received six balls on arrival at a tournament and six if they made the cut. Gloves and shoes were luxuries only given out at the Open.

'I tell you, I hear stories about players saying, "If you don't give me a couple of hotel rooms, I'm not going to play",' says Hobday. 'To me, they should be burnt at the stake. They should be putting things back into the game.'

Hobday might feel strongly about that, but he doesn't think there is anything wrong with Tour players taking advantage of the comfort zone created by the increase of prize money, and merely playing to make a living. 'If they're good enough to make £50,000 or £60,000 then it's a good job, isn't it? So I take my hat off to them. They still have to work bloody hard because it's the toughest job in the world, in my opinion. If they can make £60,000 a year playing golf, then they deserve everything they can get.'

We picked up our drinks and negotiated bar stools, exhuberant locals; Ross McFarlane and Vijay Singh, who were engaged in a battle to the death on a space invader machine; and the wooden trellis-work that separated the bar from the restaurant. A hen party of seven monopolised one corner of the room and assorted pro golfers occupied the rest.

'That thing makes me very nervous,' said Hobday eyeing my tape recorder with deep suspicion, once we had found our table. But on the table it stays. I decide that it's high time he dispensed with the small talk and opened up about his chequered past. 'First,' says Hobday guardedly, 'tell me what you've heard.'

Well, among the more infamous Hobday-abroad stories is one which took place in Crans-sur-Sierre, Switzerland, venue of the European Masters.

It was a bitterly cold night in the mountains. Hobday had made every possible attempt to warm himself, even resorting to gathering his week's supply of clean and used golf clothes from their piles on the floor (he has an aversion to doing laundry) and putting them on. Finally he decided that the only hope he had of warding off rigor mortis was to go down to the village bar and fortify himself with several brandies. This he did. But once in the bar Hobday, who was wearing more layers of protective clothing than the average American footballer, began to sweat. At intervals he peeled off individual garments.

Sam Torrance observed this with amusement. 'I bet you £5,' he said, as Hobday divested himself of a sweatshirt, 'that you wouldn't take off everything.'

Now, apart from the fact that he was four sheets to the wind by this stage, Hobday is one of those people to whom a dare is an irresistible challenge. In a trice, he had stripped naked. He then continued to drink away the evening as though everything was perfectly normal. Of course, the news spread like wildfire and eventually half the village had converged upon the bar. Old ladies and assorted voyeurs gawped. Hobday couldn't have cared less. Clothes or no clothes, it matters as much to him as it would to a five-year-old. When the management pleaded with him to at least wear his underpants, he put them over his head.

Mortified, the player who had accompanied Hobday fled the bar. Hobday ran after him, his clothes under one arm and his underpants still on his head. Rounding a street corner at speed, he came face to face with a policeman. Each did a double-take. 'Good evening,' Hobday cried gaily, deciding that courtesy was his best line of defence. But the policeman just nodded an acknowledgment.

The following morning the Tour committee tried to fine Hobday, but without success. He told them firmly and succintly that what he did in his private life was his own business.

The stories get worse.

There was that long flight to Australia, for instance. The back of the plane was full of bored, underoccupied Tour players. At breakfast-time, Hobday's neighbour came up with a plan to entertain them. He cut a hole in the bottom of his breakfast tray, unzipped his trousers and carefully inserted his member. Then he rearranged his eggs and bacon around it and garnished it with a sprig of parsley. He pressed the orange call button. The stewardess arrived, all smiles and what-can-I-do-to-help-you-sirs.

'I think there's something wrong with my mushroom!' said the wicked Australian.

Such horrendous activities must have slipped Ken Schofield's mind because he came up to Hobday yesterday and asked why he didn't try for his player's card. He said the European Tour needed more characters.

'I knew Ken Schofield when he was a virgin,' announces Hobday irreverently. I blanch slightly. 'When I say virgin, I mean when he first came on Tour; I don't mean virgin in the proper sense . . . But anyway, he's done a helluva job. I wish he had been tougher with the anti-apartheid thing but other than that the Tour has taken off. But George O'Grady was there before Schofield. I remember O'Grady when he was a virgin. He used to come and say, "Uhh . . . uhh . . . Hobday . . . You've been swearing on the course and I've got to fine you £40", and he'd blush.

'There was one particular time in Sweden. I'm going like hell with an American bloke and I'm in contention. I get to the 18th hole in the third round, and as I hit the ball my driver shatters and the ball goes in the water. Of course, I let rip. But the [American's] wife was walking with us so he pulled me in. They had to fine me. Georgie had to come and find me on the putting green the next day and he was all blushes. I said to him, "What the hell was I supposed to say?" I mean, what would he say? "Tutt, tutt, tutt?"'

In those days, Hobday had two main accomplices on Tour: Irishman John O'Leary, who is Chairman of the European Tour Tournament Committee, and Australian Jack Newton. Now one can imagine Newton sowing a few wild oats in his time, but *John O'Leary*? No one more unlike Hobday could ever have graced the professional ranks. In all the times I have encountered him he has never been anything other than the absolute model of decorum. He is softly spoken, has a calm, deliberate bearing and the most impeccable manners.

'John was a wild man,' Hobday informs me, banishing this image in an instant. 'The situations you could get into with him! He'd drink, chase women and do all sorts of weird and wonderful things in those days. He was scared of nothing. He didn't care, John, at all. He was always a perfect gentleman but he had a sense of fun, which he hasn't got anymore. He has, as you say, gone quiet.'

'What was Jack Newton like?'

'Newts? He's a great guy. One of the best . . . You should have met Newton then,' says Hobday with a grin. 'I mean, you would have fallen in love with him. He was a good looking boy and he was unbelievable with women. They'd just run at him from all angles . . . But he was a gentleman. I never saw him say no.'

But marriage caught up with Newton eventually. He and fellow Australian Bob Shearer met their wives at the same time. They were whiling away an afternoon in the tournament bar one day when they got chatting to a couple of Piccadilly girls (the old equivalent of today's Guinness girls). They decided to invite them out to dinner.

'Which one do you fancy?' said Newton to Shearer in a whispered aside.

'I can't make up my mind,' said Shearer. 'Which one do you like?'

Newton, too, was spoiled for choice. So they tossed a coin. But halfway through the ensuing evening, each realised they liked the other's partner better. They swapped over and are still married to the same girls today. 'Newton's wife, Jackie,' comments Hobday, 'is an absolute saint. I mean, she must have known he was a bad bastard.'

Hobday's wife must have married him knowing the same thing.

'Oh no, my wife used to think I was a great bloke,' insists Hobday. Her opinion was revised when Newton, then single, arrived in Zimbabwe to play an exhibition match. 'He stayed with us for 12 days,' explains Hobday, 'and every morning at breakfast there was a new woman. A brand new woman *every single day*! My wife thought that if I had mates like that, I must also be a crook. I've been in shit ever since.'

With some justification, I would imagine.

'What sort of things did you and Newton used to get up to on Tour?' I asked Hobday.

'Well, I can give you an example of madness. Tertius Klarssons, Newton and I were sharing a room in Germany one year. Klarssons had missed the pre-qualifying and Newton had missed the cut; I was lying third in the tournament. So those boys were on the tear. They say to me, "You can't stay here now, it's not even dark. You've got to come out until midnight at least." I thought that was a good idea. But at 12 o'clock I went back to the hotel and it was all locked up. I had forgotten the key. I tried throwing stones at the window to wake somebody up but I was unsuccessful. So I went and slept in the hedge.

'These two bastards rocked up at three in the morning, drunk as skunks. I said to Newton, "Thank God, you've arrived because I forgot the key." He promptly threw the key away in fun and it skittered across the road and went down a sewer. He had to climb up a neon sign, break into a guy's room and let us in. Of course, I was gone the next day. I had no chance of playing any good after that.'

And Hobday wonders why everybody thinks he's crazy.

'They don't,' I say soothingly, since the thought seems to annoy him.

'They do. I hear them in the bar. Why am I crazy? When I play I get angry sometimes. I get pissed sometimes. I chase women sometimes. Christ, what's so odd about that?'

The trouble is, Hobday just doesn't do the things that normal people do. Only Hobday would think of putting a Viking hat in his golf bag in case he won the Irish Open; only he would think of wearing it to play his approach shot to the 18th green once he knew he wasn't going to, and only he would hole it. Hobday offered the hat ceremoniously to the victor, Des Smyth, before he putted out. Smyth refused and three-putted.

Many of his adventures involve naked or semi-naked romps (when I said this to George O'Grady, he muttered something which sounded suspiciously like: 'What do you expect from a sex maniac?'). One year he stripped down to his underpants and walked across a snake-infested lake in South Africa in the middle of a tournament. On another occasion, when a player bet him that he couldn't run naked around the 18th green at Vilamoura Golf Club in 15 seconds, Hobday did it in 14.5.

Some of the best Hobday stories have arisen out of his reactions to disasters on the golf course. He once struck himself so hard on the forehead after missing a putt that the blade broke off and slid down the back of his head and blood trickled down his face.

Leading a tournament at Wentworth, several seasons ago, he began to have nightmares on the greens. The more determined Hobday became to get the ball in the hole, the more the blade tormented him and the further the tournament slipped from his grasp. He ran the gamut of emotions: he was angry, he was despairing, he was outraged, he was hysterical. Eventually there was nothing else to do but laugh.

So when the putter failed him again it got the yellow card, and at the next hole it got the red. After he had finished his round and signed his card, having lost to Ballesteros, he tied the offending object to the bumper of his car and raced off down the road. Up and down he drove, with it leaping and bounding and spitting sparks behind him. When there was nothing left of it save the head, he took it to a pub and bought it a pint.

'I'm afraid,' says Hobday unrepentently, 'I'm one of those people that lose their temper.'

He has made something of a study of the way that other players cope with the blows the game deals. 'For me, that's the highlight of the game every day I play, to watch how the other guy reacts.

'I love the delayed action guys. Let's take a nice quiet guy like Faldo, for example. Ice cool. But you can see that the ball has decided that he's going to take a beating today, and it bounces this way and bounces that way. He's got everything under control but you know he's seething. And eventually he pops. I've seen guys walk up to a tree and just smash it with their fist, and they're the quietest guys in the world. Now that to me is funny. Most guys lose their temper straightaway and throw a club or hit the caddie or whatever, and that's bad manners. But these boys, you can see them go.'

Inevitably, Howard Clark's name comes up. Towering rages on the golf course and Clark are, unfortunately, synonymous.

'That means he's extremely competitive,' explains Hobday. 'But because this is a gentlemen's game played by gentlemen, you've got to' – he imitates a player mincing round the course minding his p's and q's – 'and I disagree with that. A player can break as many clubs as he likes when he's playing with me as long as it's not on my time. He can go in the trees and whine as much as he wants. But there are times when the course belongs to me. It's my turn and I don't want to hear him swearing and cursing and shouting and screaming. Then he must bugger off. He doesn't know when to get cross, or when to throw a club, or even how to throw a club. Some guys get so angry they throw it like a javelin. You've got to learn to throw it sideways so it lands softly, face up.

'We all get cross, but you must get cross in your own time. I mean, if it's your drive and you hit it in the trees, you don't smash the marker to smithereens. That's not your time. Now the other guy's got to try and play. He can't, can he? Let him hit and then smash the thing. That's what you've got to learn.

This morning on the recommendation of several players, I went down to the range to watch Hobday practise. His swing is as classic as it ever was and his ball striking as pure. It is said that David Leadbetter, who was an assistant pro in Zimbabwe when Hobday was in his prime, based his method on Hobday's technique.

'Who told you that?' asks Hobday, embarrassed. But he admits it's true. 'All Leadbetter did was come overseas and teach them to swing like I did. But I didn't teach him how to teach.'

Like most people, he thinks that Nick Faldo would have been a good player without Leadbetter's help but not necessarily a great player. 'You must remember that the teacher is only two per cent of the player. No more than that. Leadbetter might have said, "Do that, and do it a million times." Faldo's the one who's done all the work. Leadbetter made him square at the top of the backswing and put him on plane, and that's all he's ever done. I mean, you get a diamond, you polish it and it shines. That guy was a diamond to start off with. He's got magnificent rhythm. If you took a stop watch and pressed it when he took the club away and pressed it again when he hit the ball, it would be exactly the same with every swing. The driver would take the same amount of time as the wedge, and that's the best thing you can have in the swing.'

But the best swing in the world is no use to a man with no magic on the greens. Hobday was nearly brought to his knees by the yips. That, far more than drink, kept him from reaching the heights.

'What do the yips feel like? Well, I'll describe how it feels when you've got a putt from four or five feet. You take the putter back and then it's like somebody hit you on the back. It's like an electric shock. You're afraid you're going to miss the ball. You think you're going to hit it ten feet past. Or you can hit it short. Your arms just seize up. Sometimes they hit and sometimes they don't. You can miss from anywhere. It's a terrible bloody affliction.'

'How does it start?'

'Well, to begin with you'll yip one putt in a tournament and not yip another. Then you'll yip every tournament once, then once every nine holes, then three times in every 18 holes and eventually, you don't know when it's going to happen. The worst thing you can do is yip one at the first. Then you know you're going to have a bad day. Your feet hurt when you walk on the green. It's like walking on coals. You want to get on and get the hell off as quick as possible.'

Once, at his wits' end, Hobday went to see a hypnotist, convinced that if he could only believe he was a good putter, he'd be the best putter in the world.

'The hypnotist turned out to be a woman. She put me under and when I walked out of there, I swear to God, I thought I was the best putter in the world. There was no question. Did I ever charge at those putts? I had 42 putts that day. *Forty-two*. And I still thought I was the best putter in the world. It wore off after two or three days . . . Terrifying. Now that *didn't* work.'

Hobday is concerned about my well-being. He worries that I haven't eaten enough, laughed enough, and that his stories aren't funny enough. At intervals he glowers at my tape recorder as if he might bewitch it into not participating in the conversation. His anecdotal repertoire is inexhaustable. All it needs is a key word to trigger his memory and he's off. I try 'pre-qualifying'. It turns out to be a good choice. Open Championship pre-qualifying in particular and Simon Hobday appear to be incompatible.

The jinx began at his very first Open. Hobday, who was on the putting green waiting for his tee-off time, heard the starter call his name and began to walk over to the first. In the space of some 25 yards he slipped on a rabbit scraping and snapped all the tendons in his ankle. He never hit another shot that season.

A succession of last ditch misadventures followed, but after several years Hobday managed to arrive at the 12th hole at St Andrews leading the pre-qualifying. Confident that he was home and dry, Hobday began relaying stories of past near misses to his playing partner, Klarssons. On the next hole he drove out-of-bounds. His approach finished in a cavernous bunker. At the 16th his ball hit a cigarette box by the side of the green and richocheted out-of-bounds.

'At the 17th, I made a five,' remembers Hobday. 'But by now the stories have stopped. I've got to make four up the last to get in. So I drive it up the fairway. I've got the club halfway back to hit my second shot and a man in a motorcar knocks over a kid (on the road that runs alongside the 18th). Right next to me. Hooters and screaming and brakes. So of course, I mis-hit it – right on the back edge of the green. I've got a 50-foot putt. I putted down like Doug Sanders. I thought: "Shit, I'd better hole this [next] putt to get into the play-off." I missed it by a yard but I still got into the play-off and we went round one, two, 17 and 18 three times before I got in.'

The evening wears on and the restaurant slowly empties. Only the hen party in the corner shows little sign of abating. They shriek and cackle on relentlessly. The dregs of Hobday's second lager of the evening are untouched. He has decided that if he is going to make a serious attempt at the Seniors Tour, he is going to have to stop all drinking, womanising and other forms of revelry. And once he has made up his mind about something, he is not easily swayed.

He waves for the bill. I plead for one last story.

'What about?'

'Caddies?'

Hobday acquiesces. 'I know the worst caddie I ever had . . .' he begins. He lights another cigarette, settles himself more comfortably in his chair, and prepares to do the story justice.

The tournament venue was Wentworth. Hobday had arrived on the first tee to find that all the caddies had been taken. Except one. Hobday found him skulking round the back of the caddie shack, a hippie-like character with waist-long hair.

'He was as scruffy as hell,' recalls Hobday. 'I thought he was a wino. I said: "Are you pissed?" He said, no, he's perfect. And he talked like you and I are talking now. So we set off. I've already hit my drive so we're running. We go down this mound on the first and he falls and rolls all the way to the bottom. That's where it started. He must have been on drugs. Uphill he was perfect, but downhill he just went faster and faster and faster; then his angle would change and the clubs would pull him down.

'He'd fallen over thirteen times by the time we got to the 17th. By now he's got sand on his face, his hair is thick with it, the bag must weigh 30 pounds, it's so full of sand. Every club you took out you had to wipe off. He was in terrible trouble, this boy. Now the back of the 17th green slopes steeply down to the tee. So I took him over to the side of the green while the other guys were putting out and I said: "Do me a favour, please. *Do not* under *any* circumstance come over the back of the green. Go down the pathway where the slope is nice and gentle and I'll see you on the tee." And I took my driver.

'When they finished putting out, we all went over the back of the green. We're going down the hill and the clattering starts at the back. He's decided, no, he's sharp enough to come over the back of the green. We look up and he's at the top of the hill. You had to see this guy's stride. He was doing 60 miles an hour. But every time he put a foot down the bag would come forward and hit him on the shoulder. It was giving him a terrible hiding. But the weird part was he still had the pin. He'd forgotten to put it back in the hole.

'So now he decides he's going to take a tumble and the only way he can stop himself is by putting the pin in the ground and doing a kind of pole vault. Of course, it snaps. How he didn't kill himself, I've no idea. He did a bellyflop and landed on the pathway on his nose; he's got his feet on either side of the bag. I never even picked him up. I just thought: "I told him".

'He comes hobbling along to the tee, but the clubs have given him a smack on the back of the head and he is pumping blood everywhere. Oh God, he was a horror story. He had denim dungarees which were broken by the time he was finished, absolutely broken. Torn to ribbons. The buttons were missing and there was grass hanging out the pockets. I gave him his ten pounds at the end and told him to go and take a shower. I said to him: "Go away and for God's sake get another bag. Don't come anywhere near me tomorrow."

'But now I'm sitting in the bar afterwards and every guy that comes in – because they didn't have yardages in those days – says, "Bloody incredible that 17th hole. I thought it was an eight-iron and I hit it straight over the back of the green." Because the pin is only half-height so it looks further away.'

Hobday grins. 'I kept quiet. It wasn't me.'

Chapter Twelve

THE GREEN GODDESS

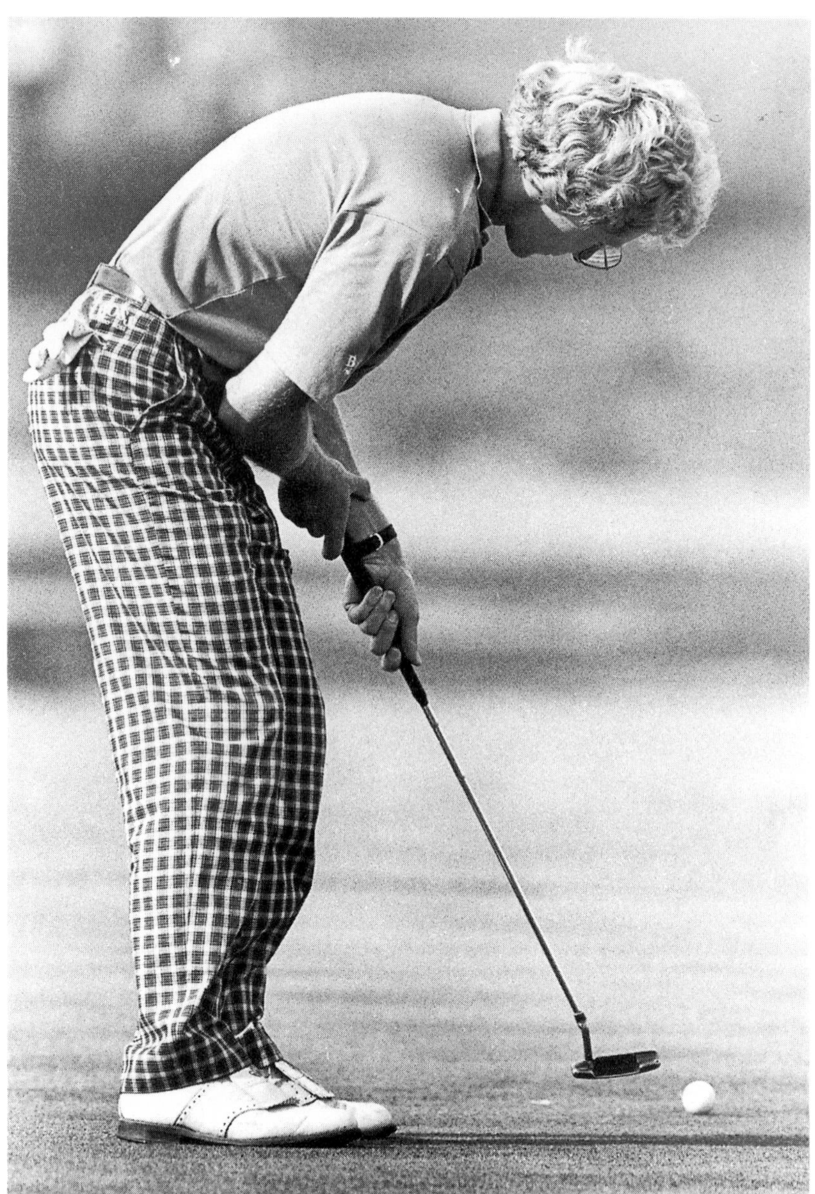

Photo: ASP, Stuart Franklin

Bernhard Langer with the grip that saved his career

GERMAN OPEN, DUSSELDORF, AUGUST 1990. THE LAST players out had left the practice range before Bernhard Langer handed his caddie one final club to clean. Half his work done, Langer then crossed over to the putting green to do the rest. This morning he shot a first round 70; good enough for the partisan home crowd, good enough for two under par, but not enough for Langer. Sometimes a 70 is the result of solid golf on a tough golf course. Today it was the product of willpower. Once more his game let him down in the area that has ended the careers of some of the greatest players who ever lived. Once more Langer found himself at the mercy of his putter.

Now, in the golden light of the German evening, Langer addresses the enigma that is putting the best way he knows how: with sheer hard work and grind. Willie Hoffman, his mentor and long-time coach, watches, white hatted and professor-like. They have two putters – a battle-scarred silver-headed one with a gold shaft, and one with a gold blade and a steel shaft – which they exchange from time to time.

Putt after putt skirts the hole. Langer stands up wearily to stretch his aching back. He watches Phil Harrison ride the pendulum action of his long black putter, the wand which is conjuring new magic into the careers of a growing number of players, and sink three 30-foot putts. Langer himself has tried it but not seriously. 'For me, trying is three months or six months. I don't expect any success in a day or two.'

Teacher and pupil exchange glances. They repair to the far end of the green to practise short putts. Those are the real killers. Even the worst yippers can make some sort of stroke at a long putt. It's those of four feet and less – a distance a top player should never miss from – where the real nerves start to come in. Hoffman waits a while before intervening, letting Langer work it out himself. Then, with a few terse phrases, he gets him putting with a peculiar kind of upper-cut stroke, which seems to impart both topspin and sidespin on the ball. It scuttles like a drunken crab across the putting surface and doesn't even glance at the hole.

Langer's face is set in grim determination. A dozen balls evade their destination. He stops and stares icily in the direction of a row of clicking photographers, the ever-present spectators at his demise on the putting green. 'It's not even funny any more,' he says frustratedly to the laconic Hoffman, who beneath the curled brim of his cloth hat wears a peculiarly benign expression.

Bernhard Langer has had the yips and recovered from them at least four times in his career. They started immediately after he joined the European Tour – 'The first week, first round'. He was 18 years old at the time. Up until that day, he had never at any time in his life experienced the tiniest twinge of fear or unease on the greens, had never had the slightest technical problem with his putting and had never encountered the affliction. He put it down to the unfamiliar pressures of playing professional golf on the European Tour. What other explanation was there?

In the initial period, he had the yips for four years '. . . on and off, sometimes better, sometimes worse'. He cured himself then by switching from putting right-handed to putting left-handed. Sometimes a complete change can do the trick – a new putter, a new routine, a new grip. 'It took a while to get comfortable,' recalls Langer. 'I had problems with distance and feel, and it was two or three months until I felt I could putt pretty good.'

The yips (a name coined by Tommy Armour, who had them) went away as suddenly as they had come on and Langer putted superbly for the next two and a half years. But as Rodger Davis, who had the yips for three years, found, 'Once you get them, you always think of them, and once you're thinking of them, the brain is so strong and powerful that it compounds the problem. You've actually got to use that to your advantage – the strength of the brain – to get out of it.' When the yips came back, they did so with a vengeance. This time Langer got rid of them within six months by adopting a cross-handed putting grip. He entered his best putting spell ever. It was to last from 1983 to 1988, and it took Langer to the top of the putting statistics on the European Tour one year, and to sixth position on the US Tour putting statistics the next.

But as it did with Bobby Jones, Vardon, Byron Nelson, Gene Sarazen and Roberto de Vicenzo, Langer's nightmare returned.

'I've gotten rid of the yips,' said Sam Snead once, 'but they still hang in there. You know those two-foot downhill putts with a break? I'd rather see a rattlesnake.'

According to psychologists, the yips – a condition causing involuntary twitching of the muscles, also affecting archers and darts players – is an entirely mental affliction. That in itself is paradoxical. Ben Hogan and Bernhard Langer, to take two people from entirely different generations who have been stricken by the yips, both became great golfers and major champions because of their tremendous strength of mind and character. Hogan, who was one of the most resolute golfers who ever lived, suffered the final humiliation at the 1954 Masters. In the lead for the tournament, he three-putted the 13th, three-putted the 17th from a yard, and missed a six-foot putt on the 18th to lose the championship.

Another strange configuration of the yips is that many of the players who get them are among the finest putters in the world when they are putting well. Langer, author of *Langer on Putting*, is a perfect example. At his best he is almost untouchable. When he won the US Masters in 1985 on the slick greens of Augusta – where the pace and borrows are such that a man need never feel embarrassed about four-putting – he didn't three-putt once in four rounds.

With the exception of pressure, which seems to be the only real common denominator, the links between those players affected and the probable causes of their affliction are tenuous at best. The yips are as likely to strike down a champion at the peak of his career as they are the rookie. Who, or why, or what might precipitate them is a conundrum as old as the game.

'My experience is that it is a building process,' says sports psychologist, Alan Fine. 'It may not be obvious to them how it happens. I know that the players I talk to can trace it back to when the problem started. 'It may be to do with putting. It may not be directly related to their putting. So often it's because they started getting anxious about their results and they started overpressing . . . As soon as you start trying too hard, you start tightening up and you lose control.'

Fine doubted that the yips came on as suddenly as Langer imagined. 'My impression of Langer's results is that they haven't been as good lately. And if you look at what came first, the poor results or the yipping, I think it would be a grey area to say that his [poor] results were caused by the yipping. I think there was one mediocre result and maybe on that day he felt uncomfortable. It often builds from one particular shot.'

One explanation Fine offers is that players get caught up in a fight or flight response. In other words, when the body is faced with a situation it perceives as dangerous, the nervous system prepares it to fight or flee. Adrenalin sends a rush of blood to the muscles so the body is ready to make a positive active response to the threat.

'So here we are on the putting green,' imagines Fine. 'We perceive it as a threat: "This is very important", or, "I might miss". If you perceive it as a large enough threat you go into this disresponse. Well, if you get all the blood pumping to the muscles and adrenalin going like that, you're going to start shaking anyway. That can produce the yips.'

'I don't know anything about the yips and I don't want to, I honestly don't,' says Mark McNulty, acknowledged maestro on the putting green. 'If somebody's got the yips, he must go back to basics – make sure he takes the putter back and comes through at an accelerated pace. I've tried to tell Bernhard that. You've got to go back to basics.'

Players like McNulty, Seve Ballesteros, Jose Maria Olazabal and Sandy Lyle, all of whom have exceptionally good minds and simple, solid putting styles, would no more entertain the idea of getting the yips than they would of flying.

'There's no mental approach to putting apart from getting the ball in the hole,' says McNulty firmly. 'Some people ask what I think about when I putt. I think about getting the ball in the hole. I mean, everybody does, but it's when they start thinking about too many other things, that's when they start missing putts.'

Try telling that to Langer, who five-putted from four and a half feet on the penultimate hole of the Open Championship at Royal Lytham (he shot 80 and finished 68th). Or Sam Torrance, who has had the yips since the European Open in 1986: 'It's the worst feeling in the world. I had a putt at Montpelier to tie second place from only a few feet away, and it didn't touch the hole. I knew I wasn't going to hole it before I hit the putt. It was hellish.' Or Simon Hobday: 'You see, the one hand fights the other. The right hand is pushing and the left hand is jammed. So eventually the left gives way and the ball goes ten feet past the hole. I've never actually had a fresh air, but I've been close a couple of times.'

What keeps a man going when he has to face such mental endurance tests daily? Langer always looks to the same place for comfort: his faith.

'The first thing that kept me going was my belief in Christ. The second thing was that I knew I could putt because I'd done it before, and I believe that whatever you've done before you can repeat. I also knew at the time it started I was a fairly good ball striker. I knew that if I could just get the putting somewhere under control – I didn't have to be the best, just mediocre – I could make a pretty good living. But, you know, I never gave up hope because I knew that if I just improved a little bit, that my confidence would grow and then I would get better and better.'

Optimism is its own reward. Time and time again, Langer has conquered what many people consider to be unconquerable.

'I'm not sure that the yips are incurable,' says Langer, who tried out 50 different putters on the putting green at Wentworth two years ago in a desperate search for one that would bring back the magic stroke. 'A lot of players I know on the American and European Tours have had the yips [and recovered from them]. I mean, Hubert Green said to me he has had the yips five times, and he's still playing and putting very successfully at times. Johnny Miller had it several times. Even a guy like George Archer, who is one of the so-called best putters – which he is at times – says he has a lot of putting problems. And a lot of guys have. They're just not known for it.'

For Sam Torrance and Peter Senior, the answer has been Harold Swash's (Wilson's putter designer) broomstick putter, which is 13.5 inches longer than a standard 35-inch putter. The top of the shaft is held against the chin by the left hand and the putter-head is controlled by the right hand, which grips the lower half of the shaft lightly between thumb and forefinger. The basic principle behind it is that if you separate the hands they can't oppose one another, which is basically all that happens when a player yips.

Torrance tried a multitude of cures before he discovered Swash's putter, including a version of the putting grip which has helped Langer. 'Bernhard actually grabs his arm which must lock all the nerves. 'I put my thumb against it, which worked for a while but was never sound. What I'm doing now is a solid, sound method. It just makes total sense.'

'It depends how you define cure, really,' says Fine. 'You can definitely learn to control the yips. You can do it two ways. You can learn to control the mental state with breathing techniques: if you focus your attention on breathing out as you swing through the ball that stops your mind doing the things that cause the fight or flight response. You can also work with a hynotist. There are ways of reaching into the subconscious and dealing with the fear that is there so it doesn't emerge.

'Because in the end you start to question your own ability, and once you do that then you're into that same philosophy . . . where one particular shot becomes a big deal . . . If you're questioning your own worth because of the yips, you've potentially got great problems. No one shot is an indication of total ability as a player.'

English Open, the Belfry, August 1990. The door of suite 442 in the Tony Jacklin Memorial (prematurely) House, is opened by Bernhard Langer, unfamiliar in a suit. 'Sit down wherever you like,' he says in his soft, flat voice, gesturing toward a grey selection of chairs. We perch on opposite ends of a couch long enough for six people. The room is neatly disordered.

'What are you reading?' I ask across the Dralon expanse.

'Oh, just a Christian book.'

He hands it over obligingly for me to look at. It was Langer who started Christians on Tour, a group of players and wives who gather weekly during the season for prayer meetings. 'A lot of the willpower comes from believing in the Lord. I believe he wants me to be out here. I think that's how I can be most useful to his cause.'

Christianity is not something he ever pushes on people but he is quick to acknowledge the part it has played in his success. 'If there is one thing I'd like people to know,' he says in his biography, *While the Iron is Hot*, 'then it is that it takes more than talent to be a success, it is a gift from God.'

Off the golf course and out of the golf club environment, Langer is reserved and quite extraordinarily relaxed and unhurried. Everything he does and says is deliberate, considered; even his humour is slow and unexpected.

'He's a real genuine type of person,' said caddie Pete Coleman when I talked to him about his employer. 'You know where you stand with him.' Gavin Levenson, who roomed with the German when he was starting out, says exactly the same thing. He says that in all the years he has known Langer, through success and failure, he has been constant; never pretentious or conceited, never puts on airs and graces, never been anyone but himself.

'I think over the years he's learnt the language more,' says Coleman. 'He knows what people say now and the little jokes they make, and he's probably become a nicer person through it. He seems to give the time of day to a lot more people . . . Trouble is, with him not understanding the language over the years, it's made him sit in the back seat and just mix with his own type of people. But over the last few years he's come out because he can understand it. He seems to mix a lot more than he did.'

All of this just makes Langer's attitude to appearance money harder to understand. Of all the top players, he is probably the most unbending in his stipulation that he must be paid or he won't play. Later on in the year (August 1990), an experiment was tried at the German Open. The sponsors declared that no player would receive appearance money, and that every penny would be put into the prize fund, which would take it to £500,000 and make it the richest tournament in Europe. The plan backfired, for the simple reason that some players will not play for any amount of money if they are not paid to tee-up. Most of the top players simply took the week off. An exception had to be made of Langer, since it was felt that you couldn't have a German Open without Germany's top player. ICI paid him his usual fee.

But whether one agrees or disagrees with Langer's feelings about appearance money, no one could argue that if anyone deserves the financial rewards the game brings, he does. On the golf course and on the range, Langer is the hardest worker, without any question. If you had to single out the players who have done everything humanly possible to maximise their talent, you would have to look to Faldo and Langer first. 'It's the old Teutonic disposition,' says Dave Musgrove. 'Single-minded, etcetera, etcetera.'

'He's made everything out of everything,' seconds Coleman. 'He couldn't do any more than what he's done for his ability.'

Too often in the world of professional golf, we judge players by association. Think of Ballesteros, think of eighteen phenomenal drives into eighteen separate wildernesses, and eighteen Houdini-like recoveries. Think Sandy Lyle, think simple, and think of effortless one-iron shots disappearing into the blue. Think of Woosnam and towering drives, Ronan Rafferty and brilliant short iron play, Eamonn Darcy and unorthodox golf swings. And think Bernhard Langer, think superb iron play and think of the yips: the three are synonymous.

'Isn't it frustrating to play great golf from tee to green, and then be reduced to mediocrity by your putter?'

'Yes it is, but on the other side I've had weeks and years where I've hit the ball poorly and I've putted tremendously well and my short game's been pretty good. You see, people don't see that. They give you one label, like I've got the label that I can't putt and I have the label that I'm one of the greatest iron players in the world, which I might have been for a year or two, but not always. I mean, my swing can go and I don't know where the ball is going. Can't find it.

'Take America, where I played from '85 through '89 as a full-time member. They keep statistics about everything and I was never in the top 80 out of 200 players [in driving accuracy], and I was never in the top eighty in greens in regulation. Never even in the top 100, which means my ball striking was awful. But I was in the top ten in the Order of Merit. Now if you're a bad player from tee to green and a bad putter, how are you going to be in the top ten in money? No way. So my short game was tremendously good to make up for the missed greens and the missed fairways.'

But statistics generally are misleading. Even a player's score, taken at face value, can give a totally wrong impression. Take, for example, Langer's final round in the French Open at Chantilly in June. He had only 23 putts as compared with Mark McNulty's 32. Ostensibly, it would seem that Langer had an excellent day on the greens, which he did, but more importantly it means that he missed so many greens that he spent more of the round salvaging pars or making birdies with his sand-wedge than he did with a putter in his hand. McNulty, on the other hand, hit virtually every green and holed every putt in regulation.

Ever since Langer injured his back in Australia nearly two seasons ago, he had been struggling with his irons. He admits it now with a curious relief as though he would rather people turned their attention to the defects in his iron-play than dwelled any longer on his putting miseries.

'If I've played 65 tournaments in two years, there have only been ten weeks when I've struck the ball well; the other 55 I haven't. The problem is the way I turn, the way I take the club away. I've got a very strong grip, so I've got to account for that to start off with. My clubface gets shut a lot of times which causes a hook, or . . . I come over the top, which creates a pull hook, or I start blocking it . . . It's like a chain reaction. You do one thing wrong and in two weeks you've got 15 faults because of that one thing which started it off. You've just gradually got to work your way back.'

Practice has always been Langer's panacea.

'I've always believed, like Gary Player, that the harder I practise the luckier I get. I've always felt that if I want to be better than the others, then I'll have to work a little more than the others. You don't become the best in the world by not working.'

At the US Masters with Sam one year, Bob Torrance can remember watching Langer at work. 'He was on the practice ground in the morning, went to the putting green, played a round of golf, came off the golf course, sent his caddie for a sandwich and then went back to the practice ground and back to the putting green. He just did that all day. He was just going about it like a man of business.'

'I feel that the more I put into it, the more I can expect,' says Langer. 'I am a hard worker, that's the way I grew up, and I'm not talented enough not to be.'

'You are enormously talented,' I say in surprise.

'I know I'm talented, but it comes with a lot of work. I've known in the past that if I don't practise I find it very difficult to play very good. Also, if I take two or three weeks off on the trot and then come back and play, I'm not playing well. I need a few days to get into it. Whether that has something to do with technique, I don't know. It probably is, because I've found it easier in the last few years to do that . . . my swing's getting a little more grooved these days.'

'Do you think it's true that some people need to hit more balls than others, whether or not they are good players?'

'Some people need to hit more balls because their technique is not that good, I think, and they don't feel comfortable if they don't. But I know very few people who can get away with hitting very few balls.'

Langer used to be as fanatical about practising as Vijay Singh, and as conscientious as Hugh Baiocchi, who has played golf seven days a week for the last ten years. Now when he is at home in Anhausen, Germany, he will usually only practise three times a week. There is a practice net in the cellar of his house where he hits balls for an hour or so in between sessions on the range – 'just to keep the muscle memory there and the feel'.

'Generally,' explains Langer, 'I'm a feel player – I like to just feel things. But sometimes I feel things differently to what they really are. That's when you have to break it down to technique. It really changes every few weeks or months. When you feel comfortable, you don't think about certain details in your swing, you just let it happen. And other days it feels so awful that you have to work out why.'

At such times he turns to Hoffman, who has coached him on technique and golf course strategy since the early seventies. 'He taught me how to measure the course and what to look for. They used to laugh at him. He was playing tournaments in Germany 20 years ago and he was the only guy measuring the course. All the other guys were just eye-balling it.'

It is extremely difficult to get Langer to give of himself, or to make him open up at all. He never embellishes his answers or expands on any topic voluntarily, but if pressed, can be quite surprisingly forthcoming. Bill Elliot, his biographer, says that Langer doesn't feel he is an interesting person and therefore can't understand why people should be interested in him.

'Have you ever been to a psychologist?' I ask.

'No.'

'A guru?'

'I don't really know what a guru is. What's a guru?'

'I think it has a fairly wide definition.'

'No, I haven't.'

I was puzzled because I had been told by two separate sources that he had been to see both a psychologist and a guru in the shape of an old woman, at various times. I forced the issue and still he denied it. I felt embarrassed that I could make a mistake of that magnitude and more than a little bit confused.

'I've been to a sports psychologist,' said Langer suddenly, 'If that's what you mean.'

I thought: 'Where have I been for the last five minutes?'

Playing in America five years ago with close friend, Joey Sindelar, Langer got talking to Sindelar's sports psychologist. A lot of what he was told Langer felt he already did. 'You have to be doing certain things otherwise you wouldn't be out here.' But there were one or two aspects which he felt would help him on the golf course which he wasn't already doing.

'Like what?' I ask, since he has left the subject hanging in mid air again.

'Like switching on and off, like not trying too hard, like just letting it happen. Relaxing, instead of forcing it.

'You know,' says Langer all of a sudden, 'the thing is, you can only do your best. Sometimes your best is 82. One thing he says is don't be mad at yourself that you've hit a bad shot. As long as you know that you've tried your best, that's all you could have done. And that's easier said than done. Because in golf, you only hit three or four perfect shots a round; all the others are not right. So you always think you can improve. You're always mad at yourself for not hitting the perfect shot.'

'You are a perfectionist, though.'

'To some degree. I think I used to be more of a perfectionist than I am now. I learned that I'm never going to be perfect.' Spontanteous and infectious laughter bubbles up in him. 'I can only try to get as close as possible.'

Starting out on Tour, Langer's main goal was to keep making the cut so that he wouldn't have to prequalify for tournaments each week. Then he aimed for the top 60 and automatic exemption, for tournament victories and the European No.1 spot, for the US Tour and finally, for a major. Every year, with every achievement, he aimed his sights higher. 'Then at some point I hit the wall,' says Langer quietly, 'and I went down a little bit.'

He says that with a calmness of demeanour and an acceptance which he would never have had years ago when discussing the possibility of not reaching those heights again. It is partly the result of his new philosophy towards life and the game. Like a lot of the top players, he has learned the value of not being one-dimensional. This year he has taken more time off than ever before to be with his wife and his son, born in May, and to pursue his golf course design projects, his hobbies – skiing, tennis and watching sport – and to get more actively involved in Christianity. Like Lyle and Faldo, he has also resigned his membership of the US Tour. He felt that his health and his family life were suffering because he was playing and travelling so much.

'I used to be that way for some years,' says Langer, meaning one-dimensional, totally immersed in his career. 'That's all there was for me – golf, golf, golf and nothing else. I found out that it's not good that way. You need other interests and you need to grow as a person. There's more to life than golf. One day you're going to wake up not playing good and that's the end of the world for you because there's nothing else. You know what I mean? If you only have golf in your life and you keep shooting 76s every week, then you're so depressed because there's no other thing in your life. And then to change once you're 40 is much harder than doing it gradually.'

Bernhard Langer intends to start now.

Chapter Thirteen

THE DEVIL DAY

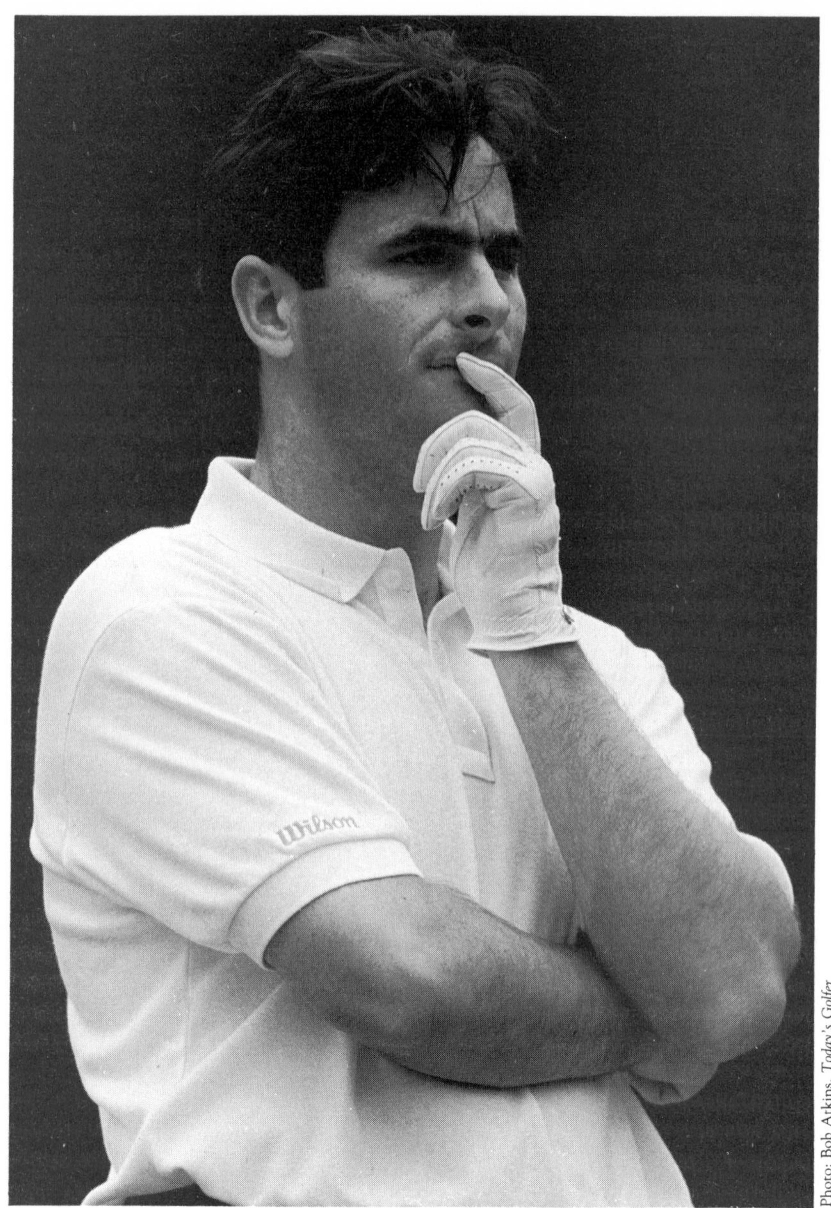

Photo: Bob Atkins, *Today's Golfer*

David Feherty: 'Golf isn't a nice game at all'

VOLVO PGA CHAMPIONSHIP, WENTWORTH, MAY 1990. IN A world full of people saying what they think they should say instead of saying what they really think, David Feherty is refreshingly, often disturbingly, frank.

Take an innocuous subject like pro-ams.

This is one Irishman who is not going to wax lyrical, insincerely, about them. 'I have fairly strong views on pro-ams,' says Feherty, setting the record straight from the start. Tousle-haired and black browed, he is seated on a bucket beside the putting green in front of the Wentworth pro shop. 'Well, it's the nature of the game, really. Golf spectators are different from other sporting spectators in that they are, generally speaking, actively involved in the sport that they watch. Not like football. I mean, most people that go to watch a football match don't play football any more. They did it when they were children, or whatever. But this is a game where people can participate till the lights go out. That's why we have to play in pro-ams, basically.'

Every Wednesday is pro-am day. Four-balls made up of three amateurs and one professional taken from the top 50 on the Order of Merit play better-ball, Texas scramble and other such formats. Most players have mixed feelings about them, some absolutely loathe them, but for the most part they accept that pro-ams are one of the main reasons for the game's commercial success. Golf's unique selling point is the fact that it is the only sport that allows an amateur to compete with the best professionals in the world on an equal level. In other sports they can't. They couldn't play a game against Steve Davis or Ivan Lendl; they couldn't play football with Diego Maradona. But because of golf's handicap system, an amateur can play 18 holes with Greg Norman or Seve Ballesteros or David Feherty.

'Tennis players don't have to play in pro-am's,' says Feherty resentfully, although he knows all these things are true. 'Can you imagine what John McEnroe and Ivan Lendl would say if they were asked to play a quick five-setter with a few of the boys from the local club the day before Wimbledon? But we do it every week . . . It's the most destructive thing possible for your game, you know, before competing in a major tournament, to have to play in a pro-am. It's a helluva undertaking. I think that's why a lot of the boys get upset about it.'

At 32, David Feherty, winner of five tournaments on the European and South African Tours, is one of the best, but also one of the most unconventional players on the circuit. Born and bred in Bangor, Northern Ireland, Feherty is the golfer with a passion for music – he has over 600 records in his collection ('Puccini is my favourite composer of all time') – who keeps a medicine chest in his golf bag, has a fetish about lip-ice and washing his hands, and who once dreamed of being an opera singer. This last has been a favourite talking point where Feherty is concerned, since the day he turned professional in 1976.

'You know what it's like being in the media,' says Feherty, whose face is arresting in the same way his character is, because it is so defiantly different. 'People get their teeth into something and they think, "Christ, it's a little out of the ordinary; we can write about that." Really it was blown out of all proportion and it always has been. I mean, this has plagued me for years.'

He imitates a reporter – ' "Oh Christ, you were the opera singer, weren't you?" Anyone that ever heard me sing knew I wasn't going to be an opera singer. I did a year's training after having sung for a long time in church choirs and school choirs, and a couple of radio broadcasts. I trained with a Polish lady in Belfast. I heard myself one day and I thought, "No. That doesn't sound very nice. I think I'd rather play golf." '

Which is why he is here now – playing in pro-ams. And why Feherty finds himself driving down the M25 on a Wednesday morning trying to prepare himself mentally for the day ahead.

'I get to the golf course late, as usual. I say to myself: "Just go through your normal routine. Get there at least half an hour before your round, get spiked up, hit a few shots and get going." But you know, with Shey [his son] and all that business, and phone calls, you get there less than half an hour before. You don't get the chance to go out and hit too many balls.

'I've got my ball in my pocket after two holes. It's a no return, which, to be perfectly honest, isn't that uncommon an occurrence. In a pro-am I just concentrate on the team score – not that that worries me to a great extent either, but I'll do my best for the three that are out there. I'm not all that worried about my own score.'

It is Feherty's firm belief that the approach of most amateurs to pro-ams is fatally flawed. 'Nearly always, they are under the misapprehension that if I miss a six footer, I'm actually going to be worried about it. I'm going to be worried about the team score, obviously, but I'm out there for a practice round and I'm out there to give them a good day – if they behave themselves,' adds Feherty with a wicked laugh.

'The way to play a pro-am in a lot of ways is actually to say nothing at all, because anything that you say is nearly always going to be the wrong thing to say. There's one in every group that says, "Good shot" every time the ball leaves the clubhead without waiting to see where it finishes. So that would be point number one: wait until the ball has stopped moving before you decide whether or not it is a good shot.

'Then you get the guys who want you to read every putt . . .'

Playing in the Epson Grand Prix at St Pierre one year, Feherty was asked by one of his pro-am partners to read a four-foot putt at the first. Reading putts, incidentally, is something he is quite prepared to do. He squatted down and lined it up. 'Inside left,' he said.

The man was sceptical. 'I was going to hit it right lip,' he informed Feherty.

'Honestly,' said Feherty patiently, 'it's an inside left putt.'

The man accepted the advice grudgingly. He crouched over his putter. He eyed the hole. He froze over his putter-blade. He checked several times to see that the hole hadn't moved. Finally, he took a full backswing and hit the putt four feet outside left. The look he shot Feherty was nothing short of murderous. 'I would have holed that if you hadn't opened your mouth,' he said bitterly to Feherty.

Feherty managed to restrain himself. 'Well, that's fine,' he said in a perfectly normal tone. 'You read your own putts from here on in.'

'And the bugger holed everything,' Feherty says now, relaying the story. 'That was the worst.'

'Does that kind of thing happen often?'

'Oh, you'd be surprised what they say.'

'How do you feel about playing in pro-ams?' I asked Grant Turner once.

'Well, some of them are okay, some of them are difficult. Necessary part of the job.'

'Is that the way you think of them?'

'It's the only way to think of them. Makes it more bearable. A lot of them are okay if you get a good team and decent people. Sometimes it's difficult when your team doesn't speak English and they don't play golf either.'

'Pro-ams,' says Zimbabwean Tony Johnstone, 'are something – whether you're drawn with a good team or not – that has to be done . . . and from the sponsor's point of view, may be the most important aspect of the week. That's his PR day for his clients. And if it wasn't for pro-ams, we wouldn't have sponsors. There are a lot of guys on Tour that hate pro-ams . . . and treat the amateurs badly, then wonder why the sponsors pull out. I can't say I'm a lover of pro-ams but pro-ams are the reason we make the money we make. If you're lucky enough to get three guys you get on with, pro-ams are great. It's a good practice round, you can have some fun and some social golf, win a few bob if you play okay. And if you happen to get a team who are a bunch of idiots, well, it's just something you've got to do.'

Feherty played in a five-ball in Sweden one year with four amateurs, two of whom had never been on a golf course before. The first of these initiates stood up on the first tee and actually managed to hit the ball. The second fresh-aired it several times.

'I played in one of the pre-tournament pro-ams in England with a Dutch guy who had never been on a golf course and had never held a golf club before. He had five swipes at it on the first tee before he made contact. Eventually, you know, walking down the fairway I said, "Where do you play?" He said: "Here. This is my first time."

'So you end up giving him a lesson. Picking his ball up and saying, "Well, okay, we'll try it again on the next." It's just a nightmare for any professional person to have to go through that. It's hard to think of an equivalent, you know, in the business sense. Imagine being an accountant or a dentist, or something, and somebody comes in, and you're saying: "Here, have a go at that. No, no. That's not right."' Feherty chuckles malevolently at the thought.

What is most surprising, perhaps, is that of all of the things Feherty finds abhorrent about pro-ams, the one he minds least is his amateur partner's standard of golf.

'That's another major misconception. They all come out here expecting me to give them a hard time . . . Nobody has a fault as a player, I don't believe. I mean, the game's so severe – it's such a horrible experience at times trying to play this game – that I would never criticise anybody for playing badly. It's just that the behaviour patterns are so weird sometimes . . .'

According to Feherty, amateur players who take part in pro-ams come under several distinct categories:

THE TRIER: 'I think the very worst is the trier. The guy who comes in and says, "Right, chaps, let's really have a go at this now. Come on, team, I think we can win this." And then they go off and make a three-pointer at the first and a three-pointer at the second and they reckon they're on a roll then, and they can be a dreadful pain in the backside for the rest of the team, not just the pro.'

THE MOUSE: 'He's the one who says, "I won't get in your way." And that's nearly as bad. He tries so hard not to get in your way that he tap dances on your line three times at least. He doesn't want to finish out and isn't really all that keen on participating.'

THE BANDIT: 'You get a lot of them in Ireland and things like the Four Stars. A lot of dodgy handicaps in the Four Stars. And that's embarrassing if everybody is playing off dud handicaps and you know you're going to end up winning by six shots.'

THE CHEAT: 'I played with the president of a golf club in Spain once. He was a persistent trier. You know: "We're going to win this at all costs." And at all costs meant: "I'm going to tee it up in the rough. I'm going to tell you I had a four when I actually had a five." That sort of thing.

'There's a fair amount of funny business that can go on. I wouldn't call it cheating, but there's a general sort of ignorance of the rules – of marking the ball and slovenly behaviour that we just wouldn't put up with on the Tour. Every now and then I'll pull somebody up. I'll say, "Look, you just can't mark the ball like that, I'm sorry." And they look at you like you've got two heads. Like, "What the hell are you saying? I'm in *your* team."'

THE INTERROGATOR: 'You get the stock questions: "How do you get backspin?" With 15 years' practice, mate. "Is Ballesteros really a nice guy?" "I suppose you get all your expenses paid?" "Are you making a living?" "Do you have a shop?" "Do you have another job?" "Is this all you do?"

'You always get asked as well, "Do you enjoy playing in pro-ams?" And every single professional who is playing in that pro-am – if they told the truth – would say, "No. I don't. This is a real task. I'd rather be at the dentist. I'd rather saw off my leg than be playing in this pro-am at this particular time."'

CAPTAINS OF INDUSTRY AND ENTERTAINERS: 'These are people who know that they are not supposed to play the game well and, generally speaking, they're a pleasure to play with. If you're playing with the manager of a certain company, for example – he's a confident man in his own field and he knows that you would be uncomfortable trying to run his business for a day – and he goes out there with that attitude. They don't expect anything of themselves in terms of golf, even though they can be very competitive. There's no one more competitive than Jimmy Tarbuck, or Bruce Forsyth for that matter. But we don't expect anything of them, in the same way that if I were to go on the stage at the London Palladium, people wouldn't expect me to be funny.'

'They'd expect you to sing,' says David Jones, who is practising his putting within earshot.

Feherty bursts out laughing. 'They'd expect me to sing, the bastards would.'

Last year Feherty played with Forsyth in a pro-am at Kingswood. He felt desperately sorry for him, the way he was constantly harassed and hounded by the media and the gallery. 'He's expected to be Bruce Forsyth all the time,' says Feherty. 'He's not allowed to be a normal person the way he is at home. He got attacked in the press room a couple of years ago for snapping at somebody on the golf course. It was a big celebrity pro-am and there were autograph hunters all over the place. I'm playing with Forsyth and he decides to go for a pee somewhere down the bottom of the course. He goes into the woods and eight people follow him. You can imagine the situation. He's going to turn around and say, "Piss off", you know. "Can't I take a leak?" Next thing it's in the papers: "Bruce snaps angrily at autograph hunters." That's what happens here. You're not allowed to be a real person.'

In June, the only four-round celebrity pro-am included in the European Tour schedule is held at Moor Park Golf Club, near Rickmansworth. Hosted by Terry Wogan, Jimmy Tarbuck, Ronnie Corbett and Henry Cooper, it is run as a Tour event but a Pro-am Better Ball competition runs concurrently. The celebrities are people like Shakin' Stevens and Meat Loaf, who attract vast crowds of non-golf fans, all of whom run amok across greens and fairways in frenzied pursuit of autographs with patent disregard for the professionals who are trying to play the tournament.

To Feherty, the whole idea of a four-day pro-am is anathema.

'The Four Stars is a real attitude adjuster in a lot of ways. You have to really set your stall for that one. You've got to start off at the beginning of the week and say, "I'm going to be hassled here this week. It's not going to be easy but I'll just play as well as I can and get through it." I've had an incident at the

Four Stars playing with a guy where we're on the 16th tee, I get to the top of my backswing and a phone rings in his bag. Frigging cellphone rings. He apologised most profusely, and to be fair to him, he just let it ring. But he did make a visitation to the bush with it shortly afterwards.'

Richard Boxall stood on the first tee at Moor Park a couple of years ago awaiting the arrival of the final member of his pro-am group. Eventually the man came running up the path, trolley bounding along behind him, all flustered and red-faced. 'Mr Lee,' he cried genially to one of Boxall's partners. 'So nice to meet you!' Then he rushed over to John Morgan with an equally effusive greeting and wrung his hand several times. To Boxall he gave a curt nod.

They teed off, Boxall feeling distinctly put out. He couldn't understand what he had done to offend the man. He wracked his brains for the possibility of a past encounter, but drew a blank. He was positive he had never laid eyes on the man before. They arrived at their balls on the fairway and Boxall took out a five-iron.

'No, no, no,' cried the amateur, making a bee-line for Boxall. He snatched the club from his hand. 'You need a three-iron from here,' he told him. Boxall was absolutely stunned. Nevertheless, he decided to let it ride. Three holes later the advice was starting to get to him. 'So,' enquired the man on the fourth, amiable after salvaging a par from a bunker, 'what do you play off?'

'Some of the weirdest things happen in that tournament,' says Feherty. 'I remember playing with Alex Higgins, who is a good friend of mine. I like Alex very much. He got on the first tee and he's scrabbling around in his golf bag like a sort of anxious rodent. Scraping around in the ball pocket – there's nothing there, down to the bottom – there's nothing there. Next thing I turn around and he's in my bag! He comes up and he's found something. It's an Opal Fruit and it's been in there three months. It's been in there so long it's ruptured the wrapper and it's sort of leaking out of one side. And he undoes it and it's down his gullet and he immediately calms down. He just needed to get something in his mouth.'

The Americans have their own pro-celebrity tournament: the hugely successful Bob Hope Classic. 'I played with Telly Savalas two years running in the Bob Hope Classic,' says Feherty, 'and he hit seven people in nine holes. He was playing off 18 or 19 at the time and, of course, there was an enormous crowd of knicker-dropping old ladies following. "Show us your lolly, show us your lolly," they were shouting from the crowd. He hit so many people, so fast, they didn't have time to get out of the way. It was like an abattoir.'

In 1983, Feherty found himself playing the last round of that same tournament with Bernhard Langer, Bob Hope and Gerald Ford. It took six and a half hours to get around the course, including 18 unequal struggles between every tee and green with the marauding hordes, all of whom were desperate to get close to Hope and Ford.

'We finished about 45 minutes behind Canizares who birdied the last seven holes to finish a shot ahead of me,' says Feherty, remembering the stampedes, the screaming fans and the interminable round with a shudder. Feherty had a putt on the last green to finish outright second and to make a cheque roughly five times bigger than anything he had ever won before. It was Ford's putt first. Feherty came to, and found that he had taken the pin automatically. 'I'm standing there, I'm tending the flag for Gerald Ford and I'm thinking: "What the fucking hell am I doing?"'

'Here I am with a £20,000 putt and I'm holding the flag for this 36-handicapper,' cries David Jones, imagining Feherty's dilemma.

'Exactly,' shouts Feherty. 'With three broken knees.'

But even Feherty admits that pro-ams do have their good points, the main one being that he has made a lot of friends through them.

'Bruce Forsyth,' says Feherty, drumming up a list of his favourite pro-am partners, and naming one of the nicest and most down-to-earth celebrities you could wish to meet. 'He's a very keen golfer. He's passionate about the game. I remember feeling that way . . . I know it just doesn't feel that way anymore. I just couldn't wait to get out on the golf course. I can see that in him.'

Here we go. Next to pro-ams, this is Feherty's favourite hobby horse. He likes to maintain that he isn't particularly fond of golf as a game. 'I play to make a living,' he insists.

'You're joking?' I said in amazement the first time I heard him say that.

'No, I'm not. I don't even think it's a very nice game. Bowls is a nice game or tennis even, to a certain extent. Golf isn't a nice game at all. You can get out there and you can knock your pan in, day in and day out, work your nuts off, and get kicked in the face for it time after time after time. And you've got to do that and keep doing it; keep swallowing the shit that it throws at you. And eventually you'll get a chink of daylight, and you'll get a big cheque here, there or wherever, and that's nice. Most of it isn't very nice at all.'

'In that case, what would you do if you had your life over?'

'I'd do exactly the same thing. Not because I enjoy it; it's what I'm good at. I mean, to say I don't enjoy the game . . . I enjoy my life. But when I'm on the golf course and I'm working hard and under pressure, or whatever, I don't really enjoy that. That's work.'

'What do you like most about being a professional golfer?'

'The freedom it gives me,' said Feherty. 'Nobody tells me what to do. Nobody gives me a hard time except me and that's quite enough, because I give myself a hard enough time. You keep your own hours. You do what you want to do. If I don't wanna go and play, I don't play. If I wanna take a week off, I take a week off. If I wanna take a month off, I take a month off. Plus I can make a lot of money at it, which is the bottom line.'

I brought up a conversation I had had with Gary Player, where Player was saying how much it annoys him when sports commentators quote professional golfers' winnings, and accompany it with a remark to the effect of: 'Gary Player has just earned £20,000 for his week's work.'

'It's a lifetime's work,' said Feherty. 'I mean, I've been working in a pro shop and in a golfing environment since I was nine years old. You put your time in. Anything anybody makes out of this game they deserve. No question about that.'

Today, however, seated on his bucket on the putting green, David Feherty is in a particularly mellow mood. 'It's not that I don't like golf,' he is saying, 'but golf is my work . . . If I didn't have to work I wouldn't play golf. I can think of other things I'd rather do. I don't feel I owe the game anything at all. Quite the reverse. I don't think anybody owes the game anything. People say that people who have made millions out of the game should put something back into it. That's not necessarily true. People who've made millions out of it deserve those millions because this is tough.'

'But what would you do if you didn't play?'

'I'd love to be able to do nothing. I think I could do that quite comfortably. I tell you what I would do, I could caddie. I could have a ball around here. I'd get a real kick out of that. What do you think, Harry?' Feherty says to his caddie. 'Wanna play?'

'Right,' says Harry. 'You're on.'

Chapter Fourteen

OF RAGS AND RICHES

Photo: ASP, Stuart Franklin

Power golf: 'There's no bits and pieces to Ian Woosnam's game,' says coach Bob Torrance. 'It just flows'

MONTE CARLO, JULY 1990. TWELVE HOURS AFTER WINNING the Monte Carlo Open, Ian Woosnam is still celebrating – with a cup of coffee at Nice airport. According to the monitors, the Heathrow flight is indefinitely *retard*, and air traffic controllers rarely make exceptions of champion golfers, even if they have just won the Monte Carlo Open and broken three long-standing records in the process.

Beside him, his caddie Phil Morbey, Sam Torrance's caddie Malcolm Mason, and Michael McLean give Ian Wright stick about the inebriated woman who has attached herself to him. 'So you're the famous one,' was her opening remark to Woosnam. Clinging to the back of his chair to steady herself and breathing a heady combination of champagne and beer fumes over him, she had demanded his autograph. Woosnam laughed it off good-naturedly, but was obviously relieved when her attention was diverted by the ribald comments of the caddies.

McLean stops tormenting Wright to address Woosnam.

'So what's the secret?' he asks suddenly, referring to the Welshman's dramatic return to sparkling form, resulting in a last round 60 at Mont Agel. 'What's the reason you're suddenly playing so well?'

Woosnam looks surprised, the way he always does when someone calls into question something which is as natural to him as breathing. 'No reason,' he says. 'I'm not hitting the ball any better. I'm just holing a few putts.'

Of all the top players Woosnam is the least arrogant about his prodigious talent, the least pretentious, the least impressed by the idea of his own importance. As wealthy and famous as he is, to this day he would rather go down to his local in Oswestry, Shropshire, than all the fancy places his money could take him. That's just the way he is. At the end of 1987, his most successful year on the European Tour, he still had his feet firmly enough on the ground to say of his native town: 'I know everybody here, I've grown up with everyone. It's when I go out of the area that people say, "Oh, there's Ian Woosnam," and I feel like a superstar. But when I'm here I just feel like an ordinary person.'

Some players change as inexorably as the tide as they cross the divide between star and superstar. It may be a gradual process – a steady erosion or corrosion of certain values, or it may happen overnight. They might wake up one morning believing in their own media hype.

Ian Woosnam, elevated in a single year to millionaire and subsequent superstar status, has never been in danger of forgetting where he came from.

'I think a lot of it comes from his roots,' explains Phil Morbey. 'Because he had to work so hard when he was a young kid,' he adds, referring to Woosnam's childhood, spent driving tractors, milking cows and tossing hay bales on the family farm. Woosnam left home having acquired two things: the certain knowledge that he didn't want to be a farmer, and extremely strong forearms, hands and legs.

The third son in a family of four children, his was a youth devoted more to sport than study. He excelled at soccer and golf, and was torn between which to choose as a profession. But when he left school at the age of 16, golf, by dint of the fact that it offered a longer and physically less destructive career, won the toss. What would he have done if he hadn't been a Tour player? Ask most pro golfers that same question and they will spin stories of bents toward accountancy or engineering. Woosnam, now 33, just grins and says candidly: 'God knows. Nothing special, I can tell you that.'

Two stories.

When Woosnam was nine years old, the family went on holiday to Butlin's camp in Pwllheli. Harold Woosnam, Ian's father and one of his strongest influences, was a boxing enthusiast and he entered Ian in the camp competition. Being something of a veteran fighter as a result of all the bullying he received at school, Woosnam saw off his opponent without expending much energy and won a free holiday for the family. He did this for two consecutive years.

It was while the Woosnam family were enjoying their free holiday the following year that they were informed that Ian had just won the swimming competition. 'That's impossible,' cried his father in disbelief, 'Ian can't swim.' But Ian had. Given a choice between sinking and swimming he had swum. And won.

From an early age Woosnam possessed, in large measures, aggression, resolution and guts. Rough and muddy scrambles on the football pitch and long hours in the bar afterwards, boxing victories over people twice his size, playing golf for money when there was none in his pocket; these are things which have shaped and moulded his character. Inveterate are his down-to-earth manner, his humour and his fiercely competitive nature. But his background also bred into him a deep-rooted provincial loyalty. When he came on Tour in the mid-seventies his approach to life was determinedly blue-collar; you work hard, you play hard.

Fourteen years later little has changed. His closest friends are still the people he travelled with when he first came out on Tour, players like D. J. Russell and Joe Higgins. Tournament or no tournament, he goes out when and where he wants to, spurning the careful diets and early nights favoured by other top players. A whole mythology has grown up around him as a result. You will hear that he likes to drink and that when he drinks he likes to fight. The former is true, the latter is not. Yes, he did hit Richard Boxall, but not without justification. Boxall had emerged from a restaurant one evening, spotted the Welshman walking down the road, and insulted Woosnam's wife in a voice loud enough to be heard. Woosnam only hit him once but he knocked him out cold.

Woosnam might imbibe more alcohol than most other top players do, he might, on occasion, have stayed out till all hours of the night when he has been leading a tournament (drinking helps him to deal with stress as much as anything), and he might, at times, have behaved in a manner that people don't think a golfer of his ability and stature in world golf should. But whatever he does, he does openly. He doesn't parade around pretending to be a paragon of virtue one moment and behaving licentiously the next (if he did anything to excess, he wouldn't be one of the best players in the world). He is frank, outspoken, prone to fits of temper, and incorrigible to the last. But he is himself. With Woosnam, what you see is what you get.

'He's the people's champion, isn't he?' says Jeremy Bennett, expressing the Tour consensus. 'He's the clean version of Alex Higgins. I mean, everybody loves Woosie.'

Oswestry, spring 1989. Outside a redbrick house in a tiny Shropshire town are parked several cars and a decorator's van. The Mercedes which has recently replaced a Porsche has a personalised number plate on it which reads: PRO IW. Round the back is a smaller house, just about big enough for a family of three – with two cars. That's the leisure house. That's where Woosnam, wife Glendryth and son Daniel go to relax. On the ground floor there is a full-size snooker table and a bar set up like a miniature pub. Upstairs is the video room and the bathroom with gold taps.

There was a time when Ian Woosnam could hardly afford the price of a square meal. He travelled the Tour like a gypsy in a borrowed Volkswagen caravanette, existing on a fast food diet of crisps, soup and baked beans. Long after he'd made it, the memory of those years still haunted him. Once, when asked if it would be the end of the world to him if he didn't win a major, he said abruptly: 'It wouldn't be the end of the world, no, because I can still remember the bad times and winning a major's not going to make them bad times go away.'

'I remember Ian Woosnam talking to me when we were on Tour in Nigeria in the seventies,' says Irishman Des Smyth, one of the nicest and most genuine people you could ever wish to meet, 'and he's saying, "You know, Des, I'm going to have to give this game up. I just can't make any money. Everything I've saved I've lost. I've got no money and no sponsor." And now he's one of the world's best players.'

Woosnam gave himself five years to make it from the time he turned professional at the age of 18. Months away from that self-imposed deadline, he played sufficiently well on the Safari circuit to encourage him to hold on. It was a near thing.

'I was gonna give the game up. I was going to apply for the club job at Oswestry Golf Club. I had got down to that stage. But I just kept at it, kept slogging away. I'd walk off the golf course and think, "I'm not playing again.

I've had enough of this." Then a couple of days later I'd be alright again. I'd just get over the frustration.'

With sponsorship in 1981 came a kind of turning point. 'Some days I'd have £30 in my pocket,' remembers Woosnam, who had been subsidising his income up until then by working in bars and other places which offered temporary employment. 'I used to think, God, I'm rich. It'd take the pressure off and I'd play well the next day because I knew if I didn't win I'd still have £30. You know what I mean? The more money I had the better I played, somehow.'

Woosnam's is a classic case study for anyone who thinks that pro golfers make too much money. Take the first six years of his career as an example. Beginning in 1976, he made three consecutive visits to the European Tour School at Foxhills golf club in Surrey, winning his card each time but only managing to keep it on the last attempt. His winnings from 1978, which was the first year he made any money at all, were as follows:

1978 – £284
1979 – £1,049
1980 – £3,481
1981 – £1,884

Still think you'd like to be a professional golfer?

Woosnam won his first European tournament in 1982, which took his earnings for the year to just over £48,000. Sure, it *sounds* like a lot of money. Now subtract travelling expenses, tax, the sponsor's cut, bank loans and incidentals and see how much is left. You'd earn more on the dole.

But Woosnam was one of the lucky ones. When he finally turned the corner, he never looked back. The following year he finished third on the Safari circuit money list and became exempt from pre-qualifying in Europe, which cut the amount of travelling and playing he did by half. His game profited. Confidence boosted, Woosnam played his heart out for five second places. 'I thought, "This is it. I've arrived." And I was away then.'

Des Smyth has his own explanation of the learning process that is pro golf. 'Nobody goes into school the first year and does their "O" levels,' he says. 'It takes you five years to work up to it. And it's the same with golf. Guys come on Tour, they get a card – it's going to take them five years to really be competing at the level they want . . . And every practice shot you hit and all the hours that you put in, that's all adding to your experience. And eventually, the day will arrive when you'll be out there playing in the middle of all these big time players and you'll say to yourself, "You know, I'm competing pretty good here."'

'You get yourself into that [winning] situation enough times,' says Woosnam, 'and you just learn to cope with the pressure. It takes you a while. You get a chance to win a tournament and the first few times you blow it. It takes you a long, long time to win one.'

Looking back now at the reasons why he made the transition from member of the pack to tournament winner when so many of his friends didn't, Woosnam finds that the one which stands out – alongside gaining consistency – is attitude. He names Joe Higgins as an example of someone who has never bridged the void between promise and fulfilment. Higgins is a good player who has done very well in regional events but can't get his game together in a Tour event. 'I think he puts himself under pressure,' says Woosnam, who spends almost as much time helping other players with their games as he does working on his own. 'He thinks, "Oh God, Seve's playing this week; Langer, Lyle and Faldo are playing." And it's just: "I can't beat them." His attitude is bad to start off with, I think.'

Struggling for survival in the early days of his career, Woosnam remembers being tormented by those same fears. He found a way to deal with them. He figured that if he could shoot a low score one day, there was no earthly reason why he couldn't do it another.

'When I played with Seve back in '83, he shot 73 one day and I shot 68. I thought, "If I can beat him now I can beat him any time." You've got to have that attitude – "He didn't impress me", like. You can get overawed by players, you know.'

Such lessons, once learned, are never forgotten.

Players on the lower rungs of pro golf have a tendency to look backwards all the time. They are walking down the first hole every Friday trying to calculate mentally what the cut is going to be; agonising over the bad shot they hit four holes ago when they reach the ninth on Saturday; and standing over putts on Sunday, wondering how much it will cost them if they miss.

Major or minor, Woosnam goes into every event with the same attitude. 'I just feel every week that I'm going to win the tournament. I go out to win and I go out to shoot the course record every round I play. If you've got that goal, the other ones come easier. If you're trying to lead the tournament and you're pressing, pressing, you'll suddenly think, "Christ, I'm five shots off the lead." You're making the cut easily . . . If you have that attitude, you're bound to have a good week. Stand there with the driver and just let 'em have it.'

As a boy starting out in the game, Woosnam took a leaf from his father's book. He learnt to desire perfectionism above all else. As a man, he adheres to a maxim of his own: 'You've got to have a goal and you've got to set your goal as high as you possibly can.'

The idea of setting realistic goals is anathema to him.

'I think that's absolute crap,' Woosnam says in no uncertain terms. 'If you do that you're not pushing yourself hard enough. I feel that if you push yourself hard enough, you'll get to a standard you never thought you'd get to anyway.'

Bearing that principle in mind, Woosnam set his goal in golf: to become a millionaire out of the game. By the end of 1987, aged 31, he had achieved it. Not only had he achieved it, but by virtue of eight tournament victories worldwide – including the Million Dollar Classic in Sun City – he had achieved it in a single season.

There was only one problem. By making his goal monetary, he laid himself open to criticism from every possible quarter for taking what was interpreted as an unspeakably rapacious and mercenary approach to the game. Woosnam did little to defend himself from these accusations. Instead, he added fuel to the fire by discarding the Mizuno clubs which had helped him become, arguably, the best player in the world in 1987, in favour of the comparatively unknown (in European tournament golf) Maruman. The changeover – worth one million pounds to Woosnam over three years – took place at the beginning of the next season.

As if that weren't enough, he went on to perpetrate two other offences in the eyes of the golfing world. In 1988 he steadfastly refused to defend the World Cup title he had won for Wales with David Llewellyn, going instead to Sun City in pursuit of another million. Then he flew to Japan the week before the 1989 Ryder Cup, risking exhaustion which might have jeopardised his worth as a key member of the team. Why did he do it? For one reason and one reason only. Money.

Woosnam insisted that people were being unfair when they attacked him for these capital gains. 'When you look at it,' he said, 'it's only a business, golf is. I can't just go and play somewhere for nothing, you know. Why should I? It's easy for people to criticise, but you put them in your position. What would they do?'

One question: 'Are you motivated by money?'

Woosnam held his breath for a moment then let it expire slowly between his lips. 'I think,' he said finally, 'I've always been motivated by money because I've always needed it, you know. But now, I think, I'm getting to the stage where I just want to win.' He gave a slightly embarrassed laugh. 'It's difficult to say . . . The more money you have, the more you want. It's easy to be greedy.'

Epson Grand Prix, September 1990. The billiards room at St Pierre has a dim, cavernous appearance, enhanced by stone walls, a grey cloud of cigarette smoke rising like steam to the ceiling, and low lighting. Tonight, like most nights during tournaments held at Chepstow, the tables are monopolised by golfers and caddies all playing and gambling ferociously into the small hours. The present war being waged on green baize involves a well-known foursome. Namely, Ian Woosnam and Bob Torrance versus Sam Torrance and Derrick Cooper.

'Come on, partner,' encourages Woosnam, who is casually attired in a brown tee-shirt and white cotton pants. 'Put a bit of spin on it, Bob, and you'll make the green.'

Torrance pots a red triumphantly. 'Never leave a mug a double,' he tells Torrance Jnr. Derrick Cooper enters the fray.

'Hit it while it shines,' says Bob as Cooper procrastinates.

'Watch your follow-through,' his son tells Cooper, who responds by sinking two balls with aplomb.

Woosnam takes the table. Bob Torrance goes over and holds a whispered conversation with him in the exact same way he does when he's working with the Welshman on the range. In this, as in everything he does, Woosnam wants to be the best. Once he said in all seriousness, 'I could give up golf and take up snooker because that would be another goal to go for.' He holes another red.

'One at a time's good fishing,' shouts Bob rallyingly to his pupil. Sam follows Woosnam's example by sinking a magnificent right-angled black.

'Great shot,' cries June Torrance, who is watching from the sidelines.

'At least your mother is on your side,' needles Bob.

'You know, there's nothing worse, Sam,' remarks Cooper, 'than a bad loser.'

Bob ignores him. He waits until it's Cooper's turn to play. He watches the Englishman line up and miss the pink by miles. 'Choked like a donkey!' he sings out, getting his own back.

Woosnam, whose game has been honed by matches against some of the best snooker players in Britain, takes a large swig of his Guinness, picks up his cue and begins to clear the decks. He wears the identical expression to the one he has when he is winning a tournament by a considerable margin. That concentrated, determined, infinitely confident expression.

'Ian,' cries Bob, as Woosnam pots the winning ball, 'this is the best I've ever seen you swing.'

'Thanks, Bob,' says his pupil drily.

It was around 8.30 in the evening and all four men were playing truant from a sponsor's reception which was taking place elsewhere in the hotel. This anecdote is one which illustrates several things, both about Ian Woosnam – who was in contention for the tournament at the time – and about Tour players in general.

In the first place it shows just how down-to-earth Woosnam is. How he would rather play snooker with his friends than dress up in a dinner jacket and make small talk with a lot of strangers. But since he had been paid around £30,000 appearance money to play in the tournament, he was under a moral obligation if nothing else to accept the sponsor's invitation. And therefore, it also proves just how spoilt some of the Tour players have become.

In some ways perhaps Woosnam has changed. But he has done it imperceptibly and in a strange way come full circle. When a player becomes a superstar he is often taken in hand by his management company (especially if that happens to be IMG) and will soon be seen to acquire the appropriate image: the right car, the right house, the right suit, the right haircut.

Whether it was at IMG's instigation, or whether it was of his own volition, Woosnam appeared to do all of these things. In the winter of 1988 he also embarked on a rigorous winter training schedule, which was as much to get himself into shape as it was to benefit the Spondylitus (inflammation of the vertebrae) he has in his lower back. It wasn't long before his own aversion to doing things for appearance's sake took over. The training schedule was the first thing to go – as Wobbly teasingly remarks, this last winter 'his right arm was the only thing that got any exercise' – followed by subtle alterations in his appearance. He quickly passed the point where he did things because they were expected of him and learnt to have the confidence just to be himself. And by doing so he matured and grew into the role that his golf has created for him.

His dealings with the media have followed a similar route.

'If I had my own way I wouldn't even go into the press room,' he said at the start of 1989 when his relationship with them was at its rockiest. 'I've learned, hopefully, from last year. My personal life has nothing to do with my golf. I'm here to play golf and they're here to write about my golf, not personal things.'

Now he says that he just accepts being interviewed and occasionally being criticised as a part of the pressures that accompany being a top player. His repartee at press conferences is witty and as often close to the bone as it is amusing:

'Even if I'd gone at snail's pace, I'd have caught up with the group in front,' said Woosnam at the World Match Play, when asked if the groin injury he was suffering from had slowed him down. 'You can certainly see who the slow players on Tour are,' said Woosnam with heavy sarcasm, having a dig at Nick Faldo who had been playing in the group in front of his.

'Can you take a buggy tomorrow if it hurts you too much to walk?' he was asked. But, of course, it's against the rules.

'I'd like that,' said Woosnam, considering the idea. 'You could give Nick a buggy and I'll walk and we'll still be the same speed.' Then he laughed mischievously and said to the gathered press, 'You're going to have some fun with this, aren't you?'

But the down side to success in professional sport – though still comparatively rare in golf – is that at some time in his career, a top player is going to find himself the target of the hatchet men. It happened to Woosnam, who was the victim of the cruellest kind of journalism at the Irish Open last season.

He was leading the tournament after three rounds when several tabloid stringers raised their treacherous heads at Portmarnock. They produced a story, told to them by Clifford Maudesley, an ex-professional golfer turned roofer, who claimed to be a 'friend' of Woosnam from his Safari Tour days. Entitled 'My wild birdie days', it alleged, among other things, that Woosnam and

Maudesley had gone out drinking one night in Africa, tried a bit of pot, and ended up at the flat of two girls (or something to that effect). A shocking state of affairs, really. Particularly since the incident took place nearly ten years ago, and Woosnam was single at the time.

However, that's how those sort of papers make their money. By trying to convince their readers that just because somebody is famous they shouldn't be allowed to get away with doing the things that ordinary people do.

The story was published the following morning (Sunday), and it is a credit to Woosnam's strength of mind that he still went out and won the tournament.

That, like everything else, was just a lesson to be learned.

Changing his clubs was another.

Woosnam is curt. 'Would I have changed them if I had known what I know now? I wouldn't have changed them, no.'

Rodger Davis has a reason for not setting monetary goals. He maintains that if a player sets himself a target and then reaches it sooner than he thinks he is going to, he is likely to lose his impetus.

Woosnam has found there is more than a grain of truth in that logic. After 1987 he had to come to terms with the fact that the goal he had expected to spend much of his career working toward had been reached and overtaken. A period of adjustment was required. 'I lost my motivation a little bit. I couldn't care what I was doing, you know.' You get the impression that he almost felt cheated.

It seemed obvious that he should immediately set his sights on the majors. Obvious to the rest of the world, that is. Majors have never been a particular obsession of Woosnam.

'I suppose my goal now is to win a major,' he said doubtfully at the time. 'And then, I suppose . . . another major. I s'pose to win all the majors, win 'em all. It'll take a long time to do that.' He laughed, heartened by the gathering momentum of his imagination. 'Better do two in a row, I think.'

A constant diet of the fruits of success had taken the edge off his hunger. He needed a complete break; a couple of months away from the game to drink beer, grow plump and lead a normal lifestyle. And he needed adversity. It came in the shape of a troubled 1988 season and then a comparatively poor 1989 season, in which he had only one tournament victory.

'Things have changed since then,' explains Woosnam now. His appetite for victory in one of golf's big four has been wetted by a few near misses. 'I feel like I just want to win a major now . . . My main goal,' he says to clarify the situation, 'is to win the Open Championship. I'm not really bothered about the other ones.' He hesitates, still unconvinced that his life would be unfulfilled without a major title. 'But then again, you've got to look at what you want out of your career. My first goal was to make enough money so that I could live [comfortably] for the rest of my life. I feel I've virtually done that now. I suppose I've got to look to win a major but if it never happens it never happens.'

Left alone, it seems, he would be content just to win tournaments – any tournaments. Winning for its own sake is his motivation. Not money. Not majors.

'Winning a major,' adds Woosnam, 'would just finish off my career. It would be the icing on the cake. I'm not worried about it one little bit.'

But as Sandy Lyle says, 'In the end, they judge you by the majors.' All the tournament victories of golf accolades in the world mean nothing without them. Actually, it goes even deeper than that. The recognition a player is accorded for major championship victories depends, to an extent, on how many it is perceived he should have won. Take Greg Norman, for example. If it is generally reckoned that a player of his stature in world golf should be able to win five majors, for argument's sake, and he retires from the game with only one, then he will never be ranked alongside the Arnold Palmers and Gary Players of this world.

In spite of himself, Woosnam recognises this. One of the main reasons he would like to win the Order of Merit this year is that he will move further up the Sony Rankings, thereby ensuring he gets invitations to all four majors next year. As usual, he qualifies this statement the moment it is uttered with: 'I'm not going to push myself to win the Order of Merit. If I win it, I win it. I'll take it as it comes, it's better that way. You can enjoy it a bit more.'

At this point in time, he is lying just behind Mark McNulty – whom he will supersede if he wins this event – on the money list. With only four big tournaments left between now and the end of the year, the fight for European honours has developed into a two-horse race. A healthy rivalry between McNulty and Woosnam has sprung up during the course of the season, each taking turns to outdo the other narrowly. McNulty finished second to Woosnam's third at the Open Championship, and then last week, Woosnam defeated the Zimbabwean in the final of the World Match Play.

'Obviously, Mark's playing great,' said Woosnam, prior to meeting McNulty in the final. 'But if I play like I did today, it just puts a lot of pressure on him. I hit a lot of greens in regulation and put pressure on the other guy to keep holing putts.'

'Do you ever get nervous?' a reporter asked Woosnam the next day, after he had overcome McNulty.

'Oh yes,' Woosnam assured him. 'I might not show it but it's eating at me all the time. I do a lot of deep breathing. You've got to be nervous to play good golf.'

'To come down the 18th,' said McNulty in admiration, 'I think I would have had to be playing my best golf. I've always felt that Olazabal is one of the best iron strikers in the world. Ian follows close behind. Now obviously, Ian's weakness is his putting. When he's not putting well he loses a lot of confidence.'

One of the main catalysts in Woosnam's prosperous season (rivalling 1987 for consistently high finishes) – in which he has thus far won the American Express Mediterranean Open, the Monte Carlo Open, the Bell's Scottish Open and the World Match Play – has been his new Ram Zebra putter (ladies' model). Golf is a game where feel is everything and this new blade has made all the difference.

'That's something players do,' explains Woosnam. 'They mess about with different putters to get different feels. You're always looking for something. The grip on this putter is over to the left-hand side, which is weak, and the face is slightly open, and it seems to be getting the ball on line. It's getting the ball to come off where you want it to come off – on the line you see. Whereas, before [with the Ping putter], it wasn't coming off on the line that I was seeing, now I can stand up and just hit it naturally and the ball goes where I see it going. That's half the battle. I'm not having to fiddle around and do something to get it on line.'

The same cannot be said of his clubs. For some time now he has felt that he is having to work to get the ball on line. The problem reached crisis point around the time of the US Open earlier this year. 'There's no point in me going,' said Woosnam miserably, just prior to the event. A natural drawer of the ball, he had reached the stage where he couldn't hit the ball left if he was facing in that direction.

But golf is a game where expectations can be changed by a single round. At the start of the week, Woosnam, who walked off the course during a practice round with Jack Nicklaus, would have been glad to string 18 holes together.

'The way I was feeling I didn't even want to play. I could quite well have gone home. You know, if I had started playing badly after four or five holes, I'd have walked in and gone home. I know I would have done. Because it's embarrassing, you know.'

Embarrassed? Ian Woosnam? Woosnam affirms this with a faint smile. 'Trouble is, you start hitting a few right and the pressure closes in on you. The fairway starts going' – he brings the palms of his hands together – 'It looks a yard wide after a while. That's why I need to just get away and work on it, then come back and start again.'

But by the end of the week he was insisting that a second-round triple bogey and a third-round double bogey, both incurred at the 17th hole, ruined his chance at victory. 'It's just that one hole,' says Woosnam in annoyance. 'It cost me a chance of being in there at the end. That's how it goes, you know. One shot here and another shot there is the difference between being a champion and not being a champion.

'Fortunately,' he says, looking on the bright side of things, 'I haven't missed a cut since we played at Seve's place [Santander] two years and [five] months ago.'

On Woosnam's scale of golfing priorities there is little doubt which takes precedence. But then Woosnam's precepts have always differed from those of other top players. In life, his family and friends come first and foremost. Then comes golf. Most successful golfers, if they were honest, would say that the reverse is true. One player informed me he had made it clear to his wife when they were married that if it ever came to a choice between her and golf, she would come off second best.

Woosnam would sooner give up the game than adopt such principles; few players have become world champions without doing so. But then, becoming the best player in the world is not a burning desire of his. He feels the same way about it as he does about the majors – if it happens, it happens. As he points out without ambition or conceit, 'If I played like I did in '87 every year, I'd be Number One in the world by far.'

Making an effort to do so is not on the Woosnam agenda. Currently ranked fourth in the world, he simply isn't prepared to do what a player like Nick Faldo has had to do to get to that position.

'Nick Faldo's different, obviously,' explains Woosnam, as though the Englishman has been beamed down from another planet. 'His life is totally dedicated to playing golf. My life isn't. If you're Number One in the world, you've got to spend hours and hours on a practice ground beating balls, beating balls. I think I've reached the stage in my life where I don't want to keep bashing balls. I've been bashing balls for 20 years near enough now, so I don't want to keep on doing that.'

Even now, at the peak of his golfing career, he is toying with the idea of retiring. Not for a while, mind you, but very possibly when he gets to 40. 'I'll see how I feel,' says Woosnam. 'But you know, I've been a pro for 14 years now. By the time I'm 40, that'll be another eight years. Twenty-two years. And I think to myself, "What's going to keep me playing golf?" It's not going to be money, it's going to have to be just winning tournaments.'

'What would you do?'

'I don't know. There's all sorts of things I'm interested in. I might do course design. I might just go fishing. Maybe travel the world, you know, and see some of the places I've been. I wouldn't just sit around, anyway.'

Right now he's quite content to leave things just the way they are: to play great golf, make more money and have a good time doing it.

'I have a couple of drinks,' says Woosnam, 'and try to have a normal family life and go out with my friends. I don't spend my time drinking Perrier water. If you want to be Number One in the world you've got to dedicate yourself to it. I want to say at least I've enjoyed myself. If I'd just drunk Perrier water and didn't go out at night; if I'd stayed in because I knew I'd got to play golf in the morning, I'd be saying, "Well, I haven't enjoyed myself."

'At least I've done both.'

Chapter Fifteen

THREE STORIES

Photo: ASP, Stuart Franklin

Longtime companions: Caddie Dave Musgrove with Sandy Lyle

EPSON GRAND PRIX, SEPTEMBER 1990. THE NEWS THAT SEVE Ballesteros has taken a local boy as his caddie this week prompted a fresh line of questioning in the press centre yesterday. Ballesteros looked relieved. The endless inquisitions of late on his form, his game, his swing and on whether or not he is going to win before the season's out, are so futile they have become boring. Ballesteros himself said as much.

He only alluded twice to his golf game. On the first occasion, he said: 'I believe I'm going to win before the season is over. If I don't, next year's another year.'

And in reply to a question on whether his concentration on the golf course was improving, he said: 'It's getting better, getting better. I see myself now more with the game than before, but still I'm not there. My mind is not there.'

Then, thankfully, we moved on to the subject of caddies.

The more one thinks about it, the more extraordinary it seems that a player with Ballesteros's record and of his stature in world golf should choose a young boy who has never caddied in a professional tournament – indeed, who may never have caddied before – over a professional Tour caddie. It defies logic. Yet it is not the first time he has done it and it won't be the last.

In this respect, he differs from the other top players. Almost all of them have had the same caddie for anything from two years to ten years. Ian Woosnam has Wobbly, Bernhard Langer has Pete Coleman, Jose Maria Olazabal has Dave Rennick, Sandy Lyle has Dave Musgrove, and so it goes on, right down the rankings. Ballesteros, on the other hand, has had Nick de Paul, Pete Coleman, Dave Musgrove and Ian Wright (for the last two years), interspersed with his brothers and a hybrid collection of other bag carriers.

Given this track record, one has to reconsider the importance of a good caddie to a player. At his press conference, the question was put to Ballesteros.

'Well,' he said, 'I can give you an example. At the French Open four years ago, my cousin was caddying for me for the first time; and for the first time he was walking on a golf course. He didn't know anything about golf. And I won and I shot 62, the course record. It shows something there.'

He smiled triumphantly, pleased to have proved his point. But he went on to admit that a regular caddie can give a player confidence, and generally knows what to say and when to say it on the golf course. 'It's not a major factor for me,' Ballesteros insisted. 'I like to do all by myself. This is my decision.'

'What do you look for in a caddie?'

'Basically, what I want from a caddie is to stay quiet, have the right yardage, be there on time and keep up with me on the golf course. Some of them, they walk way behind.'

'This young boy, Jonathan, is he just carrying the bag this week?'

'That's all he do,' replied Ballesteros with a grin. 'He haven't make a mistake yet!'

Ballesteros is a notoriously difficult man to work for. He demands a high level of efficiency and is particularly intolerant of mistakes of any kind. 'He's like any golfer,' remarked Ian Wright, while he was still in the Spaniard's employ. 'When things are going well, you don't have to do a lot . . . The hardest part is when things are going wrong and you've got to try and turn that round into something of a reasonable round.'

Wright found himself on the receiving end of Ballesteros's temper on more than one occasion; most famously at the Open Championship at Royal Lytham in the final round, when he handed Ballesteros the wrong club at the 12th. 'He didn't hit it very well,' said Wright. 'But the thing is, he's not going to turn around and say it was a bad shot. I just stood there and he talked in my ear.'

Nick de Paul, the Pennsylvanian who caddied for Ballesteros when he won the Masters in 1983 and the Open Championship in 1984, also had numerous flaming rows with him.

'Well, I was hard on Nick a few times,' explained Ballesteros, 'because he was wrong a few times with yardages . . . and I mean, once you are a professional [caddie] and you charge so much money, you should be a hundred per cent right.'

In his interview, Ballesteros was asked whether, in a critical self-analysis, he would describe himself as a hard man to caddie for.

'I think you'd better ask Nick de Paul and Peter Coleman and Ian Wright. I think I'm very fair. Sometimes I get upset when they make a mistake but that happens to everyone. I'm fair, I would say.'

'But you're a perfectionist.'

'I know.'

As far as Ballesteros is concerned, the only thing that a caddie does – and he specifies that he is only talking for himself and not for other players – is save time. He is perfectly capable of doing his own yardages, but if he has a caddie who can do them quickly, then it saves him work and allows him to concentrate more fully on his game.

'The caddie's not a problem,' said Ballesteros finally, making it clear that the subject was closed. 'It's not my problem. I work with good caddies and I work with caddies that never know anything about the game. I don't really care about that. I think I can do all by myself.'

DAVE MUSGROVE: **caddied for Sandy Lyle since 1981**

The Zum Zum fast food bar which has taken up residence on the practice ground this week has done more business with players and caddies than the hotel restaurant and golfer's bar combined. It exudes smoke and the assorted smells of bacon, onion and hamburgers which reach all but the furthest noses on the range. For that reason, there seem to be far more people eating than there are working. Even Dave Musgrove, to whom I was talking, was devouring a curry pizza with relish. We were regarding a rather ironic spectacle. That of Sandy Lyle giving a lesson to Seve Ballesteros.

Musgrove jerks a thumb in their direction. 'What's he giving him a lesson for?' he says.

'Why not?' I asked reasonably.

'Well, it's just one less to beat, isn't it? We're not here on bloody holiday.'

Dave Musgrove, formerly of Kirkby-in-Ashfield, near Mansfield, and author of *Life with Lyle*, glances sideways at me with an unholy gleam in his grey eyes. This might be the only life he has known since he gave up his job as draughtsman for the aerospace engine division of Rolls-Royce in 1972, but there are few more intelligent men on this Tour. As a raconteur he is unrivalled and his wit is razor sharp. He adds yet another twist to the riddle of why people abandon normal life and good career prospects in favour of humping golf bags round the world.

'It's the open road, isn't it?' says Musgrove, providing the answer. 'The chance of a big cheque and the freedom of the road. And if you've ever worked in an office, you'll know the difference.'

Musgrove does. The vast majority of players don't. Most of them have never worked in an office, have never held down a mundane nine-to-five job, have never commuted, and are unlikely ever to know what it's like to have to deal with the stresses particular to that kind of environment. It sometimes seems, therefore, that they have difficulty appreciating how incredibly fortunate they are.

Three things stand out in my mind:

(a) David Feherty's insistence that no player owes the game anything.

(b) A young player in his first year on Tour, ranting and raving and generally behaving in a contemptible manner for nearly two hours in Cannes because his luggage had been moved to another room without his permission. When there are people who would give anything in the world to spend a week in a luxury hotel on the Cote d'Azur, it seemed a remarkably petty thing to get hysterical about.

(c) A conversation I had with a golfer in Monte Carlo, where I commented on how lucky Tour players are to be able to do something they love, and have the opportunity of competing for the kind of money they now play for. 'I don't think I'm lucky,' he said in all seriousness. 'It's my talent that brought me here.'

'No,' says Musgrove now, considering the failure of most golfers to appreciate the aces fate has dealt them. 'They don't. They've no idea. They've no clue. They don't appreciate what it is to have a talent because they've never been without it. It makes you angry when you see them abusing the talent, the ones that do. And when they complain about conditions after playing and that, I say, "Well, my mates have to get up at 5.30 in the morning and work down the pit eight hours, and when they come up they play nine holes in anything, whatever the weather is. They go and play, just 'cause they can. And you're complaining about playing for a million dollars every week." '

Musgrove gives a disgusted laugh.

He started caddying, aged 12, at Hollinwell golf club. At the time, he had no idea that he would ever do it professionally, but it taught him a good deal about the game and he still plays off single figures. Robert de Vicenzo was his first bag, followed by Vincente Fernandez, Seve Ballesteros and Lyle.

'You've worked for a lot of the top players,' I say to him. 'What do you think they all have in common?'

'Egotistical, if you like,' says Musgrove. 'Self-centred. They have to be, you see. It's very hard work to keep winning. You've got to believe in yourself, haven't you? You can't keep looking at other people and admiring 'em. You can't beat 'em then, can you? It's no good looking at other people and being in awe of them. Seve never was. If the bloke had never been heard of, or he was a household name, he'd got to beat him the same. He didn't look at anybody any differently.'

'I wouldn't have said that Sandy's selfish.'

'Oh . . . not selfish, I don't mean particularly, but . . . how can I put it? . . . Well they've got to be, haven't they?'

'*On* the course.'

'Well, you just don't switch it on and off, do you?'

'He just seems the nicest.'

'Oh, yes – of the top players. Langer's a good bloke and Woosie is. Langer's a real good fellow. He's got a good sense of humour. You don't realise that. I make him laugh, any road.'

But Langer, like Faldo and some of the other big name players, has very little time or patience for people who aren't confident or don't excel at what they do. It seems to be one of the traits of successful people. Blaming their mistakes on the golf course on anyone or anything, rather than admit that it might be their fault, is another. I have a theory that it has to do with maintaining a certain level of confidence and self-belief. Musgrove argues that it is much more of a weakness to be dishonest. He says that in his experience, good players might shift the blame at the moment of crisis, but will admit that they did do something wrong and analyse the reasons for it after the round.

'At the time, when they hit a bad shot, they'll say, Oh, so and so moved, or I shouldn't have hit that shot or that club, or whatever. But a week or so later – or even that night – they'll say, "Oh, I was frightened of hitting it left or hitting it right and I rushed that shot." Because in the end, they have to work out why. A lot of them go through their rounds very carefully afterwards.'

'Is that what Sandy does?'

'Yeh. Very carefully. How many putts he had, how many greens he missed and how many fairways he missed. Sometimes, if they think they've not played well, they'll go over their round and they'll say, "Well, I hit every fairway, I hit nearly every green. I didn't play all that bad. It must be the score." So you've got to be honest afterwards, haven't you?'

Rodger Davis says as much. He believes that unless a player studies his own statistics – as opposed to the published statistics – then he isn't necessarily going to know which areas of his game he needs to work on to improve. And he feels that it is only by understanding the components of his scores and correctly assessing the strengths and weaknesses in his game that a player is able to set himself realistic goals.

Musgrove did a survey of every shot Lyle hit for an 18-month period, beginning in 1984. He didn't like the existing method for working out statistics, which counts a shot hit to 15 feet not actually on the putting surface as a green missed, while a shot which may be 40 feet from the pin on the putting surface is counted as a green hit. Stephen McAllister says that every time he misses the cut, he appears at the top of the statistics the following week. Musgrove did his own statistics, breaking down scores into long-irons, mid-irons and short-irons and clubs used. The only conclusion he came to was that the better Lyle's bunker shots and chip shots, the better he scored.

'What do you think was the main cause of his slump?'

'Well, it all started with his marriage,' says Musgrove, contradicting Lyle's answer to the same question. 'It was when she [Lyle's ex-wife] got married again. Then he got married again. I mean, we always used to say if they get married they're no good for a year. That was one of our old caddie theories. Big change in your outlook. Especially if you've got to be single-minded to be at the top, and all of a sudden you've got somebody else to think of.

'But you see, apart from that, I can't understand how golfers, especially when they've been very successful, can keep going. Sandy hadn't really had a long break [during the winter of '88/'89]. But he'd been going on and on, winning no end of stuff, you see. And me, being idle, I'd want to say, "Bugger it." Wouldn't you? What's the point in playing and winning all this money if you don't do anything with it? Seve's never played more than 25 tournaments in his life in a year. Never. Ask him. And Jack Nicklaus is the same. It's 17 or 18 – has been for donkey's years.'

'That's because their whole year is geared around the majors.'

'Well,' says Musgrove, and the word is resonant with scorn. 'What's a major? Define a major. I don't believe in all this majors business.'

I was astounded. Odd how, when confronted with a statement like that, all sensible lines of defence evaporate from your mind. The only thing I could think of to say was that majors were important to the players. Musgrove said that he didn't think they were. He said that their importance was a product of media hype.

'Well,' he said, in support of this claim, 'you go and have a look at them in the States when they're playing for a million dollars a week, and see whether they care what the bloody title is.'

'But majors are the most important thing in life to people like Faldo,' I squeaked.

'Yeh,' says Musgrove scathingly. 'You go and ask him to lend you a fiver. Then you'll find out whether he thinks about money or not. They're all the same when it comes down to it, 'specially when they've got a wife and kids. You think the wives don't think about money? You're kidding! Every bloody ha'penny. That's what it boils down to. How much in the bank, Frank? It's not how many pots you've got on the mantlepiece. You don't pay the mortgage with them, do you?'

Several moments went by while I digested this. In the end I said rather lamely that you could only spend so much money.

'What keeps tycoons going? What keeps Arnold Palmer going?' demands Musgrove who, in spite of this heated verbiage, manages to retain a perfectly calm exterior. Passers-by observing us sitting in sunshine beside the putting green would think we were discussing nothing more consequential than the weather.

Musgrove struck up a conversation with Palmer's 25-year-old caddie at the Masters earlier this year. The man said that he had spent 30 weeks on the road during the 1989 season, including tournaments, exhibitions and skins games. He was worn out. He recalled one occasion where he had arrived home in Orlando, Florida, at 4 a.m. from Phoenix. When he walked into Palmer's office at 9.30 the same morning, the first thing the 61-year-old man demanded was: 'Where have you been?'

'Palmer gets up at 7.00, does his exercises and he's in the office at 7.30 every morning. And how much money has he got? He comes on advertisements in the States on the television and they don't even say who it is. No names mentioned. Palmer comes on. Rattles it off – in his own voice . . . That's what a tycoon is, isn't it?'

Musgrove's steely eyes stare cynically out at me from under a grey thatch of hair.

'What happened when Sandy was disqualified at the 1989 Nestlé Invitational?' I ask to divert him, because he is obviously warming to this theme.

Musgrove says that Lyle was simply fed up. The clubhouse was closer than the green, so that when the Scotsman hit his second shot on the 18th into the lake, he opted for the shortest distance between the two points and walked in.

'If he'd said – like the Americans nearly all do – "Ooh, I hurt my hand on that shot and I don't want to risk it for the TPC next week", you know, crap like that, they'd have believed him. But he didn't say anything. Too honest.

So they fined him.' He laughs bitterly at the injustice of it all. 'They fined him for being honest.'

'When would you say he began to lose form?'

'At the Nabisco. When he had all that trouble about going tŏ Australia. When he tried to withdraw from the Ashes. He was worn out then. You come to a point where you just have to have a rest. And that's what he's been having.'

According to Musgrove, Lyle got progressively more tired mentally as time went on. He himself became exhausted by the strain of it all. 'I mean, last year, I could cheerfully have had two years at home and not batted an eyelid – if I could have found something to do . . . It makes you wonder why you're there, you see, if they're not playing well. "What am I doing here, miles away from home, wasting my time?" But I feel like going again now.'

'How much help is a caddie to a player?'

'Oh no, I think it's the other way around. I think you can be a hindrance. If you're not a hindrance then you're helping, aren't you? You can make a nuisance of yourself if you're not bothered about what's happening, not concentrating on the game. You're not exactly going to hit the ball, are you? It's the bloke that's got to hit the fairway off the tee and hole a four-foot putt, nobody else. What can you do to help him do that?'

'But with the amount of money they're playing for now, if a caddie can save his player two strokes a tournament, then surely he is helping him.'

Musgrove gives me a frustrated glance. 'But what I'm saying is, he's still got to hit it. If he doesn't feel like it, been out chasing women. How many times do they come on the tee, they've been shagging all night? Can't hit a bloody ball. Even when they've been in the lead. It's happened to me a few times.'

'The top players don't –'

'They're very strict,' says Musgrove firmly, cutting me short. 'They've got to be, otherwise they wouldn't be at the top, you see.'

'Have you worked for Faldo?'

'I worked for him for four months. He was very workmanlike. He'd just got over the shock of going to America and nobody taking any notice of him, and then he realised that it was the perfect time to get stuck into his game and get hardened to it. Which is what he was doing. He won about £4,000 a week, which in 1982 was good.'

'He's a perfectionist, isn't he?'

'I s'pose that's one way of putting it,' says Musgrove, suddenly taciturn. 'That's what everybody says.'

Silence. Musgrove looks out into space. 'Why should I have to worry about him?' he says at length. 'Why should I have to rack my brains about him?'

And when he looks round at me, his eyes glint with such devilry that it occurs to me that he just may have been sending me up all this time. Then his laugh rings out across the courtyard and he is gone.

PHIL MORBEY: **caddied for Ian Woosnam since August 1987**

Ballesteros might deny that he has any need for a good relationship with a caddie, but there must be something to be said for it. One of the most successful partnerships in European golf owes much to the fact that player and caddie are close friends.

Philip Morbey, alias Wobbly, has worked for Ian Woosnam for the last three years, the most productive of the Welshman's career. He and Woosnam are so compatible that they even room together at American and Australian tournaments. 'It gets so boring for both of us,' says Morbey in explanation (it is almost unheard of for a caddie to room with a top player), 'that if you didn't, you'd be in your room thinking, "What am I going to do?" We do different things: watch the TV, play pool, play table tennis and generally relax.'

With his tangled mop of brown hair, tanned face and Maruman endorsed clothing, Morbey is the embodiment of good health and achievement in a profession where one finds precious little of either. He was born and raised in Selby, North Yorkshire, and in his way is as staunchly down-to-earth as Woosnam is. He is, however, rather more hyperactive and noisy.

'We don't just talk about golf on the course,' he is informing me now, shouting in a broad Yorkshire accent above the racket in the golf club bar. 'We talk about general things. How his car's going, maybe, or about football – although he's not the keen football fan, I am. Sometimes it helps in between shots, or if you've got a long wait on the tee, if you can talk about something else – take your mind off it for five minutes. Then you're fresh when you start to concentrate on your shot again.'

He realigns the pencil behind his ear, a permanent fixture.

'Do you think that that is where a caddie can really be of help to a player, psychologically?'

'I think that's one of your main jobs, really, trying to psyche him into playing good shots. It's just a knack. The more you caddie for one person, the more you know when he is in a good mood or when he is approachable. If he's in a really bad mood, no matter what you say, it wouldn't help. You've just got to wait till he's cooled down a little bit then try to get him going again . . . It's important to know what to say and when to say it.'

'Would you say that Ian is a perfectionist on the golf course?'

'Oh, very much so,' says Morbey enthusiastically. His effervescence obviously has a positive effect on Woosnam, in the same way that Fanny Sunesson's does on Faldo. 'He thinks he can hit it to a foot, two foot all the time. So sometimes he can get a bit disappointed when he hits it to 15 feet . . . He'll get a bit naggy and he might say: "Oh, if I'd taken a different club I'd have hit it closer."'

Woosnam will ask his caddie's opinion before he selects a club on every single tee shot, approach shot, pitch and chip shot. He tends to read his own putts unless he is really unsure of the line or lacking in confidence with his putting stroke, in which case he will collaborate with Morbey. 'He works very much on confidence,' says Morbey. 'At the minute he's putting quite well and he gets over four or five footers and bangs them in. But just before Monte Carlo, he couldn't seem to get it in the hole from three feet. He was over the putts thinking, "Christ, I'm not going to get this in, I'm going to miss." But when he gets confidence, he's unbelievable. A fantastic player.'

One thing Woosnam has done for Morbey is encourage him to invest the money he has made (particularly when it has been a lump sum, i.e. when Woosnam won the Million Dollar Classic) in property. For a player to do as much for his caddie as Woosnam has done for Morbey is rare. I can only really think of one comparable example, and that is Jose Maria Olazabal and his Scottish caddie, Dave Rennick.

Rennick fell asleep last season at the wheel of a car which crashed and killed two caddies. Sadly, he has recently been convicted and sent to jail for six months. On hearing that a jail sentence was a realistic probability, Olazabal assured Rennick that he would have a job to come back to. John Graham, Mark James's caddie and Rennick's friend, is going to work for Olazabal over the winter and plans to share any percentage money he earns with the Scotsman. Something else which is rather extraordinary is that, although Rennick was unable to caddie for Olazabal in the Lancome Trophy which the Spaniard won, due to the fact that the police were holding his passport, Olazabal still paid him his wage and a percentage of his winnings. Now that is unheard of.

In the bar, Wobbly considers the qualities of the top players as employers. Although he has never caddied for Ballesteros, he says that the Spaniard is one of the most temperamental golfers he has ever come across. 'I wouldn't work for him, not for a day. It just wouldn't appeal to me. I could work for someone like Olazabal or Greg Norman; though Greg's a hard man to work for. He gets uptight with his caddie. But I'd never change unless it happened that I finished with Ian, because he's such a good player, such a good friend.'

'What do you think makes Ian such a good competitor?'

'The thing that makes him so good?' There is a pregnant pause. 'Well, he's got no fear of anybody,' says Morbey at last. 'You know, he'll play with Greg Norman, he'll play with Jack Nicklaus, and he'll go out there to beat those fellas. Whereas, you get other players, if they played with Greg, they'd be overawed. They don't play their best game. But when Woosie's playing well, he knows he can beat anybody. I think that's what makes him as good as he is.'

PETER COLEMAN: **caddied for Bernhard Langer in 1980 for a season then began working for him again in 1983**

Grey sheets of rain sluiced the courtyard at St Pierre, smudging the outlines of the rain-suited figures on the putting green. Only those players who were almost on the tee were out there, cursorily tapping putts into brimming holes. The rest skulked in their bedrooms, delaying the inevitable, while their caddies hung about in the cold stone hallway of the hotel. They packed and repacked their golf bags with extra towels and sweaters and peered dismally out into the gloom between the bars of white water which spilled from the roof.

'Does Ian warm up for long when it's like this?' I ask Morbey, who is standing impatiently in their midst. 'Ten minutes,' he says with snort of laughter. 'Funny how they have to go out an hour when it's a nice day and when it's like this, it's ten minutes and they're ready.'

We watched Bernhard Langer and Pete Coleman disappear under the arches on their way to the range, a full hour and 20 minutes before their tee-off time. For Coleman, rain or no rain it's business as usual. Usual, that is, if you caddie for golf's hardest worker.

According to Coleman, on days when he isn't actually competing, Langer practises for an average of eight hours. 'Bernhard,' says Coleman, with wry affection, 'he's one of them guys, he'd never miss a Tuesday [practice day]. He'd feel like he wasn't prepared properly . . . And if he made a bad showing that week, he'd blame it on the fact that he didn't practise enough, or do something enough. He's that dedicated.'

As an accessory in Langer's search for the grail, Coleman shares the load. For him, those long Tuesdays are the hardest, five and a half hours spent resolutely trudging after Langer. Listing under the weight of the golf bag, Coleman weaves an erratic path down the fairway after numberless practice balls, clocking up extra miles, bending and straightening, bending and straightening.

In a game where the best players are separated by their exacting standards on and off the golf course, Langer's legendary attention to detail sets him apart even from them. Both he and Coleman carry yardage books, thus eliminating the possibility of error under pressure. 'Sometimes,' says Coleman, 'we'll even argue over one metre, which doesn't mean a thing golf-wise. One metre is only sort of one-tenth of a club. It's just strange. But that's how particular he is . . .

'It used to be in the way he paid me as well. I mean, in America, if you made \$649, you'd expect a cheque for \$650. But he always used to be spot on; never round it off. Everything was done so you didn't have no comeback. Everything was done precisely.'

Money was the bone of contention and the reason for his resignation when Coleman first worked for Langer. The situation has subsequently been resolved to their mutual satisfaction.

'Now he asks you what you think and he comes up with the money,' says Coleman, who used to drive a Porsche on his earnings. 'You know, Seve was the same. He was never generous in respect of money, and I mean, he was Number One for quite a few years and getting more appearance money than anybody else when I worked for him.'

When challenged on this issue, Ballesteros has always maintained that five per cent of what he earned was a lot of money. 'Ten per cent of nothing is nothing,' he likes to say.

But Dave Musgrove says that the Spaniard is just mean with money full stop. He tells a story about the Scandinavian Open one year when Ballesteros, despite the fact that he was putting for second place in the tournament, was in a fit of pique and cursing Musgrove for his own loss on the 18th hole. Finally, Musgrove could stand it no longer. He dumped the golf bag on the green and walked off the course.

When Ballesteros had recovered his good humour, he came to find Musgrove and apologise. 'Come out to dinner,' he wheedled. 'I will pay.'

So Musgrove and he, and Canizares and his caddie, went out to eat. As they walked into the restaurant, however, a friend of Ballesteros spotted the foursome and insisted on buying them dinner. By the time Ballesteros emerged from the restaurant, he was on top of the world. But he was absolutely determined not to end the evening without buying something so he insisted on taking them all for a coffee. The bill came and Ballesteros inspected it. He dug in his wallet and produced some change.

'No, no, no,' said the waitress and held up four fingers. The bill was only for one cup of coffee.

There was a moment of silence while Ballasteros absorbed the full import of what she was saying. First he went white with anger. Then he went red. Then he erupted. 'Do you know how many pesetas that is?' he screamed. 'Do you know how many cups of coffee I can get for this in Madrid?'

'The thing is,' says Coleman on the subject of caddying for Ballesteros, 'after you've been with a person like that for a few years, you should be making a reasonable living as well . . . If you work for people like Seve, Langer and Lyle, who are getting appearance money, what's wrong with them giving their caddie at least some extra money to give them a good life? If I was working for a firm for nine years, I wouldn't still be office boy; I'd probably be manager.'

With Langer, Coleman's living is more than reasonable but, even so 17 years of caddying is a long time. And while he enjoys the camaraderie of Tour life, he finds himself at 49 with few alternatives. 'At my age, I can't really down tools and do anything else and get any sort of money. And that to me is the only reason for caddying. There's no real appeal in walking round a golf course non-stop. But at least I feel I know what I'm doing when I'm out there.'

This is the time when a life spent flitting around the globe as carelessly as a butterfly begins to lose its attraction. In caddying there is no security; no pension fund or financial guarantee accompanies the job. Unless a caddie is one of the tiny minority who have made a fortune out of the game and invested it wisely, then he is going to have to look around for alternative employment eventually.

'Which you wouldn't do,' insists Coleman, who is reluctant to return to his old job as electrical worker for British Rail. 'You wouldn't make a lot of money out of it . . . I'm not going to give this up for another five or six years unless ill-health comes by. Then I don't know what I'm going to do, actually. In the meantime, I shall just go on for as long as I can.'

Chapter Sixteen

TO BE THE BEST

Photo: Phil Sheldon

The public and private face of Greg Norman – good humoured and genial. Here he shares a joke with caddie Bruce Edwards

DUNHILL CUP, SCOTLAND, OCTOBER 1990. THIS AFTERNOON a white ball split the blue at St Andrews, took two bounces on the out-of-bounds tarmac road, parting unwitting passers-by and spectators like chaff, and landed 15 feet from the pin.

The unluckiest player in golf just got lucky.

'Is that my ball?' The tone was one of amused disbelief, a rich Australian twang which I heard before I saw the broad smile, red sweater and blond head of Greg Norman looming above the gallery beside the 18th green. On a day like today, with a strong wind behind, this short par four is easily drivable for prodigious hitters like the Shark, even without the use of artificial aids. And without luck. I thought to myself: where is good fortune when you really need it? Coming down the 72nd hole of a major championship, for instance.

Holing out for birdie in the pro-am where it couldn't matter less, something similar must have crossed Norman's mind.

Used to be that the nickname Great White Shark was one of endearment and a tribute to Greg Norman's aggression on the golf course, his fearlessness, and the ruthless manner in which he hunted down his opponents and went in for the kill. No more. Now, as these things often do, it has become a term of derision. Switch Shark for Carp: the fish that let all the big ones (the majors – golf's indisputable measures of greatness) get away.

That's what happens when a man fails to live up to other people's expectations of him.

Within two years of turning professional in 1976 at the age of 21, Greg Norman came to be regarded as the brightest, most incandescent manifestation of Australian genius since the Sydney Opera House. Not since Arnold Palmer had a player combined such power and flair on the golf course with such charisma and charm off it. In the first year of his career, Norman overcame Jack Nicklaus, his hero, in the West Lakes Classic. In his second, he won two tournaments, in his third, he won four. Since 1977 he has only once had less than three victories in a year, and on five occasions he has had five or more, his best season being 1986, when he notched up an incredible ten titles.

Who could have guessed that 14 years down the road, Norman would have won just one Open Championship, the 1986 Open at Turnberry, and not a single Masters, US Open or US PGA Championship. His 61 other tournament titles, which – most damningly in the eyes of the Americans – only include nine on the US Tour, mean little in a sport where a champion's worth is assessed by one method and one method only. The majors. All the near misses in the world don't count.

Just to reiterate, Norman:

1986 – Bogeyed the final hole of the Masters to lose to Jack Nicklaus.
1986 – Lost to Bob Tway in the US PGA after the American holed his bunker shot on the last.
1987 – Was beaten by Larry Mize on the second extra hole of a play-off for the Masters when Mize holed his chip shot.
1988 – Bunkered his drive on the 18th in the play-off for the Open Championship at Troon to lose to Mark Calcavecchia.

Cynics would add that he also lost an 18 hole play-off for the 1984 US Open to Fuzzy Zoeller; that David Frost holed a 50-foot bunker shot to beat him in the USF&G Classic earlier this year; and that Robert Gamez holed an improbable seven-iron on the final hole to win the 1990 Nestlé Invitational.

When a player comes within a hair's breadth of victory that many times and doesn't win, you've got to start looking for reasons. Either he isn't destined to win another major, or he doesn't have another major left in him.

'Do you think fate owes you a major?' Norman was asked after the play-off at Troon.

'Shit,' replied Norman with feeling, 'it owes me four.'

In direct defiance of the above statistics, given the importance of major championships in the game of golf, Norman rose to the top of the Sony World Rankings – an elaborate system of points instituted in 1986 – and took up an unassailable position there. He was briefly deposed by Seve Ballesteros in 1988, but Nick Faldo, who accumulated four major championship victories during the course of Norman's reign, failed to dislodge the Shark until August 1990 (and then for only six weeks).

In light of this, the credibility of the World Rankings has come under close scrutiny. Administered by IMG, they are calculated on a scale whereby all four majors have a guaranteed number of points a player can gain; the Players Championship in America and the PGA Championship in Britain have a minimum number of points; and in the 60 other tournaments included in the ranking system, the number of points awarded depends on the strength of the field, which is based against the top one hundred players in the Sony Rankings. This means that the top players (eight in the top 20 in the rankings and 16 in the top 50 are managed by IMG) can inflate the points value of a tournament simply by competing in it, thus perpetuating a kind of chain effect whereby they are the only ones able to make realistic advances in the rankings.

When it was felt that Norman had outstayed his welcome at the top of the World Rankings, a peculiar trend started among observers of the game almost to hold him personally responsible for monopolising the Number One spot. Part of this was resentment that a player who only had one major victory to his name should be rated above a man with four, and part of it was because, as an IMG client, Norman was the golfer most obviously reaping vast financial rewards as a result of being 'the best player in the world'.

Paradoxically, the world rankings don't even mean very much to the Australian.

'Never have done,' says Greg Norman positively.

The reason? Because unlike other professional sports which have a world ranking system, i.e. tennis and motor-racing, golf has no world tour. '[The ranking system] doesn't work and never will work until we have a world tour; until we have all 120 players playing in different tournaments round the world under various conditions all the time.'

'Do you think that it would ever be possible to have a world tour?'

'I would love to see it, personally. Whether you could ever get the Schofields, the Bemans, Japan and Australia, to all sit down and be sensible, and not be self-centred and selfish towards their own tours . . .'

But until such time as there is a world tour in golf, he feels very strongly the Sony rankings are an unacceptable method of assessing the rating of players, particularly when there are bonus schemes and contractual benefits resulting from them. 'Ever since the inception of the world rankings, I've been fortunate enough to have been at the top of it to be able to voice my opinion,' says Norman, who has always been their most outspoken critic in spite of the fact that he has most to gain from them. 'But it's amazing when I'm Number Two now people are writing differently about it. I won't say very much about it anymore because it sounds like sour grapes.'

Tall, golden and larger than life, Greg Norman makes himself at home in his suite at the Old Course hotel. In the short space of time since he found me sitting forlornly in the foyer (dwelling on luck and the general unreliability of professional golfers), he has made dinner arrangements with a friend, read a fan letter on the way up in the lift, divested himself of shoes, waterprooofs and sweater, answered two questions and dispatched his caddie, Bruce Edwards, to fetch a couple of lagers. At last he settles down, the picture of relaxed contentment.

It is 6 p.m. Twilight is falling over St Andrews. Norman has just completed a five-hour round in a gale-force wind, and satisfied the demands of his pro-am partners, a crowd of pen-wielding autograph hunters and several reporters, but he couldn't look less harassed if he was lying undisturbed on a beach in the Bahamas. On the contrary, he seems to be enjoying himself thoroughly. Nothing is too much trouble for him, no phone call a nuisance, no question too direct.

'What is your feeling about appearance money?' I ask, with the latter in mind.

'Well, you see, appearance money as far as I'm concerned is totally up to the sponsor,' says Norman immediately. 'It's his money. And I get offended when somebody tells me what to do with my money and how I should spend it. Dunhill, for example. If they wanted to go out and pay a million dollars to get Faldo or Ballesteros or whoever to play, that's their money. They feel they can justify it . . . that they'll get exposure from those players . . . So it's not an issue for the Tour administration to handle. It's an issue for the sponsors. Now if the sponsors all get together and say, "Hey, we're not going to pay appearance money", now it might be a different deal.'

Appearance money has been a contentious issue for over a decade since it was first paid to players such as Seve Ballesteros. A criterion was established for the giving of it: a player had to have won a major, or have topped the Order of Merit. What it basically means is that a golfer is paid to play in a tournament regardless of how he subsequently performs. How much he is paid depends on his perceived value in terms of how much media coverage, gate entrance money and brand or product awareness he will bring the sponsor. A player like Ronan Rafferty might get £20,000, Jose Maria Olazabal (who, it should be noted, has not met either criteria) is paid in the region of £30,000, Ian Woosnam, £40–50,000 and Nick Faldo and Ballesteros, around £60,000. The Spaniard, who is unquestionably a European sponsor's biggest draw card, has received over £750,000 in appearance money in 14 starts this year – as compared to £148,000 in prize money.

The situation was fast approaching the stage where players were effectively holding sponsors to ransom by refusing to play unless they were given appearance money. No longer. At the time of writing, the PGA European Tour were forming a subcommittee to deal with the problem, and appearance money will soon be outlawed. Sponsors will be notified that they face elimination from the 1992 Tour schedule if they are caught paying appearance money to a player.

'The people who pay are the problem,' said Ken Schofield, in his press conference on the issue, 'not the player. He just takes the cheque.'

'It'll never happen,' says Norman with certainty. 'I mean, as tough as the US Tour is about appearance money, it still happens over there. You know, if a sponsor wants you to go and do an outing for him in another city away from the tournament, and he says, "Hey, here it is [appearance money], go and do it on Monday." He's happy and you're happy. So whether it's blatant or whether it's behind someone's back, it still goes on.'

The principal argument against appearance money in whatever guise has always been that once paid, a player is not necessarily going to be driven to do his best. In his own case, Norman refutes this emphatically.

'I think – I know this is a fact – I play better when I get paid because I don't want to let the person down who paid me. If I get to a tournament in the States and I think I'm not really playing that great, you know, my system's not ready to play, I don't play. But if I feel the same way going into a tournament in Japan and Australia, I get up and I grind my arse off, because I don't want the sponsor to think: "Look at that Norman! Comes over here, takes all the money and runs."'

It's a shame there aren't more players with Norman's values. Mark Calcavecchia, for example. He was paid to play at the Dutch Open earlier this season, but when he missed the cut after having played two atrocious rounds of golf, he lashed out like a spoilt child and broke a sponsor's advertising board. Cursing and shouting, he left the course and the country, appearance money in hand, never – if justice is done – to return again.

That kind of behaviour incenses Norman.

'I don't want to do that because it ruins it for somebody else coming behind me in ten years' time, and it ruins the image of the game. And I'm not that type of person,' he adds.

It is this conscientiousness in honouring his commitments, combined with rugged good looks, a down-to-earth manner and excellent business acumen, which has helped Norman become the second-richest player in the world. Arnold Palmer is the first. According to a survey done by *Golf World* (November 1989), Palmer's off-course income, including endorsements and appearance money but excluding prize money, media fees, course design fees and non-golf business investments, totals $9 million, while Norman's is in the vicinity of $8 million. The Shark's world-wide published earnings prior to the 1990 Open Championship were $7,296,921.

When your own annual income is barely more than the last four figures in that number, it can be hard to imagine what would motivate a sportsman to keep going when he has scaled the financial and physical heights that Norman has. Where does the desire come from?

'I honestly believe that I have not achieved what I want to achieve in the game,' says Norman, instantly dismissing the idea that he has reached a sporting peak. 'I think once you reach your pinnacle, there's only one way to go and that's downhill.'

But a decade and a half on the road is a long time. The pressures which accompany professional golf at world-class level don't lessen with age. They increase. The travelling becomes tougher and lonelier. Playing a tournament schedule which criss-crosses four continents becomes more of a drain on a golfer's mental and physical resources.

'It's just a fact of growing up, I s'pose,' says Norman resignedly. 'When you were 25, you really didn't care. You just went out there with one objective: to play golf. Ten years down the line, so much more has happened, so much is happening around you, that you have to pay a little bit more attention to it. I mean, you have to watch what's going through your own office now. You really can't just say, "Okay, go ahead and look after it, guys", and let it go.'

For Norman that means that every day he is in the country he leaves his home in Lost Tree Village, Florida, and goes straight to the office, where he will take the time to understand the complexities of his business empire. Golf is the next priority. Norman plays and practises out of Grand Cypress, Orlando. Only when he has fulfilled all of his obligations can Norman go home and relax with his wife, Laura, and his children, Morgan-Leigh and Gregory.

Is it any wonder that a laid-back pro-am day like today seems a comparative stroll in the park?

'You wake up every morning and go through the same routine so it gets kind of monotonous and boring. Sometimes you just want to say, "I'd love to walk away from it for three months." But you can't. So you're always walking this fine line. And that's what the unfortunate thing about it is. A lot of the media don't see that. Because you can see it in the articles they write, and a lot of the spectators believe what the media write. So the person who gets hurt in the long run is the player, and then the game eventually.'

There is a knock at the door. Norman bounces up still in mid-flow and lets Edwards in with the lagers.

'What time shall I come in the morning?' asks Edwards, when he can get a word in edgeways. A dark-haired young American with designer stubble and the same friendly manner and easy smile as Norman's, he declines Norman's invitation to stay for a drink.

'Come around 11.00,' says his boss. 'Come and have lunch or a snack, if you like.'

'It's sad,' says Norman, resuming the conversation without a pause, 'because we're not all as bad as what a minority of the press would like to make us out to be . . . I read articles, not only about myself but about other players too, and you think, "Well, I know this guy and I know he's not like that" . . . But that's what happens and it disappoints you.'

It turns out that he had this identical conversation with some friends of his last night. Norman's friends said to him that the press couldn't see how sincere he was or how much he did for the game behind the scenes. When Norman does something – like dedicating his 1988 Heritage Classic victory and giving away the trophy to Jamie Hutton, a young fan desperately ill with leukaemia – it is because he wants to do it and not because he thinks it will make him look like a hero in the press.

'Success is wonderful,' says the gregarious Australian who, until recently, had always taken fame in his stride, then he adds, 'but it can also be very painful.' Norman copes with it in the best way he knows how. By being himself. 'I've been pretty good with it,' he says, 'but, I guess, in the last 12 months it's been a lot harder to take . . . People have been a lot more critical.'

There comes a time when being a nice guy and behaving like a good sport when the chips are down is no longer enough. A sportsman who is the best in the world at what he does is expected to win the championships to prove it. If he doesn't – if he continually stumbles at the last or loses tournaments through outrageous streaks of misfortune – then sooner or later he's going to have to pay a price for that. He's going to be pilloried by the media and criticised by spectators.

Norman tried to turn his back on it. He stopped reading newspapers. He cancelled the golf magazines which he had sent to his house from all around the world. This morning, going out for his round, he said to Edwards: 'You know, I'm fed up. I'm just going to mind my own business from now on. I'm not going to try and help anyone' – which is not true because he will because he's that type of guy. 'But you get to a point where you think, "What the heck's the point? Why am I banging my head against the wall?" '

He sighs with frustration.

'I love the game with a passion. And that passion sometimes gets to a point where you wish other people would realise what the game is all about and do the same thing. Put a little bit back into the game.'

Unlike most of our games, golf is not played on a regulated pitch or field, rolled flat and measured identically from Kidderminster to Timbuktoo. It is played on golf courses as diverse as St Andrews and Shoal Creek, it is influenced by, and at the mercy of, all weathers, and it involves a stationary ball. This last once caused Ted Williams, a ball player, to remark to Sam Snead: 'Golf's not that hard. The ball doesn't move.'

'Yes,' retorted Snead drily, 'but we have to play our foul balls.'

These three factors, when taking into account the enigma that is the golf swing, combine to make golf a capricious and unpredictable game which requires at least as much good fortune as a Chihuahua would in a pen full of crocodiles. But the question regarding the plight of Greg Norman in the majors is whether ill-luck has always played a part in his downfall, or whether he has made serious errors of judgement when it has mattered most.

'You can always say you made a mistake,' says Norman frankly. 'Everybody focuses their attention on the dramatic last two shots, or whatever, and if you go back one or two holes, you think, "That's what I did wrong." Some people call it unlucky. Some people call it fate.'

There is a pause. A slight tightening of his mouth is the only visible sign of tension. He says suddenly: 'I mean, it's kind of tough because I'm the only one it's ever happened to – and had it happened twice back to back. And you think, "Well, the law of averages says you win 50 per cent of the time, not lose one hundred per cent of the time." But you know, I really don't call it bad luck because I really don't think of it that way.'

'Well,' I said, 'it doesn't necessarily have to have been bad luck on your part. It could have been good luck on theirs.'

'True,' says Norman, surprised. 'That's true.'

And he laughs, revealing a perfect row of white teeth, and the moment of unease passes.

'Oh yeh, anytime you reflect on something, you say, "Well, if I'd done this or I'd done that." I really don't do that. Because you really can't change what's happened . . . Sometimes it's beyond your control – like what those guys did to me. So when it's beyond my control, then I feel a little bit better about it because I had nothing to do with it. The only way I can control my own destiny is the way I execute the game of golf. And I play the way I feel like I should play, not the way some other guy in a magazine or newspaper tells me I should play.

'I mean, the 18th at Troon, for example. I still believe to this day, if that had landed six or eight feet left or short of where it landed, it would never have reached that bunker because that bunker wasn't in play all week. Now you'll sit back and read where people say that bunker was in play; it's always been in play. I know exactly how far I hit the golf ball, but it was just one of those things. I've watched the replay and slowed it down. It landed right on top of a hard mound and skidded. But, you know, that's seaside golf. That's the way the game crumbles.'

Norman's graciousness in defeat and perpetual good humour in the face of disaster has been the reason for his perennial popularity, and has earned him the admiration of his friends and rivals. After the Open Championship, it prompted Sandy Lyle to remark in his artless fashion, 'I think a lot of people respect Greg an awful lot.'

Norman says that he believes you have to take the blows golf delivers on the chin. Ostensibly, he has done that. Only he will ever know how deep the cuts still run, how complete the mental healing.

'You go off and try to resurrect it and start all over again. But the whole crux of the deal is as long as you believe in yourself and don't believe fate's against you and don't believe in bad luck . . . If you believe in your own ability and you love the game with enough heart to say, "I can bounce back from whatever they throw at me", I can come back. I know I'll be back. Whether it be next year; whether it be the year after that. I know somewhere down the line I'll be able to do it. And things'll turn around and maybe I'll hole my second shot, or something like that.

'If I didn't believe in my ability to be able to say, "Yes, I'm going to play for another ten years and do what I want to do", then I'd probably walk away from the game tomorrow,' says Norman, blue eyes determined. 'It's my belief in myself and how much I love the game that is why I keep playing it. I mean, the money's great, sure, but I don't play for the money. I play for wanting to win and the winning makes you successful . . . That to me is the test of the true character of an individual, how you win and how you lose. Probably more, how you lose.'

Are such characteristics intrinsic or learned?

As a child Norman says he was introvert and shy. I look at him now, the absolute epitome of confidence and self-possession, and my imagination fails to make the necessary mental leap between the two extremes. 'Even when I came on Tour in '76, I was very introvert and shy,' insists Norman. I think the disbelief was showing on my face. 'But I could see that it wasn't going to do me any good being that way, because you're going to miss the boat in a lot of things. I actually had to change my whole personality and attitude to become successful. And so one thing leads to another; if you do it off the golf course, then it happens on the golf course.'

There is another knock at the door. Norman springs up to answer it and he and his manager, Hughes Norton, greet each other with delightful cries.

'How ya doing?' shouts Norman exuberantly.

'Great, great, great,' responds Hughes with equal excitement, followed by, 'I've been better, I s'pose.'

Having introduced us, Norman sits back down and picks up the threads of what he was saying with barely a pause.

As long as he can remember, he has always had a competitive nature. 'I've always wanted to be the best. Always wanted to be the first off at the traffic lights, stuff like that.' The Shark laughs wryly. 'Everything I do is exactly like that. Having a talk with Hughes –' he glances over at his manager, merriment dancing in his eyes, '– I always want to have the final say.'

'What d'ya mean, you want to,' says Norton indignantly. 'You do.'

'That's the way I am,' confesses Norman with a grin.

When Greg Norman walks on to the first tee in the morning, he wants to feel one overriding emotion: nervousness.

If he can feel the adrenalin pumping through his veins, if he is filled with the desire to play well, he knows he is in for a good day. That is his barometer. But if he walks on to the first tee and those butterflies are missing, invariably it means he is going to struggle to concentrate and get himself motivated.

'If you're already down,' explains Norman, 'it's hard to bring yourself up. How do you get yourself over it? Do you talk to yourself or be really hard on yourself? But when you're up, you can bring yourself down and then you automatically get up again because it comes to crunch time and you've got a score to post. When you're flat . . . you're only hoping for one or two birdies. But when you're flying, you're looking at six or eight birdies. It's an amazing feeling to have. It's very difficult to explain to anybody unless they've really experienced it . . . It's something way beyond anybody's comprehension. I've felt it outside of golf, but that's just the way I am.'

'Doing what?'

'Well, I've felt it driving a car – you put yourself on edge. Anytime you go beyond your limitations, right , your comfort zone – everybody has a comfort zone, no matter what you do – now you really feel like you're naked in the street. And now you don't know where to go because you've got no control. You've never done it before. It's like winning your first golf tournament. Once you learn to win, you're comfortable with it. You think, "Let's go ahead and do it." But if you haven't won it's like walking into a dark room; you don't know where all the obstacles are. You walk in there and you kick the table and you stumble and make a couple of bogeys . . . That's what happens when you lose your comfort zone.'

According to Norman's theory, the best players are the players with the widest comfort zone parameters. They are players who can adapt to situations to such an extent that they can play badly and still win. As an example, he cites his own victory in the Memorial Tournament at Muirfield Village earlier this year.

'I played horrible golf. Probably the worst golf I've ever played, but I won the golf tournament. I figured out a way to win the golf tournament. Yet there's times when you've played great – the Masters and tournaments I've been beaten in – and you've lost. Now which way would you rather have it? That's the final argument.'

Walking this tightrope between triumph and adversity, engaging in bloody head to head battles, and challenging himself to win the tournament when he might be ten shots in arrears, these are the reasons why the Shark is inextricably hooked on golf.

'I couldn't give up this game,' says Norman with conviction. 'Even though I could, I couldn't. That's what you would miss after a period of time, that feeling of getting in there and coming back, or playing just one [perfect] shot.'

This is testimony to golf's addictive powers, of how the love of the game is never really destroyed by its cruelty. Not even when it brings a player to his knees time and time again. Not even when it breaks his heart and steals his dignity. I find myself thinking back to that grey day at the Open Championship when Norman shot a 76 to Faldo's 67.

'What really happened in the third round of the Open?'

Norman doesn't hesitate. 'I lost my rhythm with my putter,' he says. No excuses given or sympathy asked for. 'The putt I missed on the second hole, I guess, was a very makeable putt, but I just hit it too hard and hit it through the break. And the next putt I missed a couple of holes later, I hit too soft. So now I'm second-guessing myself on the line and speed, and as time goes by I'm getting myself worse and worse in a hole in the way I feel about my putting. Then I hit a good drive on 12 which I thought was perfect and it trickles into the bunker, and I hit a drive on 13 which I thought was perfect and it rolls into the bunker.

'And that's where, to me, the whole tournament changed – the tee shot on

12 that fell in the bunker. I lost my momentum. I lost it even though I was only a couple behind Nick . . . Nick putted extremely well the whole week, there's no question about it. He was making everything that he looked at and he had a lot of confidence. And he kept the momentum going. So that's what happened: it was the ebb and flow of momentum.'

'I've seen so much of it happen in negative terms,' says Norman. He is speaking of losing. 'It saddens me. If somebody beats you, heck, he beats you. He's better than you on the week. You've got to say to yourself, "Well, I'll go out there and work harder and beat him next week."

'Sure, your confidence can go down very quickly. It's happened to me over the years. But you know deep down in your gut it's just a superficial deal. Three months will go by and you'll be bouncing right back into the game. You'll think: "What went wrong for three months?" But that's always going to happen because of the mental and physical parts of your game. Your mental fits your physical and vice versa. So it's an amazing contrast of passions because your mind is so strong. And if it's strong in the negative side then you'll never play great golf, but if it's strong in the positive side then you're going to be around for a long time, no matter what people say or do to you.'

Yesterday, in driving rain and a force nine gale, Norman worked for two hours on his game on the practice range at St Andrews. For only the second time in his career, he has flown his coach of 18 years, Charlie Earp, over from Australia. Norman is a self-taught player and if his swing is in the groove it rarely alters. But lack of practice caused him to lose his swing plane. 'I got my hands too high and that meant I wasn't swinging down the line. I was dropping too far inside the line and the club was going out.'

One day of working with Earp and Norman is swinging the best he has in a long time. 'You know, if you're going to maintain a level of golf, you have to practise every day. No question about it. Whether you're playing good or playing bad you have to practise. And I didn't. I kind of took it easy. I didn't really hit the full six hundred balls a day that you need to groove your swing. I've hit about three thousand in the last week.

'See, that's what I love to do,' explains Norman with a grin. 'I love staying out and hitting balls because I'm in my zone, you know, I'm in my element. I can control what I'm doing. I don't have anybody out there saying, "Come, we've got to go and do this, we've got to do that". I'm there. I'm locked in for three or four hours and I love it.'

'What are your biggest strengths in life and in golf?'

'In golf, I would say my biggest strength is driving the ball. I'm long and I'm fairly straight so I have an advantage there. As a person, I guess, my self-belief. I won't do something unless I believe I can do it. I think I'm a very, very honest person. If somebody asks me a question, I'll give them my honest answer. Now whether the truth hurts somebody, that's their problem, not mine. I always stand up for my own beliefs. If somebody challenges me and I know I'm right and they're wrong, then I'll go and talk to them about it. I won't let it stew, I'll get it off my chest. And I never hold a grudge.

'That's the way I am,' says Norman quietly after these frank admissions. 'I mean, I'm not putting on any pseudo face here.'

I have never been more certain that someone was being absolutely straight with me.

His inability to say no, he admits is a big weakness. Most other top players wouldn't think twice about refusing to do an interview, for example. 'I won't do that,' insists Norman, 'because I've always believed that life's a two-way street. If somebody wants to ask you to do something, then that's a reflection on you and your ability . . . And, you know, it's time, but heck, what's time? Time's something you can use for you and you can use against you.'

'How do you manage not to spread yourself too thin, to still have enough time to concentrate on your golf game?'

'Well, you see, the down side to it is that these people, when you do say "No, sorry, I can't. I've got another commitment", they see that you've done it forever. You've always been willing to give an interview and when you say no, they get kind of pissed off. I had it today with some guy on the putting green. I wanted to go and get ready for my game. I've got things to work on, and here he is asking me questions. I felt like saying, "Hey, God dammit, imagine if I walked in when you were writing and deep in your concentration." But I didn't. But I was short enough with him that he knew and he walked away. Now when I see him again it'll be interesting to see what kind of reaction I get.'

The psychology of the media is a complex one. Being continually affable and amenable as Norman is is no guarantee of good press, just as – perversely – behaving like a prima donna doesn't necessarily mean that a player will receive more than his share of bad press.

Immediately after his round with Faldo at the Open Championship, Norman went to the putting green to work on his stroke. There he was approached by the Championship press officer who said that there was no time for Norman to give a press conference, and that a few quotes from him would suffice. Norman willingly complied. But due to a general lack of communication in the press centre the situation was misconstrued and Norman was reported as having refused to be interviewed. It wouldn't have occurred to many journalists to double-check for the simple reason that players flouncing off after bad rounds and refusing to be interviewed is commonplace.

'Yes, well, I'm not a Seve,' says Norman tersely when I point this out. He has never refused to go into a press conference in his life. 'I'm not a Faldo – because I know Nick has done that a few times. If things don't go their way they're not acceptable. And I'm not that way. I mean, I bite the bullet and accept that you have your good days and your bad days.'

Norton rang Norman immediately after the Open Championship.

'Look,' he said to his client, 'you've got to get rid of this image.'

'What image are you talking about?' said Norman in astonishment.

'What are you doing turning down press conferences?' demanded Norton, and faxed Norman an article out of the *Wall Street Journal*.

'You know, I've even sat down in the press room and waited for 30 minutes for somebody to finish, and I've thought, "What the hell, I'd rather be out there practising," ' says Norman bitterly. 'But you have to do it. It's an obligation you have to fulfil, and if you don't fulfil that obligation, then you're missing a lot of steps on the way to doing the right thing.'

The phone rings for about the fifth time in the last hour. Norman hops up and answers it without a murmur. It's Nigel Mansell.

'You win a race, you come second, you sign a deal and then you call me!' chides Norman, his voice deep with affection. He reclines in one chair and hooks his feet over the back of another. He is going to be there for a while.

Norton has returned to his chair and we talk sporadically. He is the overall client manager for IMG in the States. He shows me a newspaper advertisement for a tournament organised by Norman in the States, in which about 20 golfers play for a million dollars with as much going to charity.

Snatches of Norman's discourse with Mansell drift over. It seems that the Australian has been plagued by reporters asking for his theory on Mansell's decision to postpone his early retirement and sign with Williams. 'What am I? Your press agent?' demands Norman.

Norton tells me about a book on Norman's mental approach to golf which is soon to be published.

'Oh shit!' laughs Norman, recovering from one of Mansell's quips. 'Don't give me that. I know you too well . . . How's the family?'

His manager, meanwhile, is explaining to me how in-depth interviews like this one, given gratuitously by Norman, can devalue his worth in the book publishing trade. Potential publishers might begrudge paying him to do what he has previously done for nothing.

'Do you know what the problem is with you?' Norman is asking Mansell teasingly down the phone. 'Nobody gives you a fucking hard time. So I've got to sit back here and do it.'

At length he rings off and settles down once more. He and Mansell have been best of friends for years. They share a love of fast cars and golf. At the 1988 Italian Open at Monticello (which he won), Norman, who collects cars, bought two Ferraris: a limited edition F40 and a Testarossa.

'Golf and racing car driving – there's a very good correlation between the two, believe it or not,' explains Norman. 'Hand–eye co-ordination and feel.'

'Do you think that is the key to a good swing?'

'Buy the book,' shouts Norton from the doorway of the bedroom where he is practising his putting. 'We also have a video.'

Norman laughs good-humouredly but ignores him. Fundamentals, he says simply. Basic fundamentals and natural hand–eye co-ordination. Most professional golfers have the ability to feel the distance between the ball and the pin. The best players – most notably, Ballesteros – are just people who have been endowed with more of that feel.

Norman's brown hands grip an imaginary club.

'A very good friend of mine in Australia,' he says slowly, 'once told me that when you play golf, it's like making love to your hands. You can feel it. It's just there. You can just feel the clubhead and you can go, "I'm going to put that clubhead on that ball and put it to within a foot of where I want it." And you're making love to your hands all the time when it's on the clubhead. That's when you're playing well.'

The twilight has turned to darkness. Norman seems oblivious to the inky blackness of the room, content not to turn on the light. The silence is heavy, the only sound being the muffled click of balls as Norton putts tirelessly in the glow of a bedroom lamp. I look at my watch and start guiltily. Two hours have gone by. Norman doesn't look in the least bit perturbed, or if he is, is too polite to show it.

So I ask one last question.

'What goals can be left for a player that has done everything short of win the Grand Slam?'

'To be the best I can be,' says Norman, smiling his easy smile. 'As simple as that. Now how good that'll be, time will only tell. You know, you can set yourself goals and go about trying to attain them, but you can also just say to yourself: "I want to be the best I can be. I don't want to settle for anything less."

'If you settle for second best, then you're a loser.'

Chapter Seventeen

ZEN AND THE ART OF GOLF

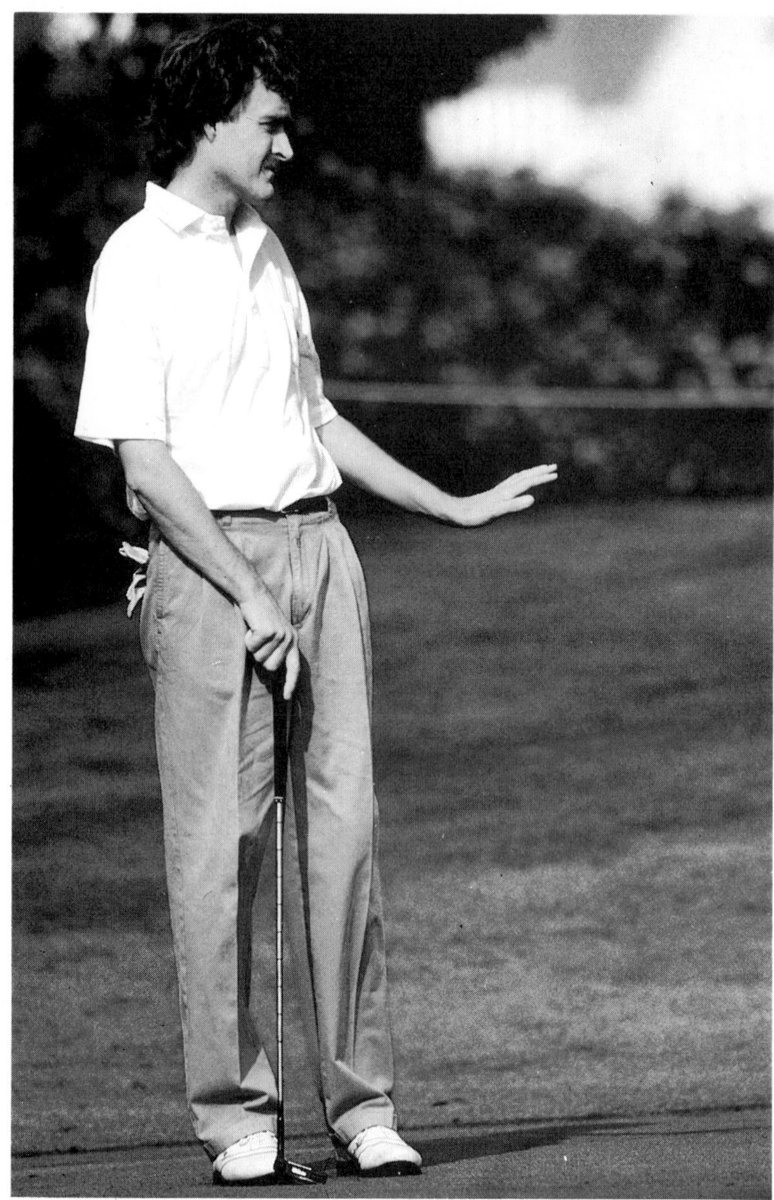

Photo: Phil Sheldon

Zen master: David Jones talks to the ball

MONTPELIER, MARCH 1990. ON AN EVENING STROLL DOWN A pleasant street in what in all other respects is a good residential area in Bangor, Northern Ireland, the casual passer-by would be struck by the contrasting spectacle of the door of a certain house. It is a door which one might expect to find in a shanty town: sadly neglected, shedding splinters and paint peelings, with broken window panes. Even the postman on his morning rounds approaches it with caution and, arm outstretched, inserts letters gingerly through the rusty flap.

That's David Jones's door. He finds it cheaper to maintain and more effective than a burglar alarm.

Six foot four, with overlong hair, David Jones is the most extraordinary person I know. He is the kind of man who, having been seized by the urge to visit all the cathedrals in Britain, would stop *en route* and buy ten books on Zen, Taoism and Mao Tse Tung; or who would carry a golf club and a bag of practice balls up to the top of Mount Kenya, and spend an enjoyable half hour hitting them into oblivion.

Six years ago Jones again defied convention and went to a sports psychologist at a time when it was considered taboo. *The Inner Game of Golf*, Timothy Galwey's book on mental strategy on the golf course, had recently been published and Jones, David Feherty, David Llewellyn, Peter Tupling and Gary Cullen got together and decided to pay Alan Fine a visit.

'In that particular era it was almost a closet thing,' says Jones. 'I mean, people didn't like to let it be known that they needed help with how they thought on the golf course and how they concentrated. Anything other than pure hard work in the strictly golfing sense was viewed with suspicion. Whereas now, a very few years later, it's all very open. People don't feel guilty or embarrassed about revealing that they've had hypnosis to get over yips, or that they play tapes to themselves when they go to bed.'

'Do people do that?'

'Yes, Seve does it, Langer does it, a lot of people do it.'

Fine was the first person to make Jones aware of the type of mental preparation and exercises he could do to help focus his attention on the golf course, and prevent his mind from wandering ahead to potentially dangerous holes, or from dwelling on disasters.

'Until that time I had never come across the techniques that made an individual identify what actually was negative and positive on the golf course. People mistakenly thought, and still think, that positive thinking is simply standing up on the tee and saying, "I'm going to make a birdie here", when in actual fact that's not what positive thinking is about. Standing on the first tee of a tournament and trying to convince yourself what you're going to be doing on Sunday at five o'clock is going to have absolutely no effect whatsoever on the way you're going to make contact with the golf ball on Thursday morning . . . Alan Fine was the first person to bring home to me that the whole business of being mentally efficient is being mentally aware of the very moment you're in on the golf course.'

Fine's approach to the Inner Game deals strictly with mental interference and how to shut it out. He works on three basic areas: visualisation, mental tricks, and negative vibes.

The principle behind visualisation is that the use of mental imagery – picturing the shot you are going to play – will help a player physically to hit the shot. Visualisation highlights one of the main difficulties of the Inner Game – that of assessing its effects on your physical golf game. For instance, if a player stood up on the tee and visualised hitting his ball down the fairway and hit it in the rough, then did the identical thing on each of the next three holes, his immediate reaction would be: 'This is a waste of time.' But mental techniques have to be practised just the same as physical techniques do before they can be perfected.

The second area is that of introducing tricks to occupy the mind. For example, if a player is reciting "Mary had a little lamb" to himself, or concentrating on the movement of his big toe, his attention will be concentrated on that rather than worrying about poor shots or problem holes, past or present.

Fine's theory on the third area of the Inner Game is that, in order to do better, a player has to deal with the negative thoughts in his head, like the voices which tell him when he is having a bad day: 'You'll never be any good at this game.' Fine has an Inner Game exercise, which he gives players to do, where they have to give all of these negative voices a human perspective.

'Who's telling you these negative thoughts?' Fine would ask Jones.

'Well, he's sort of like a schoolmaster that tells me what to do all the time. "You've got to make four here," he says.'

'What do you want to say to this alter ego?'

'Fuck off out of my life and leave me alone to play golf!'

Fine would then instruct Jones to change chairs and play the other part of himself. 'Right,' he would say, 'what do you want to say back?'

'Well,' said Jones in the role of the schoolmaster, 'I'm only trying to help, because I was rooting for you last year when you took six at the last and cost yourself £2,000.'

'So you get this dialogue going,' says Jones now, 'and it's actually an amazing thing to try. And people have learned a lot about themselves, because the vast majority of golfers – I'm not maligning them – are not deep thinkers.'

But as these sessions progressed, Fine began to delve deeper and deeper into the cause of Jones's insecurity on the golf course, which at that time was his personal life, until it reached the point where Jones felt no longer able to confide in him. Some people find it easier to unravel their psyche before another person than others. David Feherty, for example.

'He's absolutely fantastic,' enthuses Feherty, who has been working with Fine for the last six years. 'I go to see him quite a lot. I just go to empty my head of whatever crap is in there. The trouble is, we know each other so well now that I know what he's going to ask me . . . I'm very familiar with the techniques, you know, and I'm very familiar with him. And he knows more about me than my mother. You know, you have to be perfectly honest. Let him know what bothers you and why it bothers you. And it goes deeper than golf very often, before you can winkle out what it is that's actually distracting your attention from what you're trying to do. So the sessions with Alan have been very helpful, both for my golf and just for me.'

Understanding Jones's inner struggle with this invasion of his privacy, however, Fine redirected him into areas in which he felt Jones could help himself – one of which was Zen. But Jones's interest in Eastern philosophy and sports psychology was such that eventually he found he began to get sidetracked from his original purpose, which was to use it to play better golf.

'It almost became a religious thing. I began to see, or thought I began to see, that if I was going to change this way of thinking, I not only had to change it on the golf course, I had to change it in a lot of other ways as well . . . I was in a very difficult situation at the time with my marriage, you see, and that sort of changed me as a bloke.'

Now I've never known Jones to be anything other than easy-going and relaxed about life, calmly dispensing advice in a manner that elucidates the most complicated and perplexing problem, and I find it almost impossible to imagine him with the totally different attitude and set of values he says he had.

'I was very much into material things . . . and at that stage I was very well-off. I had all the trappings of a successful young man. I had a wife and kids and a lovely home. I had a nice car and a pile of money in the bank. Everything was hunky dory and that was how I measured myself as a bloke – how my image was. Now once things got rocky in my private life, my whole ability to lead that kind of life went rapidly downhill. I wasn't playing well; I gave my job up because I wasn't enjoying it; my marriage broke up. In the terms I had set myself, I was no longer a successful person.'

Jones woke up one morning shortly after his divorce and the inevitable legal wrangles and found he had lost everything he treasured: his family, his house and his money. 'So all of a sudden I realised that all things I had learned to value [success and material possessions] were completely meaningless. Now I've still got them, but I don't value them at all.'

Richard Boxall comes bouncing into the lobby of the hotel where we are conducting the interview and, seeing us, comes over to investigate.

'Your eyes are very red,' accuses Jones.

'I haven't had a beer all day,' says Boxy indignantly.

'What do you think, Richard?' I said. 'Is golf a very mental game or isn't it?'

'I believe it's very, very mental,' says Boxall in a professorial tone. 'I believe – and I'd just like to quote this – "The ball is round and scientists rule the world".'

And he departs in the general direction of the hotel bar.

'So that was how I changed,' says Jones, picking up the thread of the conversation. 'I was never aggressive, bad-tempered, wild; I was never a womaniser or a raving lune. But I had a completely different set of values, and a completely different image of what I had to do to be seen to be a good fellow . . .

'You see,' says Jones, returning to the original point of the conversation, 'the Inner Game is an attitude of mind. You can't be an Inner Game player of golf and be a psycho in your everyday life. If it's going to work successfully to improve your golf or realise your potential, then it has to apply to more than just your golf. You can't go around being a bad-tempered, grumpy individual, who drinks and smokes and eats badly, and then suddenly on Wednesday thinks: "I'm going to be an Inner Game player for the next four days".'

Not every player sees it that way. Mark James, for example, sees the game as a purely technical examination. He doesn't believe that the game is more than five per cent mental at most. Yet he is one of the most mentally tough competitors on the European Tour, one of the best front-runners in a tournament and one of the best players under pressure in professional golf.

'He's at one end of the spectrum,' explains Jones. 'At the other end, you get people like Fred Couples, who willingly succumb to the pressure and who don't appear to attempt to do anything about it. Then you get the people in between, who either accept their limitations or don't accept their limitations – like Seve at the moment. He can't accept that at this particular time he's not capable of doing better. His outlook is that he's been the best in the world and he's still the best in the world, and that there's one thing that's going to snap him back to where he was. Whereas, there's got to be some sort of progression back.'

'How do you explain people like Gary Player or Lee Trevino, who are enormously successful and have tremendous mental attitudes, and who have never given the Inner Game a second's thought?'

'I think Player's a witch,' says Jones with a grin. 'Trevino, I don't know. There are people out there who are not Inner Game thinkers, who don't conduct their lives in a proper way, who don't understand the swing, but they're world-beaters. You don't have to be a nice bloke, you don't have to be into good karma, you don't have to be anything to be a great golfer anymore. You've just got to be good at golf.'

'So what are you doing at the moment? Zen?'

'Well, I know it sounds a bit kind of sycophantic, but I actually regard my life as a sort of meditation in a way. I just try to do, in as far as I can, what I perceive to be the right thing all the time. I never do anything because appearances demand it. I don't go to places, see people, dress in certain ways, go to services, funerals or marriages, or whatever, because I ought to be seen there. I don't do anything unless I think it's the right thing to do. I try not to.'

Epson Grand Prix, September 1990. Rick Hartmann is having breakfast. Muesli, fruit, whole loaves of wholewheat toast and several pots of tea are being dispatched. No eggs, no bacon, no sausages, no soft drinks. Sports psychologist, Dr James Loehr, has talked him out of them.

Was he health conscious prior to their meeting?

'Oh no,' says Hartmann. 'I ate crap all the time . . . Now I try to eat as well as I can. But that's another thing where, in the beginning, I took it to extremes. I do have to be good, but he says: "Listen, if you have something bad, don't worry about it. You feel guilty about it? Fine. That's good enough." '

Concern about his diet wasn't the only reason Rick Hartmann went to see Dr Loehr. He had slipped from 47th position on the money list in 1987 to 146th in 1988, which he took as a definite sign that he needed mental attention. 'You couldn't go from the top 50 in the Order of Merit to 146th just for technical reasons when there hasn't been that much change. If anything, you'd improve.'

At the time, however, Hartmann, who had been making multifarious and complex changes to his golf swing with the assistance of David Leadbetter, thought his problems were entirely physical. Two things happened to convince him otherwise. First, David Frost and Wayne Player gave him some notes they had received from an American sports psychologist on focusing and thinking on the golf course. Hartmann worked on those few principles for the duration of the 1989 season and finished an encouraging 79th on the money list. Then David Leadbetter, who will often suggest that his pupils see sports psychologists, gave Hartmann a book written by Dr Loehr. Hartmann read it and considered it. He was in dire financial straits at the time. He had lost his sponsor through playing badly and was looking for anything that might help him do better. Loehr's book convinced him that a trip to Florida to speak to the sports psychologist in person certainly wasn't going to make matters worse. It might just be the answer.

'Most sports psychologists work on what you're supposed to do on the golf course,' says Hartmann. 'But I wanted to know why I think the way I do. I've always wanted to find someone who wanted to get inside my brain, really. I know I'm supposed to do A, B and C, but there's a lot of things getting in the way of A, B, C so I can't do them. Jim gets right inside your personality and looks back to when you were a kid . . . He tells you what kind of person you are, so you get an idea of your strong points and your weak points and how to cope with them.'

It's Loehr's theory that a person's strong points can also be his weak points – if he doesn't have them under control.

'That was the case with me,' admits Hartmann. 'Just to give you an idea, I am an extremist. Everything has to be perfect. Even my luggage has to be unpacked in a certain way. That's just what I am. I'm a very neat person. I never leave the house without making the bed, you know, things like that. When I work on technical things in the swing, I go to the extremely perfect. And when I go on the golf course, if everything's not perfect, then I don't think I can play.'

This is the point at which Loehr began. Hartmann had to learn to relax on and off the golf course, and he had to learn to subdue his perfectionism to the point where it wasn't a controlling factor.

There are numerous Inner Game methods of dealing with perfectionism. Loehr, like Ted Pollard, believes that the key to mental strength is physical fitness, and therefore he works on the premise that the best way for a player to cope with mental interference of any kind on the golf course, in order to maximise his potential, is with an intense dietary and physical regimen off it.

He believes, according to Hartmann, in the big picture. Not the little picture of what you do on the golf course.

Loehr, who until the start of this season had mainly worked with tennis players, now works with Mike Clayton, Bryan Norton, David Jones, Peter Fowler and J. C. Snead. For every player who sees him, Loehr devises an individual schedule. In Hartmann's case, he concentrated on the following areas:

(a) **Scheduling**: Most of the tennis players Loehr works with, i.e. Andre Agassi, Martina Navratilova and Gabriella Sabbatini, schedule their season around the major championships. 'He feels that you can have control over when you play well,' says Hartmann. 'I mean, look at those [golfers] who play well in the majors every year [Jack Nicklaus has had 13 top three finishes in 18 Open Championship starts], they must do something to schedule that.'

(b) **Technically**: Hartmann wanted to take a week off mid-season to go and see Leadbetter, for example, but Loehr advised him not to. He said that because Hartmann gets so analytical, it would be better for him to do it over a month in the off-season.

(c) **Diet**: Loehr believes that certain foods and the times at which they are eaten will have a positive or negative effect on a player's performance. For instance, drinking excess amounts of coffee will make him jumpy on the golf course, while carboydrates are energy-giving and will help him to think well. Or if a golfer has a large meal late at night, then his digestive system uses up all his energy reserves while he is sleeping and he wakes up with none. The same principle applies if he eats a big breakfast. His body uses up so much energy digesting it that, if he gets into a crisis situation on the golf course, he hasn't got any in reserve to help him handle the pressure.

(d) **Exercise programme**: Different people have different ways of dealing with stress. Loehr felt that Hartmann would benefit most from aerobic exercise,

particularly running, which makes the body release chemicals that deal with stress hormones. Mike Clayton has found that running has made an incredible difference to the way he copes with stress, on and off the golf course. Prior to seeing Loehr at the Irish Open, Clayton had never made more than five consecutive cuts. Subsequently, Clayton has made 15.

(e) **Caddie**: 'He believes that the caddie is extremely important,' says Hartmann. 'He actually said that it could be one of the most important things for a golfer, because a caddie can also be a coach. In tennis, the coach can sit in the stand but he's not allowed to say anything. You're actually allowed in golf to have a caddie there to talk to you, whether it's to slow you down, to relax you, or to get you more hyped up.' Hartmann got along so well with the caddie he was using at the time of their meeting that Loehr encouraged him to keep him. 'My caddie's been a big part of my doing well,' says Hartmann.

Contrastingly, Loehr told Mike Clayton to fire his caddie the first time he saw him. 'Well, Michael knew he had to do it,' explains Clayton's wife, Debbie, 'but he just needed someone to push him over the edge. Michael wasn't unhappy with him, he just didn't suit him at the time. It was good for both of them, it wasn't all tragedy and drama. But Michael needed someone to confirm his own feelings and push him to do it because Michael procrastinates too much – "Oh, it'll be alright" – when he knows it really won't be.'

Clayton found himself a new caddie immediately after the Irish Open. At the very next tournament, Clayton made a mess of one hole and lapsed into his old habit of swearing and cursing. Mick, the new caddie, turned around and said curtly to the Australian: 'Shut up.' Clayton was stunned. 'All the anger just drained out of me,' he said. 'That's what I needed from a caddie. Too many of them don't say anything when you start playing badly. They just go quiet.'

(f) **Family**: Loehr works on a programme for Claudette, Hartmann's wife, because he feels that she is the closest person to him and, apart from the fact that she has to deal with the stresses that accompany being married to a professional golfer, she also has the ability to help him. 'She knows my highs and lows,' explains Hartmann, 'but also, from her point of view, it's a very difficult lifestyle. Everything revolves around me. She's very strong-willed, so we have fights about who's in control and about all the stuff she does for me, and when she's going to get her time.'

Loehr suggested that it might be an idea for Claudette to do something that she was interested in, rather than always depending on Rick. Claudette, who talks to Loehr regularly on the telephone, told him that she had always had ambitions of being a fashion designer, and he encouraged her to go out and buy a sewing machine. Now she designs and makes her own clothes.

'I found in the early days of our marriage, I made the mistake of trying to play psychologist,' says Debbie Clayton, who went through much the same thing as Claudette Hartmann has, 'and only saying things that I thought were beneficial to his psyche when he went out to play. And in the process I was getting more and more frustrated in myself, and more and more depressed. Eventually I thought: "I'm going to say I've had enough, I don't like this financial pressure, and what the hell are you doing out there? Do you know what you're doing?" And once we'd got over that, and I wasn't playing psychologist any more, we were much happier.

'I think that's a trap you can fall into. Of suspecting that if you say you're unhappy, it's going to hurt him on the golf course. You get a heightened awareness of how they're thinking, or how you think they should be thinking, so you end up being a sports psychologist instead of a wife.'

The main principle behind Loehr's Inner Game theory is that there are four main mental states: high positive, low positive, high negative and low negative. By focusing on all of the factors directly and indirectly influencing his game, Loehr helps a player to create the perfect arena for the optimum performance state – high positive. In Hartmann's case, Loehr found that the best way for him to achieve a high positive attitude on the golf course was through relaxation.

'At the Irish Open I was lying fourth coming down the last hole,' recalls Hartmann. 'Obviously, I was quite nervous, and something I like to do is talk. . . . The more I talk, the more at ease I am. . . . Coming down 18 I was joking with the steward walking down the fairway instead of thinking about my golf game and probably making bogey or worse. This way I made par quite easily. Didn't make birdie, but I could have. It's just a step that he's taken me, from trying too hard to trying less in a better way for me.'

At Portmarnock, Harmann told Loehr that he was struggling with his putting.

'What do you think about when you're on the green?' asked the sports psychologist.

'Visualisation,' Hartmann told him.

'Let's try this then,' said Loehr, who talks to Hartmann on the phone for 15 minutes daily for a week, once every fortnight. 'I don't want you to visualise it going in the hole. I don't want you to try. I want you to look at it kind of nonchalantly, think about it, have an idea, and just go up and hit it.'

Hartmann's putting improved overnight. Practising is another area of his game where he has found that less is more. At the Lancome Trophy he only hit balls once the entire tournament – for half an hour. The rest of the week he played tennis every day. Hartmann was so laid back that he wrote in the diary he keeps of his moods and emotions in order to study how he feels when he plays well: 'I think I might be too relaxed this week.'

He finished fourth in the tournament.

'Obviously you can go too far,' admits Hartmann (who finished 39th on the

1990 money list), 'but I haven't gone that far yet. Because of the make-up that I am, it's very difficult for me not to care about something. That's why this psychology of not trying to make the putt is great for me because it's impossible for me not to try. He wants me to get to the point where I don't try and I can't do it. It's amazing.'

Cannes, 1990. Among the players with more unorthodox approaches to the Inner Game is Jeff Hawkes, a Scientologist. Hawkes has proceeded down the Dianetic route to golfing nirvana so far that Simon Hobday's joking assertion that he is 'ready for the State House for the Bewildered', is not as far removed from the truth as it first appeared. Nevertheless, he is a good player, a nice guy, and it has never done his golf any harm. It has, however, led to some bizarre situations on the golf course. Apart from talking to the golf ball and believing that he can move the ball with his mind – which, let's face it, we all do at times – the oddest phase he had been through is one where he would repeatedly ask his caddie to tell him where he was.

'Where am I, Guy?' he would say to his caddie.

'You're on the 18th fairway at Wentworth, you've got 157 yards to the pin, and you're playing your second shot,' would come the dutiful reply.

Hawkes was playing the Sunshine Circuit in South Africa one year when he hit his ball into the branches of a thick and leafy tree. His black caddie, Foley, was made to scale the tree trunk and begin a rather fruitless search for the ball. He was hot and flustered and tired of telling Hawkes his whereabouts on every second hole. He scanned the crevices listlessly. Hawkes, meanwhile, had watched Foley ascend the tree and vanish into the foliage. After five minutes he grew impatient. 'Where are you, Foley?' he cried plaintively.

Down came the muffled reply: 'I'm on the 12th hole at Germiston Golf Club, I've got 240 yards to the green, and I'm up the fucking tree.'

David Llewellyn's approach to the Inner Game is slightly more familiar. He believes that if a man can alter the blinkered way he looks at things, then he'll see things in a wider perspective and, in doing so, will realise that they aren't as important as he first thought they were. He will stop trying so hard then and, as a result, will do them better.

'It's very difficult to apply just to golf,' says Llewellyn of this philosophy. 'You have to apply it to the whole of your life, and if you put things in perspective, then golf is a very tiny part of your life.' He gestures toward the players on the practice range. 'They think that golf is their whole life,' he says. 'Now isn't that ridiculous.'

Llewellyn, who once thought exactly the same way, learnt to his cost just how ridiculous it is. 'David Llewellyn,' says David Jones, 'is one guy who, having given up golf because he couldn't face the thought of actually going on to the golf course, came back into the game, tortured himself over a period of time – even though he's a really happy kind of individual – and really through introduction to Zen, turned his life around.'

'Why did you leave the Tour?' I asked Llewellyn.

'I left the Tour because (1) I couldn't play well. (2) If I'd stayed for another three months, they'd have taken me away in a strait-jacket. They'd have put me away in a white room padded with mattresses. I really was bad. I was horrendous. (3) Because I had no money and I had a family to support.

'It literally was driving me insane. I'd come off the golf course having bitten through my tongue and not known I'd done it. I'd have big knots in my stomach. I just decided to give up. And when I started again seven or eight months later, I got the same type of feelings. That's when Gary [Cullen] introduced me to Alan Fine [September 1984].'

'What made you come back?'

'Because Bridie [his wife], she kept saying to me, "You'll be back because you love it." '

At that time Llewellyn flatly denied it. He spent two years working at a golf club in Malta, and another year at a golf course in Britain. He rebuilt his swing completely, continued to play in local events, and when finally he had the chance to play on the European Tour again, took it. Llewellyn found that, although he still got those funny feelings on the golf course, with Fine's help, he could control them. His interest in Zen was a natural progression from his sessions with Fine. According to Jones's definition, 'Zen is a form of Buddhism. But really, it's a very individualistic form, which just works on the basis that, if you're going to get the most out of anything, you've got to put yourself in harmony with your surroundings, the people around you and the world in general.'

'It's impossible to describe, really,' says Llewellyn, whose wife bought him a weekend course in relaxation and meditation at a Buddhist Monastery for Christmas. 'I suppose it's an attitude of life . . . but that doesn't describe what it might be. I don't know what it is. It's like saying, "What's nature?" Put it this way, whatever Zen is, it's changed my perception of life.'

Like Jones, Llewellyn disagrees with the traditional concept of positive thinking. 'You see,' says Llewellyn, 'I don't understand what positive is . . . You know you're not doing so well and you've got to try and make the best of a bad day. How do you do that? You do that by standing on the first tee and trying to do your best. And when you've hit that one, you walk up to it and you do your best again. Until they say stop, which in our game happens to be 18 holes.'

English Open, The Belfry, 1990. Not everyone finds that the Inner Game is the answer to their prayers. Gary Cullen, who had been on the Tour for 15 years, went to Alan Fine to find out how he could play better golf and discovered that he didn't want to play the Tour at all. Practising beside David

Jones one day, Cullen turned to his friend and said: 'I just don't want to do this any more.'

'Well, stop then,' said Jones.

It was a casual remark but it stopped Cullen in his tracks. The possibility that he could, and maybe should, stop, had never occurred to him until that moment. So he stopped.

'Gary's now got a deep-sea fishing business on the east coast of Africa,' says Jones. 'Happy as Larry. Never plays golf.'

'What happened to Peter Tupling?'

'Peter . . . used the Inner Game as something to really beat himself up with and it had a very adverse effect on him. He gave himself a very hard time about his inability to play well under pressure, and that just blew him away. He lost everything, you know. He lost his game and he lost his whole equilibrium, as regards golf, and was sort of driven out of the game by the fact that he played so poorly for a period of time.

'I think he's still involved in the game and still plays a bit. A different sort of character, you know. A much more gritty, down-to-earth character, who really had to struggle to come into the world of golf and be successful. It sort of embittered him slightly. I've only seen him once or twice in the last five years, and I sort of got the feeling he isn't happy with the way it went.'

Golf destroys more dreams and lives than any other sport, because it has the capacity to make addicts out of the people who play it.

'It requires a huge amount of dedication and self-discipline,' says Jones. 'Any pro sport does, but because it's such a singular existence it has a very catastrophic effect – less so now because the facilities for having companions with you are much greater – but it takes a terrible toll on your relationship with a woman, your marriage, your life in general, because it demands so much of you.

'You know, it demands that you go and you spend 40 to 45 weeks of the year playing and practising golf, four, five or six hours a day. You invest anything up to £30,000 – £40,000 a year of your own money or somebody else's into pursuing this career. You have to travel all over the place, whether you want to or not, to places that you may not like, in an effort to play the Tour. And that takes its toll if it doesn't provide some financial success. It's very easy to get an unbalanced attitude about what you've put into it and what you've got out of it. What I'm saying is that the game doesn't necessarily reward the effort. It's a combination of effort and skill, and who's to say what balances what out . . .

'I mean, what is golf?' asks Jones. 'Golf is only a game. I know there are pros you could say that to who would shoot your head off. But it is.'

Chapter Eighteen

AN IMPERFECT GAME

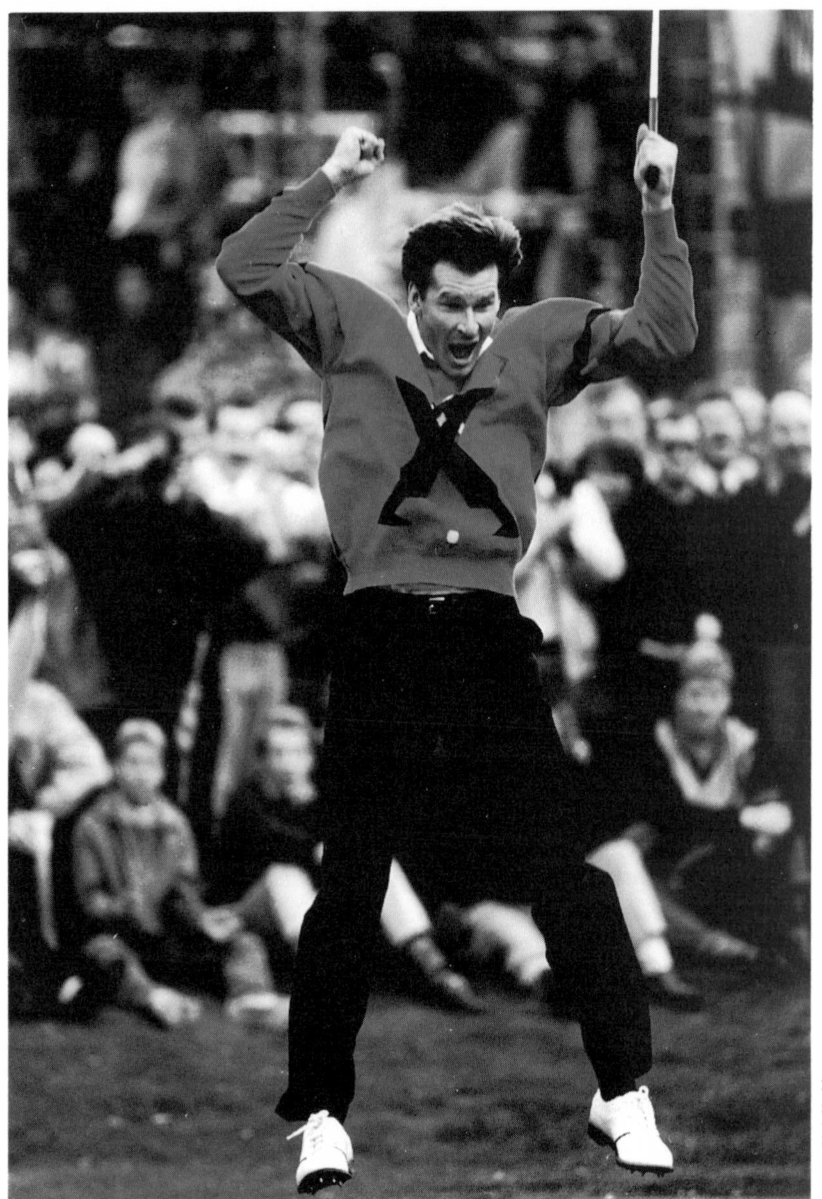

Photo: Phil Sheldon

Victory: Nick Faldo leaps for joy as he holes out to win the 1989 World Match Play

THERE IS A STORY ABOUT NICK FALDO.

David McNeilly, a multi-linguist Irishman with a passion for French Impressionist poetry, tells it – he used to caddie for the Englishman. It goes something like this. Walking beside Faldo at the golf course one day, McNeilly noticed Faldo's eyes drop to his shoes, one of which had begun to smile at the toe the way shoes do when they reach the end of their lives.

'You need a new pair of trainers,' said Faldo, regarding McNeilly's shoes with distaste. McNeilly agreed wholeheartedly, but said that he wasn't in the position financially to go out and buy any just then. Faldo stopped. He took out his wallet and examined its contents. McNeilly stared at him in amazement. Surely, Nick Faldo wasn't going to buy him, David McNeilly, a new pair of trainers? But it appeared he was. A delighted McNeilly prepared then and there to take back everything he had ever said about the man.

With some deliberation, Faldo took out a sheaf of mint notes from his wallet and fanned through them cursorily. He removed the elastic band which bound them and handed it to McNeilly. 'There,' he said. 'Put that round your shoe.'

Frank Nobilo, the affable New Zealander, once remarked to me that, in his opinion, the best way to form an accurate impression of a player was to speak to the people closest to him, rather than to the player himself. It struck me that this was the perfect way to set about unravelling the tightly bound defences of Nick Faldo. To approach the subject laterally, as it were, rather than directly.

Golf is a game well known for its capacity to reveal a man's true character, yet Faldo has remained stubbornly masked throughout. Thousands of column inches devoted to the dissection of his personality and private life have failed to elicit more than a few shadowy outlines of the man. Pieced together, these images ambiguously reveal an intensely private man, a perfectionist and an assiduous grinder: as equally capable of being benevolent as mean, candid as unpredictable, and gracious as unbearably arrogant.

Throughout his glorious career, Faldo's footsteps have been dogged by controversy. Long before he abandoned his golf scholarship at Houston University after only ten weeks in favour of returning to Britain and turning professional, Faldo was inciting criticism and incurring wrath. The list of his culpable offences is long and varied. It includes a vast banquet of sins, all of which have been reheated for breakfast so many times that they have become positively unhealthy.

Those most commonly dredged up are:

The Safari circuit incident in Kenya, where Faldo caused Lyle to be disqualified by pointing out to an official that the Scotsman had illegally put sticking tape over his putter-head to stop it reflecting the sun; that was the foundation on which a case for their rivalry was built.

The World Match Play incident, where Faldo won his match against Graham

Marsh after his ball, which flew the 16th green, was deflected by the crowd back on to the putting surface.

But the 1989 Dunhill Cup incident was and is the most notorious, and probably the most hurtful from Faldo's point of view. His semi-final match riding on the results of the last hole, Faldo took the decision not to play his final pitch shot to the 18th green because mist had obscured the landing area. He applied the same cool logic to that situation as he would to any other on the golf course. And for that he was vilified. In a sport where hooliganism and booing of players is rare, Faldo could induce it.

The students of St Andrews University took it upon themselves to punish him for what they deemed was a contemptible and unsporting action, waving anti-Faldo banners and hurling vitriol. It was a discraceful display of behaviour which, at the time, seemed an over-reaction of the animal rights campaigners injecting poison into Christmas turkeys variety. But there was more to it than that. It was a release of the pent-up irritation of a generation of golf followers, all of whom had grown up on a steady diet of reports about Faldo's *faux pas*.

The problem has always been one of communication. From the first, 33-year-old Faldo, born in Welwyn Garden City, Hertfordshire, kept himself to himself, resisting the pull of the Tour's family circle. Where other young players were drawn routinely into the social pleasures of life on Tour, Faldo chose the practice range or quiet evenings out with close friends over their company. He gave the impression of being cold and aloof. He was considered a loner.

In the early stages of his playing career, he also suffered from an affliction common to quite a few of the good players, whereby, having been denied an adolescence by his dedication to golf, followed by sudden elevation to stardom, he was emotionally retarded. To make matters worse he had an unfortunate sense of humour – the kind which offends more often than it amuses – and a habit of putting his foot in his mouth which was distinctly unendearing.

This career-long melodrama has been played out against the starkly contrasting backdrop of Faldo's genius on the golf course. With a golf club in his hand, Faldo's ice-cool manner was acceptable. He could be disdainful. He could be inscrutable and remote. He could be whatever he wished as long as his exquisite talent was on display and it was praised as concentration and single-mindedness. For those four precious hours Faldo's solitary crusade was its own reward.

The path to greatness can often be charted. By tracing the patterns of a life back to childhood, one might find some instance, someone, or adversity of some kind, which might have sown the seeds of a champion. In the study of Faldo's youth, one event has always lent itself more easily than the rest to being the landmark in the spawning of a career: a summer's day in '71.

Faldo, who was at that time a fanatical sportsman, running, swimming, cycling, and playing football, cricket and basketball every hour that God sent, was drawn to a television picture of Jack Nicklaus at the US Masters. He stared at it for a long time, fascinated. Witness to the battle and to the battleground – the best players in the world versus the unyielding opponent of Augusta National – he saw their trials and their tribulations, and through it all, the eagle-eyed determination of Jack Nicklaus. By the time the Golden Bear had left the screen, runner-up with Johnny Miller to Charles Coody, Faldo had been converted. From that moment on, golf was his life.

Where does that kind of unwavering dedication come from? What gives a boy, and then a man, that level of commitment, and that stubborn refusal to be diverted from the pursuit of a chosen course?

'It's just something in your make-up,' Faldo says now. 'I've always gone at everything as hard as I could, every sport I've ever done. I guess in golf I just found something that suited me. A sport I could go at as hard as I could and achieve something. The other thing is the practising. Training in cycling and swimming is very monotonous and boring, but golf is different every day. Golf is great fun. It's very easy to go out and put in hours of practice because it's so enjoyable. There's always something new to work on.'

An only child, Faldo grew up in a two-bedroomed house in Welwyn Garden City. His father, George, worked in the financial planning department of ICI Plastics; his mother, Joyce, was cutter and pattern drafter for Cresta Silks. They devoted their lives to their son's cause. As a boy, they had ambitions for him to be an actor. They took him to dancing and elocution lessons and tried to interest him in music. When it became apparent that he was only interested in sport, they put aside their artistic aspirations for him and channelled their energies into developing his athletic ability.

When a child is given everything he asks for, when he is praised, encouraged and even spoiled to the extent that Faldo was by his parents, two things are likely to happen. Either they will rob him of every ounce of drive and dedication that he needs to succeed. Or they will enhance his strengths, and instil in him the one ingredient essential in every champion: self-belief.

Faldo, in large measure, possesses the latter.

Five years after watching Jack Nicklaus play Augusta, Faldo turned professional, trailing a long and distinguished list of amateur credits. His decision to opt for golf's paid ranks rather than wait for a Walker Cup place was censured, but, as with everything Faldo has come under fire for, he did what he thought was right and best for his career at the time.

In his first season on Tour, Faldo had one top ten finish and one top 20 finish and ended the year in 58th place on the Order of Merit (winning £2,112). In his second, he had seven top ten finishes, including a victory in the Skol Lager Championship, and finished eighth on the money list (earning £23,978). And in 1978 he finished third on the rankings (earning £37,912) after six top ten placings, including a win in the Colgate PGA Championship.

Every year Faldo was improving, performing well more consistently. Then in 1979 he suddenly retrogressed, dropping 18 places on the money list (only winning £14,911). He responded to this by becoming progressively more withdrawn, almost cutting himself off from all social contact completely. His answer to the devils that played havoc with his game was to toil for long back-breaking hours on the practice ground until he had nothing left to give. He became colder and more single-minded than ever and more inclined to lash out at and use as a scapegoat anyone who got in the way of his war with his game.

It was into this tempestuous world that Andy Prodger, a reticent North Londoner, walked. On vacation from his job as golf professional at Hartsbourne Country Club in 1979, he approached Faldo and asked whether he needed a caddie for the week. Faldo agreed and they finished fourth in the tournament. When Faldo offered him a job for the season, Prodger resigned from his position at the golf club and came out on Tour.

Viewed with the benefit of hindsight, this might seem a remarkable stroke of good fortune. But according to Prodger, 'Literally nobody wanted to caddie for him because he actually had a bad reputation – the way he treated caddies, and so on.' They parted company for the first time in 1981, after two seasons and two victories. 'I don't want you to feel upset or anything,' Prodger recalls Faldo telling him at the Lancome Trophy, 'but I need to have a break. Our communication isn't there.'

Faldo went to America the following year to try for his US Tour card. Prodger went too, under separate cover, and began working for Chi Chi Rodriguez ('That was 18 months of caddying for a gentleman'), and then Tom Purtzer in 1984, with whom he won the Phoenix Open. Returning to England the following season, he was offered his job back by Faldo. 'At that time, Paul Stephens was caddying for him,' explains Prodger in his quiet, halting way. 'But Nick and Paul could never last because they're both highly strung. There was always going to be a clash of personalities there.'

Leaning forward, nervously holding his coffee cup between both hands, Prodger looks too small and uncertain of himself to have coped with the excessively demanding task of working for Faldo once, let alone twice, particularly when he had borne the brunt of Faldo's frustration with his game in the initial period.

'Well, I made up my mind that I wasn't going to listen to him anymore,' says Prodger. 'These golfers will tell you if you've done wrong in no uncertain terms so I was determined not to get upset – because the first period of time I got very upset. I was determined not to listen to nastiness and that was the way for me to keep concentrating on doing a good job. That was working fine until '89 when I made a couple of mistakes with the yardages in America. Then all year certain remarks were made. In the end I couldn't handle it any more so I started saying nothing. That's the way I go, you know. I went from being a very confident person to not being a very confident person at all. These guys can get to you in the end.'

But at the time Prodger began working for Faldo in 1985 he had just embarked on his swing change and was, with the assistance of Leadbetter, walking a technical tightrope suspended at a dizzying height. Faldo was caught somewhere between the two swings and his game ran around him wildly and uncontrollably, like blind mice escaped from a cage. According to Prodger, it was only in 1987 when he won the Open Championship at Muirfield that Faldo really began to feel his swing had changed. In the meanwhile, his inner torment and anxieties over his golf game had to find an outlet somewhere, and once more Prodger found himself the whipping boy.

'I think,' says Prodger now, 'the best way of describing Nick is to say he's a perfectionist. Nick's definitely a tunnel-visioned person. He has a tendency to ignore people when he shouldn't and say the wrong things. He's not trying to say the wrong things, but he definitely does say the wrong things.'

'Did Nick change after the Open?'

'The biggest change in Nick was actually when the family started coming along. He started to be a more relaxed person . . . Apparently he's a bit of a comedian outside golfing circles, with his own family and friends. He likes to tell jokes and play tricks. I've always said that if he could bring a bit of that into his behaviour on the course, no one would ever beat him.'

David McNeilly has another story which he tells about the time Faldo first asked him to caddie for him. On the phone to McNeilly, Faldo went through a long list of do's and don'ts and explained exactly what he expected from a caddie. Then he told McNeilly what preparations he wanted him to make before the next tournament, including how he wanted the course measured.

'Do you use a wheel?' demanded Faldo down the line.

'No,' said McNeilly. 'I always use public transport.'

In Prodger's opinion, in 1988, the year he lost the US Open, Faldo played the best golf of his life. 'The whole year he played fantastic but putted very, very bad. Certainly in the US Open, if he had putted anything like [well] in the last round, Curtis Strange wouldn't have won. There was only one person who was ever going to win and that was Nick Faldo, but he couldn't convert the chances that he had. But the whole year he was averaging something like 15, 16 greens a round and that's very impressive stuff. Unfortunately, as I say, he wasn't converting the chances. The frustration crept into his game. He knew he was playing the best he could play at that time.'

Watching Faldo in the US Masters earlier this year, Prodger could see he was beginning to swing as well as he had in 1988, much more freely. His attitude, too, was more determined.

'Last year,' says Prodger, 'he didn't play half as well as he did in '88, but he putted unbelievably. But, as I say, confidence is a very big thing with these guys, and one of the things that Nick likes from his caddie is to try and build up his confidence – keep saying, "Good shot", or "I think you've done this wrong". He likes feedback, whether it's only kidding him, but as long as his mental attitude is such that he thinks he's doing it right.'

Faldo felt that feedback was something he definitely wasn't getting from Prodger. In John Hopkins' brilliantly revealing article 'Driven by Women', he says that he felt he wasn't getting the support he needed from his caddie. 'I needed him to help me,' Faldo said, 'I couldn't understand how he could watch me miss six putts inside ten feet and not say something. I would get mad and say to him: "How many more bogeys do you want me to make before you say something?" '

Prodger realises that his silence on the golf course was part of the reason that they finally split up at the beginning of this season. He maintains that the other half was Faldo's moodiness.

'All of '89 he started becoming nasty. At the Ryder Cup I said, "Gill, can't you try and get your husband to laugh or smile. Why has he got to fight all the time?" . . . So she actually had a word with him to start to try and relax. After the next two tournaments – he could have won one of them and he finished eighth in the other – he said to me that Gill had had a word with him and he was going to try and relax a bit more. Then out in Japan and Australia, he went back to his old ways of being grumpy, grumpy.

'I've been fortunate that I've been successful with Nick,' says Prodger, who despite everything enjoyed much of the time he spent with Faldo, 'so we had what I thought was a nice working relationship. But it ended because Nick is such a perfectionist in life. If he feels something is injuring his career, he will cut it off, whatever it is.'

In Prodger's place is a caddie guaranteed to give Faldo feedback, the brisk and efficient Swedish girl, Fanny Sunnesson.

'What seems strange,' I said to Prodger, 'is how you can spend all those years working with the guy and not really know him.'

'I don't think you can. I often tried to suss him out but came up with no conclusion. One minute he can be very nice and the next, the opposite. When he actually fired me, he did it on the telephone.'

Prodger hesitates, brooding over past events. Then he says with infinite wisdom: 'To be a champion, you've got to be a diplomat as well.'

London, 16 October 1990. Nick Faldo has told us he has dreams which are in effect premonitions. 'Dream it to believe it,' he says.

Coincidentally, so do I. After months of trying to summon the courage to ask him for an interview, I dreamt that I walked up to him on the range, explained who I was and what I wanted to speak to him about. In the dream, a smiling Faldo agreed to the interview without the slightest hesitation. Inspired by this, I waited for him on the practice ground the following day. We were at the French Open at Chantilly (June) at the time.

'When will Nick be finished practising?' I asked Fanny, when she strode past swinging an empty ball bucket.

'He's not speaking to the press today,' she informed me.

'I didn't ask you whether he was speaking to the press,' I said coldly, but she was already out of earshot, noisily scooping balls out of the tractor baskets at the far end of the range.

So I waited and waited and waylaid Faldo when he had finished. He stopped, folded his arms while he heard me out, and then beaming down at me from a great height, said that he would do the interview with pleasure, but only around the time of the European Open (September).

At the European Open, I approached him again. This time he was distant. He was too busy that week, he said.

'Next week?' I asked hopefully.

'Possibly,' said his departing back.

And so began the saga of the Nick Faldo interview.

He pulled out of the next tournament, the Lancome Trophy, because he was worried about his sore wrist. I rang IMG about the interview. A message came back to say he would have to consult his schedule, but that he would let me know when he could speak to me within a fortnight. Two days later I got a curt letter informing me that, although he had agreed to do the interview, he had now changed his mind. He (in other words, an IMG secretary) knew I would be disappointed.

Well, I wasn't disappointed, I was furious. As a possible alternative, I approached Fanny for an interview. She refused point blank to speak to me under any circumstance in the world. 'I never do interviews,' she insisted.

So I confronted John Simpson, Faldo's manager and friend. Ten days and several arguments with IMG secretaries and minions later, I spoke to Simpson again, who said that for reasons of his own (none of them nasty, he assured me) Faldo wouldn't do the interview. It seemed he was too busy. During the course of the five weeks he was taking off to rest his hand, he would be so busy having treatment and moving house that he couldn't spare ten minutes.

But, like Simpson, I don't think there was anything personal in it, apart from the fact that I'm a journalist. David Leadbetter, talking about Faldo in *Today's Golfer* said: 'I think he's [Nick's] been burned a couple of times and puts up a natural wall. People say he could really afford to be pleasant and nice on the golf course, but that's just not Nick's way. He focuses and just does what he has to do. He's completely business-like about his whole game.'

'Nick has never had to put other people in his timetable,' said Gill Faldo, in Hopkin's article. 'He was always able to do what he wanted and that is reflected in the way he leads his life. He was spoilt by his mother who did everything for him.'

Nevertheless, I was determined to speak to him. When I begged and pleaded and issued veiled threats, Simpson suggested I write to Faldo. So I did. A desperate 'this interview is as important to me as a writer as winning the Open Championship is to you as a golfer' letter. The result: Faldo would be pleased to speak to me on the phone. A compromise, but infinitely better than no interview at all.

So it was with some trepidation that I dialled the Faldo household. A jovial, good-humoured and approachable Nick Faldo was in.

'Sorry about the racket,' he says, laughing at his children who are shrieking with mirth in the background.

'I don't suppose,' I ask as a final, final resort, 'that I could possibly do a face-to-face interview?'

'Not really, no,' says Faldo, and then appears to consult his diary. 'Let's see, I've got to go to town tomorrow, I've got to have treatment the next day, I've got two meetings on Friday and then I've got to get ready to go away. No, I don't think so.'

His tone manages to convey apology and the assurance that if it was humanly possible to fit me into his schedule this week, he would do so. He makes it sound for all the world as though if I had but spoken to him a day sooner, he would have seen me without a qualm. I feel partly soothed by this polite explanation, partly annoyed, partly frustrated and partly mystified – a combination of emotions which invariably accompany dealings with Faldo.

The voice on the line is debonair. A voice to charm the birds from the trees. Had I been talking to a complete stranger, I would have said that it was undoubtedly the voice of a successful man but also that of a genuine man, a contented man and a family man. Disembodied and separated from his chilling intensity on the golf course, he seems oddly human. Hearing him, you could almost imagine that the man with the practised smile and model good looks in the television advert, who would like us to believe that despite an income in excess of five million pounds a year he still uses Bic plastic razors, really does.

The 'real Nick Faldo' has always been a man disguised by his own dichotomy.

You will hear from one source that once, when a child of his fell, Faldo remained seated, leaving it to the family's nanny to pick it up and console it. But Bruce Forsyth will tell you that the time Faldo brought his daughter, Natalie, over to his house for a photo-session, he came alone. Forsyth couldn't believe how good Faldo was with her and how patient, how gently he put a golf club in her hand and explained to her what she had to do. He said it was patently obvious Faldo adored the child.

To friends, Faldo confided that he had injured his wrist when he fell down the stairs while playing with his children at home. To the press, Faldo has only ever said that it was caused through playing golf. Discussing the subject at the European Open earlier this year, Faldo said jokingly: 'It's actually Leadbetter's fault.'

These days he finds it much easier to tease the press. The good humour that Prodger talked about, which until now he has found hard to exhibit outside the company of friends and family, is now on continuous display.

'Not really,' said Faldo, amused at the press reaction to this statement, 'it's actually my fault. When I started retuning my swing, I worked a lot in the gym, but because I never worked on my arms I unbalanced my body.'

He had begun the press conference talking about a shot which had required a ruling. Hitting from a cluster of pine cones, Faldo had then put it in a bunker.

'Did you improve your lie by getting a drop?' asks a reporter.

'Yeh, the drop was better,' replied Faldo. 'But I had a bad kick to go into the trees,' said Faldo with a grin. 'I'm not accepting that it was a good drop to come out. It was a bad kick to go into the trees. Let's start with that first.'

'How was your wrist today?'

'It wasn't bad, but it's still there. Paul's [Ankers] just getting me through this week and then I'll make a decision on next week. Simple as that.' He has treatment on his wrist every night, which reduces the inflammation considerably, but he really needs to rest it for a period of time for it to heal completely.

Beside him sat Paul Ankers, former Olympic Judo champion and Faldo's physiotherapist. Ankers explains in layman's terms that the stress fracture which Faldo incurred three weeks before the Masters this year was caused by him hitting balls with much greater power and precision – as a result of Leadbetter's coaching and Faldo's own body-strengthening gym work – while his arms and hands were relatively weak.

Faldo, meanwhile, winked at the reporters and said, 'You'll get a Latin lesson if you stick around.'

This morning, just prior to our telephone conversation, and for the first time since the World Match Play, Faldo went out to hit balls. His swing is such that, after three weeks of not hitting a shot, he can pick up a golf club 'and they were all going in the right direction'. To achieve that kind of control over his swing was the whole purpose of Faldo's swing change and the subsequent work he has done. Total and absolute control over the golf swing is the ultimate aim of both Faldo and Leadbetter.

'Really,' says Faldo, 'it's a feel factor. A lot of players survive on the feel of the swing and they actually don't know very much about it technically. And that's what we're trying to work out. To break it down technically, and the idea is that you can then leave it for months if need be and get it back very quickly. It means that you can have two or three months off over the winter and have a proper rest. I proved it over the winter. I took a long break and I got it back within five days.'

In his victory press conference at St Andrews, Faldo said that he and Leadbetter had laboured extremely hard to fine-tune his swing. 'He knows my goals and he feels I can keep improving. That's the hallmark of our relationship. He knows I want to improve. If there's any small detail he feels I should work on, I will work on it until I get it right.'

'How do you feel about the fact that you have got closer than anybody since Hogan to actually mastering the game?' I ask now.

'Yeh,' drawls Faldo in response, and laughs with pleasure. 'I have my moments, but like anybody else you keep looking for improvements. When I read that I am compared with Hogan, obviously it's a great compliment and it's very rewarding after all the hard work I've done. It's nice to hear. It makes me feel good. It's better than being called a boring plodder.'

'Now that your career is totally geared around the majors, do you find you have trouble getting motivated in ordinary tournaments?'

'No. I go out there every week trying to win. But because I've been trying to protect my wrist, I just haven't been able to do that so much this year. I've had to sacrifice a lot for the majors.'

'Earlier this year, you criticised a lot of the players on the Tour for their complacency, and their willingness to just play to make a living.'

'Yes,' admits Faldo, 'that's true. But when I criticise, I try to be constructive. I was trying to rile them into thinking, "I'll show Nick Faldo that he's talking rubbish" – if that's the way they want to take it. I try to do everything that enhances my golf. Obviously, David, I feel, is the best coach in the world, and now I've got Paul [Ankers] who's helping me to build my body up. I'm trying to attune my body and mind totally for golf.

'Everybody thinks you can play golf forever,' he says. 'They look at players like Sam Snead and they think you can be competitive for a lifetime. But you're only really going to be super-competitive for about ten years. Well, to put everything you have into the game for ten years is not too much of a sacrifice. At least when I retire, I can say that I tried everything I blooming well could. I mean, I tried everything to be the best. Everything I could. But they don't. They don't work hard enough, they don't practise enough. They should be just working their butts off . . . I can't think of one sportsman who hasn't got there through hard work. Not one. If you work hard enough for long enough, you'll get there in the end.'

'But surely,' I said, 'in order to reach the top, you also have to have an enormous amount of talent.'

'Sure,' says Faldo, 'there's a talent involved. You've got to have a great gift. And maybe there's something lacking in them that they don't have the desire to be the best. But, you know, if you're not good at bunker shots you can stand in a bunker for days until you get it right. That's what I can't understand, that lack of dedication.'

'Are you a perfectionist in everything?'

The man on the other end of the line laughs delightedly. 'In some things,' he admits. 'Sometimes. Even when I try to hang a picture, I get out the spirit level. Both Gill and I have a good eye for furniture. We notice if something isn't one hundred per cent straight.'

Bill Cleary, Wilson's club designer, remembers watching Faldo regarding a joiner at work on a door frame at his Wentworth home. 'That's not right,' Faldo said to the man. 'Oh yes, it is,' insisted the joiner. Faldo went and fetched his spirit level and put it against the frame. It wasn't straight. Faldo made him take it down and start again from scratch.

'What are your goals now?'

'My goals?' asks the man who walked across the tented village at his very first Open Championship and, remembering Gary Player's words, visualised his name at the top of it. 'Well, every major you win is totally different, so it's not like you can get bored with it.' At St Andrews, Faldo said that he could understand Jack Nicklaus's view that every major victory is equally fantastic. 'I can't say that this one is better than the others. All of them mean a great deal . . . The majors are the ones where you want to win the trophies. The others you want to pay the mortgage,' adds Faldo with a chuckle.

Nick Faldo has changed, make no mistake about that.

The Virginia Water taxi driver who took me to Wentworth earlier in the season said as much. He has spent the last three or four years driving him back and forth to Heathrow. 'Nick Faldo?' he said, 'He's actually very nice. If you give him a lift to the airport or you're waiting for him, he chats to you. He's changed. Three years ago he wouldn't have given you the time of day.'

Chip Beck, who defeated Faldo in the World Match Play this year, couldn't praise him enough. 'I think Nick's to be commended,' he enthused, 'because he's obviously the best player in the world, and to stand up as a gentleman and conduct yourself as a gentleman and take defeat like a man is nice to see.'

Even the caddies and lesser known players on the European Tour are saying the same thing. He has unbent sufficiently to chat to them on the tee or comment on their game. A couple of years ago, he could have played an entire round and not acknowledged their existence.

In every respect, he has thawed, relaxed and – more than Prodger realises – learnt the value of being a diplomat. It has been a long time coming. Observing him, I have always thought that he was trying very hard to change his attitude and become a more likeable person before this year, but it is only really now that he has achieved it.

'How have you coped with fame?' I ask Faldo on the phone.

'Fame?' he echoes. 'Well, it's come very, very slowly. You don't overnight think you're a superstar, and besides, golf is a very humbling game. If you start to get above yourself, it comes and kicks you in the teeth. And then, you see, outside of it there's a lot of megastars in the world – Sean Connery [a friend of Faldo's], for instance. I mean, he's a megastar, an absolute megastar. Yet when you meet him, he's perfectly normal and you think: "Well, he doesn't put on any airs and graces." If you want to make yourself into a superstar, you can, or you can just lead a normal life. You can be as normal as you want to be.'

'Do you think you've been misunderstood by the press?'

'Oh, sure,' Faldo agrees. 'Years ago,' he says somewhat airily, as though bad press is something that happened to someone else in decades gone by. He has the cheerful self-assurance of a man at the very pinnacle of his profession who is finally beginning to win the reluctant hearts of the nation. Whether you like him or not, you have to admire him. He is, as Leadbetter says, a Champion. 'I don't think I've changed as a person. I've just learnt to express myself better over the years. It's my own fault. I could quite easily have said better things, or nicer things . . . and been Mr Nice Guy sooner.'

Right now, at his most appealing, Nick Faldo is a very nice guy indeed. But no less of an enigma for it. Once more, I find myself wondering which is the actor and which is the man? And when do the two become one?

'Thank you very much for speaking to me,' I said into the phone.

'Okay?' queries Nick Faldo, sending waves of sincerity and good will down the line. 'No problem at all. Bye now.'

I hung up, no wiser.

Chapter Nineteen

DIARY OF A TOURNAMENT

Young maestro: José Maria Olazabal on the warpath

Photo: ASP, Stuart Franklin

VOLVO MASTERS, SOTOGRANDE, MONDAY, 22 OCTOBER 1990. Night-time in Gibraltar. A slow-moving snake of traffic coils back against itself. We wait there, lined up in our silver courtesy cars, for an hour or more. Strange to think that this is the last tournament. That the whole Tour – having lived and travelled together in the closest proximity since the first day of February – will now be disbanded for the best part of three months.

Tony Johnstone, who had gone home to South Africa, has returned just to play this one event – an élite gathering of 54 of Europe's best players. He arrived at the airport sporting a gingery mountain-man beard. 'I got sick of shaving,' he explained, when we started giving him a hard time about it. 'I woke up one morning and I said to Karen [his wife], "Right, that's it. Change of plan." '

'I like to do that in the winter,' Rodger Davis tells him. 'The only trouble is, I can't stand the itchy stage.'

'Jesus,' says Johnstone in fervent sympathy, 'I went through that a couple of weeks ago. I nearly took off.' He begins to shake with mirth. 'Rodger,' he says as Davis disappears into the plane. 'It's not a question of whether you can get through the itchy stage, it's a question of whether your wife can.'

On the two-hour drive to La Duquesa, where we are staying, Adam (Smurf) Freeman, who started Golf Tours International at the beginning of this year, and Stewart Dryden, Ronan Rafferty's caddie, discuss their winter plans. Freeman used to be a caddie himself. Having given himself the season to find a niche in the Tour travel business not already covered by Traveleads and Randy Fox's Pro Travel, he has decided that it is simply not viable. It's not the fact that his venture has failed that is hurting him; at 22, the business experience has been invaluable to him and will help him in whatever career he chooses. It is the fact that if he leaves the Tour, he leaves his friends behind.

Tour life is addictive. Anyone who becomes part of it and who is accepted and included in the cameraderie finds it almost impossible ever to break away completely. An outside observer might say that if that friendship is exclusive to the Tour, then it couldn't be more than the most casual of acquaintanceships. That is not true at all. It is just that the Tour world and the outside world are entirely separate entities. You have your life and your friends on Tour, and a completely different life off it. Personally, I find it extremely difficult to reconcile the two at all.

The night is warm. At La Duquesa, the white shapes of the apartment complex are ghostly in the moonlight, the sea a silver strip. We stood under a moth-speckled lamp, waiting for the keys to our villas and talking to David Williams. His parents have come out for the week.

'You're a quiet one,' Freeman says to Williams, whose father used to be British speedway champion. 'We never hear about you but you finish about 30th on the money list every year.'

'I haven't won,' says Williams, but without bitterness. 'You have to win to be noticed.'

Later, I found my way to a bar called Cheers where I encountered Johnstone (who is virtually teetotal, except for the odd glass of Baileys Irish Cream), his caddie Grant, a young Zimbabwean with ambitions of becoming a Safari guide, and Barry Willett, who, inevitably, had the three Japanese Mizuno boys in tow. They sat there drinking large mixers, with beatific smiles on their faces.

One of the Japanese has a greater command of English than the others. He describes a recent incident where an amateur tried to get him to work on a set of irons which he could only have got from a Tour player. The amateur refused to say where he had obtained them. Mizuno clubs, you see, are only given to sponsored players on loan. Most pro golfers horde equipment like squirrels and it would be unheard of for a manufacturer to ask for anything back, but nobody looks kindly upon players who arm themselves with free clubs, balls and clothing and then go off and sell them.

Willett has heard of an instance where a player paid for a meal at a restaurant with two Taylor-made drivers. Johnstone is absolutely horrified. He opened his mouth to say so when a filthy white poodle, with a shaggy black mongrel and a Great Dane-cross in hot pursuit, came tearing into the bar and nearly knocked him off his stool. They then turned round and came at Johnstone like greyhounds. In and out they raced like yo-yos. 'Jesus,' shouts Johnstone after the trio, recovering from another fly-past. 'Am I in your way?'

The talk turns to Ballesteros, who is not playing this week. As a boy, Willett, working as an assistant to Max Faulkner, saw Ben Hogan play. He says that the Spaniard is the best golfer he has seen since then.

'He is so incredibly gifted,' agrees Johnstone. 'How can they say he's finished. He's only 34. He's just starting.'

A couple of years ago, Ballesteros and Lyle were having an argument in the Mizuno caravan. According to Willett, Lyle said that he thought the US Tour was still stronger in depth than the European Tour and that it was harder to win there. Ballesteros, who has always worn his nationality and his Europeanness on his sleeve, took it as a personal insult. He was incensed. He adamantly insisted that competiton was much tougher in Europe.

'How many tournaments have you won this year?' he demanded of Lyle.

'Two,' said the Scotsman.

'But where did you win them?' asked Ballesteros.

'In America,' said Lyle.

'Exactly,' said Ballesteros triumphantly. 'That proves my point.'

Tuesday, 23 October. This morning the sky is that magnificent, indigo blue. By nine the sun has taken the chill out of the air and I walk down to the port with Johnstone and Grant in search of a courtesy car. Johnstone, it turns out, is a fanatical gardener, something he discovered quite by accident a couple of years ago when he and his wife moved into a new home with an unkempt garden. One afternoon Johnstone had taken it upon himself to do something about it. He bought a few plants and set to work. Four hours later he returned, dirty, tired and happy. The bug had bitten.

He shows me the palms of his hands, dirt-stained and rough. 'People think that's from practising,' he says.

Mark James, as we know, is the other green-fingered golfer on Tour. Asked by *Golf World* what the biggest mistake of his career had been, he replied with inimitable dryness that he had once planted his runner-beans out too early and they had been damaged by the frost.

Refreshed by his break from the Tour, Johnstone is bubbling over with enthusiasm for the week ahead. 'I haven't been this keen to play golf for six years,' he is saying.

That is not strictly true. Johnstone, a car fanatic who drives a Morgan, won the Murphy's Cup earlier this year with a second round 61. His run of eight consecutive birdies equalled the world record held by Woosnam, Ballesteros, Bob Goalby, Fuzzy Zoeller and Dewey Arnette.

'It doesn't feel like anything special when you're doing it,' says Johnstone. 'You don't feel like a superstar. You just keep hitting every drive down the fairway, every iron shot close and making every putt. It only hits you about two weeks later. But at the time you just wonder what all the fuss is about. You think that you'll be able to go out and shoot 61s every day for the rest of your career.'

Jose Maria Olazabal shot an incredible 61 at Firestone Country Club, Ohio – one of the most treacherous and demanding golf courses in the world – in August, winning the World Series of Golf by an unbelievable 12 shots. The best players in the world were left standing. It is a feat which will grow with the years. American, Lanny Wadkins, who finished a distant second, came to congratulate the Spaniard on the 18th green. 'It's a nice win and I'm happy for you,' said Wadkins, shaking Olazabal's hand. 'Now get the hell out of here and go home.'

'Jesus Christ Almighty!' says Johnstone now, in admiration of Olazabal's achievement. 'And that course is so long and so hard . . .'

Johnstone is looking forward to tackling Valderrama. He is immensely encouraged by everything he has heard about the course. 'I've never heard guys rave about a course so much,' he says with excitement. 'Usually, they're saying it's a goat track.'

'Have you been out on the range yet?' Damien Moore was asking him this morning. 'It's so beautiful. I'm looking forward to going out to practise and I'm only a caddie.'

Aesthetically, Valderrama is everything it is made out to be. The course stretches away over the distant hills and valleys, jewel-green and dotted with brilliant white bunkers. In front of the tiled and marbled clubhouse, the

Practice range has been nurtured by the 47 green staff to state of the art perfection. You feel guilty taking a divot.

In 1985, an international financier named Jaime Ortiz-Patino, reputedly one of the richest men in the world, bought the Robert Trent-Jones designed course. He had one ambition: to make Valderrama the Augusta of Europe. He wanted a course so tough that it would, in the manner of the majors, produce the greatest champions. With that in mind, he had the course altered. He changed it to a par 71 by making the par five seventh – probably the only birdieable hole on the course at the time – into a par four. Money was no object. The fourth alone cost nearly a million pounds to build. He is allegedly prepared to lose four million a year on the course in order to pursue his somewhat sadistic ambitions. It seems that he will achieve them. At the inaugural Volvo Masters in 1988 only two players broke par – Faldo, the winner, and Ballesteros. Last year three players beat par – Rafferty, the winner, Olazabal and Faldo.

Sandy Lyle, whose slow road to rehabilitation is almost complete, is out hitting balls. He has an audience. Three greying men of contrasting build are watching him, asking his advice and investigating the contents of his golf bag. They are, apparently, friends of his. The loudest one removes the cover of his three-wood and examines the head. 'Been chewing it, have we?' he asks and laughs a smug and raucous laugh.

'It got a hiding at the Epson [Grand Prix],' says Lyle sheepishly.

'Is that Boron?' the man asks.

'I don't know,' says Lyle and the man laughs an I-thought-as-much laugh. 'It's Bridgestone,' says Lyle, reading the label. 'It's heavier, more towards conventional steel. It's a good club,' he says defensively. 'You can put some really ugly swings on it and still hit it half decent, which I always think is a sign of a good club.'

I walked away, irritated by the man's mockery and know-it-all manner. When I looked back, Lyle had stopped practising and was giving him a lesson.

Frank Nobilo and Australian Mike Harwood have already played the course and are hitting a few practice shots. 'Did you notice whether the ball was too far back in my stance this morning?' Harwood asks the New Zealander.

'No, I'm sorry, I didn't.'

'Does it look like it is now?'

'I'll tell you on Sunday,' says Nobilo, then obligingly checks it out.

'Who cares?' says Harwood, abandoning his worried contemplation of the ball in relation to his feet and giving in to the devil-may-care mood of the tournament. 'Let it go anywhere. Hit it all over the place. This is the last tournament.'

Wednesday, 23 October. Today is pro-am day. There is an air of relaxed casualness on the range which is unusual even for a practice day and banter zigzags all down the line. A group of reporters are having no trouble doing impromptu interviews with players who are just about to tee off. They approach Mark McNulty. He hits several perfect shots into the blue and studies their flight critically.

'Do you like this course?' he is asked.

'Yes, very much,' says McNulty, white-capped and pristine.

'What do you like about it?'

'It's tough. I'd much prefer to be playing a course like this than a course like Switzerland [Crans-sur-Sierre] or Monte Carlo [Mont Agel].'

Johnstone, who is practising beside him, looks up in disgust. 'I'd prefer to play a course like this even though I've won four times at Monte Carlo,' he exaggerates, mimicking McNulty. 'Even though I've won there and I've never won here.'

'You should be my press liaison officer,' says McNulty laughing. Johnstone spots David Feherty walking by. He goes up to him and rubs his beard delicately against Feherty's face and pretends to whisper something in his ear. 'On the inside thigh?' cries Feherty in mock horror. 'On the inside thigh?'

'Do you fancy your chances here?' McNulty is being asked.

'Yes,' he says. 'Because it's a tough course and on the toughest courses the best players will always finish first, second and third.'

This is McNulty's last chance to win the money list. At present he is nearly £50,000 behind Woosnam. In order to become European Number One, he has to win this tournament and Woosnam has to finish no better than third. But as McNulty admits, 'Woosnam is ten lengths ahead entering the final furlong. He is in the driving seat.'

Six or seven holes into the pro-am, there is a rain delay. The players sit around in dripping waterproofs, praying that they aren't going to be sent out again. Andy (Rod Stewart), Richard Boxall's caddie, was out on the town last night and he doesn't look well at all. His face is glowing bright red like a beacon. 'Calling all stations,' Boxy keeps saying to him.

They are still laughing about Derrick Cooper's prank at the Portuguese Open.

There is one caddie on Tour who favours an educated accent so affected that no one knows whether it is genuine or not. He has overlong hair, a smarmy manner, and is so puffed up with the idea of his own importance that he is a constant target for practical jokes. He also believes that most women find him devastatingly attractive and this has been his undoing on several occasions.

Last week, as is usual, he was trying his luck with a girl in the bar at the players' hotel. Unbeknown to him, Cooper had briefed her in advance. She led the caddie on all evening and, at a suitable moment, slipped him 'her' room key and left the bar. In due course, he followed her upstairs. He let himself into the room, stripped off in the darkness and began to tug at the bedclothes.

Richard Boxall, meanwhile, whose room it was, was fast asleep and blissfully unaware of any of this. He woke up shrieking with alarm when the caddie tried to get into bed with him. The caddie sprang back in consternation. He turned on the light to find a tousled, bemused and extremely irate Boxall between the sheets.

'What on earth are you doing?' Boxy shouted.

'Oh my God!' cried the caddie in an agony of embarrassment. 'I think I've been wound up.'

He fled the room to find half the European tour in paroxysms of laughter outside the door.

Lyle is the first player to go out into the rain and practise when we are told that the pro-am has been abandoned. The state of the weather rarely bothers him. At the Dunhill Masters in 1988, I was out on the practice ground one day when there was a sudden violent thunderstorm. Every player and caddie ran and sheltered in a tiny prefab hut at the end of the range. We were squashed in there, peering out at blue forks of lightning splitting the sky, when Lyle walked past the window. He strolled out onto the range in the rain for all the world as though the sun was beaming down. Twenty jaws dropped. 'There goes Sandy with his bag of lightning conductors,' someone said.

Woosnam is sitting on the golf club wall with Wobbly, discussing the adventures of the evil rat, Clifford Maudseley, who is now a film extra in Turkey. Woosnam has no intention of hitting balls in this weather. 'Are you looking forward to the end of the season?' I asked him.

'Oh yeh,' is his heartfelt reply.

'What are you going to do in the winter?'

'Drink,' says Woosnam mischievously.

'Are you going to do your fitness schedule again?'

'I'm going to take up Kung Fu!'

When the rain slowed, I went out on to the practice ground to talk to Dave Musgrove. He always has a story to tell.

In 1979 he was caddying for Ballesteros in the Spanish Open at Torrequebrada when they came to a long dogleg par five. In previous years Ballesteros had successfully cut the corner with his drive, but it had subsequently been altered and a hill, which was out-of-bounds, had been built as a deterrent. Ballesteros, however, was undaunted. He insisted that if he had driven the distance once he could do it again, hill or no hill. Musgrove's protests were in vain.

'I can do it,' Ballesteros said stubbornly, before taking out his driver and hitting his ball straight out-of-bounds. He refused to play another shot from the tee, setting off grimly up the slope in search of the first. Musgrove, carrying the golf bag, was forced to struggle up the hill behind him. After a quarter of an hour of fruitlessly looking for a ball in the dense rough, he decided his five minutes were up. He stamped back to the tee, face as black as coal, and scowled ferociously at Musgrove. 'Next time,' he said, 'you watch where the ball goes.'

Frank Nobilo and Johnstone have joined the pros who have decided that practising in the rain is a whole lot better than doing nothing. In spite of his assurances to the contrary, Johnstone still hasn't shaved off his beard.

'I said I was going to grow it for a month,' he insists.

'Month's up,' says Nobilo.

'I think you suit a beard,' I said to the New Zealander.

'Thanks,' says Nobilo suspiciously, 'but I'm busy tonight.'

'You'd have more chance if you had ears and a woolly coat,' says Johnstone with a grin. 'Have you got a sheepskin coat?'

Nobilo lets it ride.

'I must say, you are both very dedicated to be out practising in the rain,' I commented, changing the subject.

'I wish my coach was,' says Johnstone. Bob Torrance is hibernating in the golf club bar. 'Fortunately, I'm rifling it.'

'I'll fix you up,' says Nobilo helpfully. 'What size sheep do you want?'

There is a lot of talk about those players who have lost their cards and will be going to the Tour School at Montpelier in November. Their names – Ian Mosey, David Jones, Manuel Pinero, Robert Lee – are spoken of with sadness, mingled with profound relief that the speaker has been spared that particular ordeal this year, or for the rest of his playing life. The quiet young player now propped against the golf club railings heaves a grateful sigh that the destiny gods have seen fit to help him into the category of the latter.

On Sunday, 21 October 1990, golfing justice was done. Michael McLean won the Portuguese Open.

The man who gathered his courage and resources at the end of last year for one final, harrowing attempt at the European Tour Quyalifying School has ended this a hero. How does it feel to have entered a tournament sixth reserve, having finished stone last in the previous two events, and walked away the victor by a stroke and the holder of a five-year exemption?

'I thought I'd come here this week all laid-back and happy,' says McLean, who is going to the Dominican Republic to celebrate with his fiancée, Vicky. 'But I come here and I'm still the same old grinder.'

Golf – the great leveller.

Four years ago, McLean totted up his earnings after five full seasons on the Tour. The balance: £126,532. He decided that with the assistance of a top-class coach, he could double or treble his income.

'I thought that a good teacher could get my swing looking like Nick Faldo's and working like Nick Faldo's.'

Several years and numerous teachers later, McLean knew the meaning of the phrase 'paralysis through analysis'. So he went back to basics. 'I just tried to simplify things. In this game everybody's got a certain way of doing it and you've got to learn the best way for you. That's what I found out. You've just got to hit the ball until you feel comfortable getting it from A to B, whichever way that is.'

His five-year exemption means that McLean can now play to win rather than to make the cut or keep his card. 'If I can hit the ball consistently week in and week out like I did in Portugal, you know, I can win these tournaments,' says McLean, who arrived home to find television cameras lining the drive. 'I know I can win them now.'

McLean smiles his shy smile. 'I don't know how good I'm going to be. I could be very good. You just don't know. I've been given the chance now. It's up to me to take it.'

Thursday, 25 October. The tournament began rather dramatically when Wobbly was stricken by a bloody nose on the practice range only minutes before Woosnam teed off. Chain-smoking, gravel-voiced *Sun* reporter, Frank Clough, stepped in as his replacement. He was a hundred yards behind Woosnam at the first and an exhausted speck in the distance at the fourth when a pale and shaken Wobbly reappeared. Woosnam wasn't the only one relieved to see him.

When the range had emptied, I went to look at the Wilson van. Bryan Adams was playing on an expensive stereo system and its occupants were drinking Coke in the sun. This is a slow week for all three equipment vans (Mizuno, Taylor-Made and Wilson). The only thing that most players need for the last tournament of the season are clubs made up for them to try out over the winter.

I looked at several sets of golf clubs under repair, admired a computerised loft and lie machine and asked a few questions about Faldo, who is a contracted Wilson player.

'He's very pernickety,' says Bill Cleary, who worked with Faldo on the design of the FG49 clubs. 'Everything has to be one hundred per cent.'

In his garage at home, Faldo has his own workshop. 'He has very, very sharp eyes,' says Cleary, who believes that Faldo knows more about golf clubs than any other player he has ever encountered. Faldo's perfectionism is such that he even swing-weights his putter (D-2) and weighs the grip (52 grams). Under the grips on his irons, he used to have five layers of masking tape plus one of two-way tape. He now has 13 layers of masking tape under them. The idea is to make the grip almost the same thickness all the way down, which benefits his injured wrist.

'People say he doesn't talk much,' says Cleary, 'but I get on well with him. He's only dedicated to the game of golf. He's not arrogant. If you know what you're talking about then he's great. But if you're bluffing, then he'll spot it straight way.' The madness in Patino's methods is beginning to affect the players.

'It's like a torture chamber out there,' an angry Woosnam told reporters when he came off the course with a 74. 'They should put us off the forward tees to give us a chance. It's a nightmare – the greens, the bunkers, everything. If I had to play here every week I'd quit the game.'

'Greens this severe are not meant to be played this fast,' says Johnstone. 'And if the architect designed them to be this fast and this sloping then he's an idiot.'

Derrick Cooper shot an 81. He went straight to the courtesy car office and asked for a ride back to his apartment. 'I'm alright now I'm off the course,' he said striding across the car park. 'I'm going for some intravenous.'

'I had a mare,' said a downcast Frank Nobilo, 'mare' being a nightmare round in pro talk.

The leading scores are: Sam Torrance 69, David Feherty 70, Mike Harwood and Magnus Persson 70.

Friday, 26 October. Mike Clayton started the day birdie, birdie, hole-in-one and went straight to the top of the leaderboard with Torrance. A six on the next hole promptly removed him.

'Have you seen David's [Leadbetter] new video?' Feherty asks Ove Sellberg out on the range. 'It took me two years to get the club from here [on line] to here [across the line], and it's taken this 16-handicapper a week.'

'That's Hollywood,' says the Swede.

'You're exactly right,' says Feherty, 'that's Hollywood. He's 16 going on two. They showed this guy at the beginning of the video. He looked like a man trying to kill a snake in a telephone box!'

Lyle and Langer are discussing a new driver. 'Put that in the bag and you'll only be 40 yards behind us,' teases Lyle.

'Thirty-eight,' says Langer.

'We've got another driver,' says Coleman, 'where we'd only be 20 yards behind you.'

'We're saving that for when we come out of retirement,' grins Langer. 'For when we're old and grey.'

'Sandy's going a bit grey,' says Coleman.

'That's right,' says Lyle, regarding him seriously. 'It doesn't come cheap.'

Olazabal came in with a 69 which left him at one under par for the tournament. Level with him is Jose Rivero, the much underrated Spaniard, who shot a course record 65. Harwood and Torrance on par, and Colin Montgomerie on one over, are behind them.

Chema, as Olazabal is known in Spain, had two birdies and 16 pars and says that he missed four birdie chances. All questions and answers have to be translated into English and Spanish. Normally, that wouldn't pose a problem, but the journalists seem to be actively participating in the silly season pattern of the tournament and are arguing amongst each other and exchanging teasing remarks. One has his shoes off and his socks on the chair in front of him.

Olazabal, who is trying to speak above the row, stops in frustration. 'What's going on here today?' he says, half laughing at the schoolroom scene in front of him. The reporters sit up straight and concentrate on the business at hand.

'How important is it for you to win here?' one asks.

'I would like to win this tournament maybe in a year when it can mean a little bit more. So if I had to choose, I would win it in a year when I can win the Order of Merit. But anyway it's always important to win a tournament, and it's important to win on this course because it's one of the toughest.'

'Is it easier or harder to win at home?'

'Well, I don't think it's easier or any more difficult. It doesn't matter where you play, you still have to beat the golf course.'

'But you are playing in front of your people.'

Olazabal grins widely. 'Well, I have to say this. There are more foreigners here.'

'Do you feel that you have a duty to your [Spanish golf] federation to play in Spanish tournaments?'

'My duty,' says Olazabal, looking the questioner straight in the eye, 'is just with myself.'

'Why isn't Seve here this week?'

'Well, he played here two years ago and he will play here again. He knows that it is one of the toughest golf courses and the best players win here. And since he is one of the best . . .'

'What do you think is wrong with him?'

Olazabal gazes steadily out from behind the microphones. He seems impossibly mature and composed for his age. 'I have to be serious with this,' he says. 'He's having a bad year and everybody's been charging down on him. I don't think that's fair. In my opinion, he is still one of the best players. He's been playing pro golf for 16 years and he have one bad year and everybody comes down on him.'

'Seve says that he knows what the problem is, but he won't tell us.'

'If he knows what's wrong with him', says Olazabal, 'then he doesn't have to tell anybody.'

'Do you think it's good that appearance money is going to be stopped?'

'If they put that money in the tournament then I think that's good. I wouldn't like to see all that money disappearing. I would like to have a chance of getting it.'

'How do you feel about the fact that there's no appearance money this week?'

'That's fine. I don't need the money.'

'But then why isn't Seve playing?'

'He doesn't need the money,' says Olazabal, firmly putting paid to the idea that Ballesteros is not playing because he couldn't get appearance money out of the sponsors. 'He's at home with his wife and kid enjoying life, which is what he should be doing.'

Friday p.m. There is a bar at La Duquesa called Ryders. It is hung with black-and-white photographs of most of the players who will be found there in varying states of intoxication this week.

Tonight it is humming by six o'clock. John Graham, holding a large Bloody Mary, is looking extremely pleased with life. He is going to caddie for Olazabal in a couple of tournaments in Japan and in the Million Dollar Classic at Sun City. Today Olazabal's manager handed him a large envelope of cash with which to pay for his air tickets and hotel expenses. 'I'm so lucky, man,' he says over and over. I suspect that he is referring to the fun that he will have in the casinos at Sun City, rather than the fun he will have carrying Olazabal's bag. It will be a miracle if the money ever gets used for its intended purpose.

I went to a Chinese restaurant for dinner with a photographer and Lindsey Anderson, who is now caddying for Howard Clark. Tony Jacklin, a Chinese food afficianado, apparently rates it as one of the best in Europe. The food was excellent but took an age to come, during which time Anderson had a heated argument in defence of Clark's temper on the golf course. She loves working for him. She steadfastly maintains that Clark has never been more than slightly annoyed – and then with justification – on the golf course when she has caddied for him, that he has never shouted at a spectator or at her, and that he has a wonderful sense of humour.

Having observed Clark more closely since Anderson started carrying his bag, having heard (for once) both sides of the story, and having watched him this week off the course, relaxed and amiable, I have to say I think that she's right. I know that he badly wants to change his image, and besides, I've always thought the fact that Clark is a good friend of Mark James is a point in his favour, since James is universally respected and one of the most popular people on Tour.

Ryders Bar has changed out of all recognition when we return. In the far corner, a party of rapidly escalating volume and debauchery is in progress. The red-headed owner of the bar plays host. Dressed in an outfit we have already been treated to several times this week – a black clinging affair held together with strands of beads – she gyrates her way between the tables, breaking scores of glasses, bounding on and off laps, and, rather bizarrely, climbing in and out of the window.

A row of caddies and players watch open-mouthed as their counterparts let down their hair in fine style. Everyone goes slightly mad at the last tournament of the year because the season is over for better or for worse, there is no cut and they are guaranteed prize money. It was all good fun (though it got slightly out of hand eventually) and is the only time I have ever seen golf pros let go of their inhibitions so completely.

As Phillip Walton says, golfers are like kettles. If they don't let off steam, they just explode.

Saturday, 27 October. McNulty seems to be hitting balls with his usual crisp precision but he says that he is not at all happy with his game. Yesterday he missed 11 greens. Like Ronan Rafferty, who rarely drinks and then only a glass of wine with his meal, McNulty has approached this week with his usual degree of professionalism. I told Paul Stephens about the goings-on in Ryders Bar. 'I couldn't imagine Mark, or players like Faldo and Ballesteros, behaving like that,' I commented.

'Well, I wouldn't,' said McNulty, who was listening. 'Never. I wouldn't do it.'

'I'd be very disappointed if you did,' Stephens says to him.

'I just wouldn't,' says McNulty positively.

Feherty came in in the afternoon with a 67, which takes him to one over par for the tournament. 'This course is so uncompromising that it punishes good shots as severely as bad,' he tells us. 'It's exceptionally unfair in places, no question about it.'

As he says, there is a basic problem here, and that is that the people who run tournaments tend to hold the opinion of those who hold the purse strings in higher esteem than they do the players. The only blessing this week is that nobody gave into Patino's suggestion that the players don't wear spikes on the greens. It is difficult to imagine what he might have had in mind as an alternative. Slippers, perhaps?

'My philosophy on the game,' says Feherty, 'is that if you hit a good shot, you should be rewarded for it, not penalised. You know, games become extinct. Lacrosse is on the way out and golf won't be far behind if you keep building courses like this.'

Earlier in the week, Feherty said he thought the course was very beautiful from tee to green. 'Then there are the greens. It's as if they were built on top of elephants and sperm whales . . . You could easily ten-putt the sixth. I'm not joking.'

Today he said of their design: 'It's like building a snooker table with three humps in it . . . It's a particular Trent-Jones problem, this. It's the battle of the landscape gardeners now, it's not really about golf course architecture.'

'You've had a very good year, what's next for you?' he is asked.

'I'm just trying to get around tomorrow without being injured.'

I went out on the range next and watched Fijian Vijay Singh, tall and lean, smash balls over the horizon. Yesterday he was drawn with John Bland again. It is an on-going joke between them, the fact that the only black golfer on Tour is always having to play with a hard-nosed South African like Bland.

'We're old friends,' Bland, tongue-in-cheek, told a reporter this week when he was asked about it. Which is perfectly true. Yesterday morning while Bland was having his breakfast, Singh walked in and thumped his shoes down on a chair. 'Clean them,' he said to the South African. They wind each other up all the time like that.

Bland waited until they teed off to get his own back. Ignoring Singh, he walked over to the starter, consulted the start sheet and said loudly: 'Why have I been drawn with three caddies?'

On the range, Singh hits a shot wide.

'What did I do there?' he says to his caddie, Dave Morgan.

'I didn't really see,' says Morgan.

'Your eyes were elsewhere,' says Singh reprovingly. 'I want a hundred per cent commitment,' he tells Morgan, who is the most devoted caddie you could find.

I retreated to watch Mark Roe attempt to hit the Volvo balloon, which floats over the practice range, with a three wood. He is a brilliant trick shot artist. Hitting shots yesterday he managed to get nine balls airborne before the first one landed.

There are three joint leaders on two over par at the end of the third day of play: Langer, Anders Forsbrand and Harwood. Behind them come Steven Richardson, Torrance, Feherty, Montgomerie and Olazabal on one over par.

In his press conference, Olazabal agreed with Feherty that the course was unfair. The evidence supporting this theory is mounting. This morning, Mike Clayton hit his drive into a drainage ditch and it rolled one hundred yards down a slope and out-of-bounds. Olazabal made triple-bogey down 18 after a good drive finished behind a tree.

'It couldn't have been a good drive if it finished behind a tree,' says a reporter.

Olazabal's eyes flash with anger. 'You think so?' he says to the man. 'I bet you that if you hit a perfect shot on [the second hole] you will finish behind a tree. It's not fair to say that it was not a good shot. I don't think it was a bad shot, I'm sorry about that.'

'But you could see the tree. You could have avoided it.'

Olazabal controls himself but it's obvious he is seething. 'I had a seven,' he says. 'I agree with that. But in this game you need luck sometimes. If you have bad luck you can play great golf and it doesn't matter. If you play golf you should know that.'

Saturday p.m. On the final night, we all ate dinner at the Italian restaurant. Mark James came over during the course of the meal to say goodbye to everyone.

'Aren't you going to Ryders Bar?' queries Johnstone.

'No, I'm not,' says James. 'I have to get up early and do my hair.'

'Which one?' asks Johnstone cruelly.

Ryders Bar is quite remarkably quiet and empty. There are only a couple of golfers and caddies there playing pool. Mark (Mouligan) Mouland, who is one of the wildest players on Tour, is winning game after game with nonchalant ease. He is wearing a tee-shirt emblazened 'Don't worry – be happy', which sums up his attitude to life.

'There is only one thing more frustrating than golf,' says Johnstone watching, 'and that's this game.'

Duncan makes a speech for Mark Gardiner – Sellberg's caddie – who is leaving. 'He won't leave,' says Malcom Mason, Torrance's caddie of two seasons. 'He's a lifer.'

Mason, whose hobbies include photography and gambling, should know. Since quitting his salesman job, he has been on Tour nine years.

Gardiner, it turns out, is going to Thailand to teach golf.

'Teach golf?' echoes Johnstone in amazement. 'How can he teach golf? He's not a pro.'

'He is in Thailand,' says Mason sardonically.

'What handicap does he play off?'

'Five,' says Mason. Johnstone looks shocked. 'Well, they sell fake watches, don't they?' says Mason meaningfully.

Sunday, 28 October. Music is playing on the practice range. When I go to investigate, I find that Howard Clark is warming up for his round to the accompaniment of Genesis's *Trick of the Tale*. He has his cassette player balanced on the open glove pocket of his bag.

That's what makes life interesting on Tour – the players are full of surprises.

Malcolm Mason packs Torrance's bag for the day. It contains: chocolate, fruit, carrots, two pairs of waterproofs, 15 balls, two towels, three new gloves and six used ones.

Next to him, McNulty practises.

'Are you hitting the ball better?' I said to him.

'No,' says McNulty instantly. He points to his head. 'It's all up here.'

No matter whether he wins or loses the Order of Merit, the consistent excellence of McNulty's performance this season, and his own graciousness all through it, has earned him a respect that will last a lifetime. In 23 European starts this season, he has finished in the top ten no less than 17 times, including two victories and a tie for second place in the Open Championship, and excluding an eighth place finish in the US PGA Championship.

Brett Ogle, whose courtesy car I rode in this morning and who was extremely cheerful, is now spitting with rage. He has just been told he and Roger Chapman are two of the five people disqualified this week.

Playing the 15th yesterday, Ogle asked Chapman, who had putted out, to tap down a spike mark in his line of play. The greens here have spiked-up so badly that players have been asked to repair their spike marks when they have finished every hole; a pointless exercise if there ever was one. Chapman hesitated, unsure whether he was infringing rule 13.2 (Player Sanctions Repair of Spike Damage). When Ogle repeated the order, Chapman complied and breached the rule. Oblivious to the fact that they had each incurred a two-shot penalty, they signed for wrong scores. The error came to light at a function last night when Chapman mentioned the incident to Tournament Director, John Paramor.

Chapman accepted his fate calmly enough. He said that he couldn't have lived with himself if he had taken his prize money and then found out that he had unwittingly cheated afterwards. Ogle, however, was in a state of near apoplexy. He called Chapman, among other things, a whinging Pom.

'I will never, ever forgive Roger Chapman for being such a spoilt Pom,' he said vehemenently.

There was absolutely no atmosphere that final day. If there was a general feeling, it was one of disgust that the best players in Europe should be brought to their knees by this golf course.

'Golf is the only sport in the world where the best players are made to look stupid,' declared Johnstone, who had five birdies and 13 drop shots in four days and still finished 11th.

He was bemoaning the fact that he had come all the way back from South Africa to be put through this gruelling endurance test. 'It wasn't worth it. There are some kinds of mental punishment and torture that just aren't worth the money, and this week was one of them.'

Mid-afternoon, Woosnam, showered and changed into smart trousers and a black Boss jacket, helped himself to a Fanta lemon and came to watch television in the press room. He had shot 72 to finish with Lyle on ten over par. He made several suggestions with regard to the course, one of which was that the players force the PGA European Tour to insist that Patino alter it. Then he settled down to watch the final drama unfold.

'There's a good team going to the Asahi Glass Four Tours Championship,' said one reporter to make conversation.

'Yeh, it is,' says Woosnam. 'Who's captain? Faldo?' He gives a snort of laughter. 'Must have won more money than me. Must be appearance money.'

Out on the golf course, players are dropping like flies.

'This course is made to make you mad,' comments Woosnam. 'It's a frustrating golf course this one.'

The sanguine countenance of talented rookie, Steven Richardson, appears on the screen.

'Future superstar,' says Woosnam.

'Have you played with him?'

'Yeh. He's got a massive hook but if he sorts that out he'll be alright.'

Photographer Phil Sheldon wanders in and sees Woosnam. This morning he tried to set up a picture of the Welshman for a golf magazine to depict him as the European Number One. Woosnam refused to do it until the tournament was over and he knew for certain he had won the money list. He said he was superstitious about things like that.

'Are we going to wait until it's over then?' asks Sheldon on the off-chance that he might have changed his mind.

'We are,' said Woosnam firmly. 'Go and take some more pictures.'

Only when McNulty has finished with a 71 for an aggregate of 288, and it is certain that he won't be placed higher than third – thus taking his quota of top ten finishes to 18 and making him runner-up to the Welshman on the money list for the second time – will Woosnam agree to be interviewed as winner of the Order of Merit.

His overriding feeling seems to be one of relief. No, he doesn't think that this year can be compared with 1987 when he won the money list for the first time. 'When you do something the first time, it's always the best time,' he says.

Did he think he played better this year than he did then?

'No, I don't think so,' he replies. 'I might have played better in spells, but overall in '87 I played more consistently . . . I don't think I'll ever play as good as I did in '87. I just hit so many good shots.'

'Do you need the £90,000 bonus you get [for winning the Order of Merit] for anything special?'.

'You always need £90,000,' says Woosnam drily.

The Volvo Masters was won on two over par by Mike Harwood. It is the first time a European tournament has been won over par since the Italian Open in 1978, which is no compliment to the course. Torrance and Richardson tied for second place, and Langer, Forsbrand, Olazabal and McNulty shared fourth place.

'Obviously, I'm over the moon,' said Harwood in his victory speech, followed by: 'I suppose the best way to describe this course is it's your worst nightmare.' Like most players, he feels that with a few changes it could be one of the best courses in Europe. 'I only made one bad shot today,' says Harwood, whose goal at the start of the day was to go out and make 18 straight pars, 'and that was on the 15th, and obviously I made bogey, which I accepted. But I made a lot of bogeys which I shouldn't have had. It's a helluva tough tournament to play at the end of the year. Most guys are tired and it just knocks your brains out.'

The scene in the quadrangle outside is reminiscent of end of term at boarding school. Suitcases and golf clubs. Goodbyes and faithful promises to write. The Sanderson family, who do the scoring at all European events, are barely recognisable out of uniform as they set about dismantling the scoreboard, stacking up the names of this season's victors ready for next. A log jam of courtesy cars in the driveway as everyone tries to get away first. The top players and their caddies have already left at speed; a Lear jet will take them to Frankfurt airport and from there to Japan. Like Woosnam, for the rest of us, there's just relief. There's infinite cheer in the voices of the players from Australia and America, and even Britain, at the thought of being reunited with their families once more. At the thought of days of a different kind of cameraderie, away from the golf, the pressures, the laughter and the tears. Hooting and shouting and last minute searches for passports. Going out the drive, I turn to wave. But already they have all gone. Dispersed like seeds in the wind.

Chapter Twenty

SNATCHES OF CONVERSATION

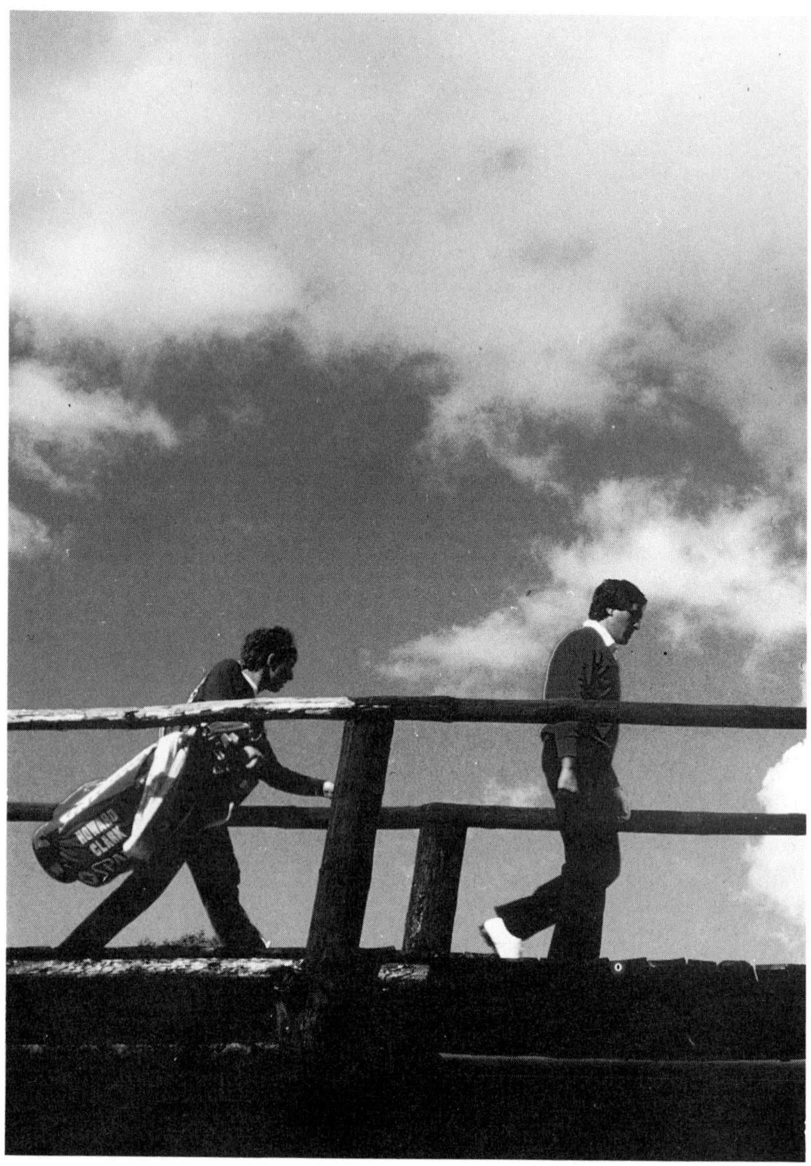

Photo: Phil Sheldon

Seve Ballesteros: 'I think over the years I've proved to everyone what I can do when I play well. I have nothing to prove anymore'

'WELL, GOLF WILL MAKE YOU SUFFER . . . VERY FEW PEOPLE understand golf. There is no game that hammers you as much as golf. Golf hammers you ten times as much as rugby does. I played rugby at school and I got honours, and I did boxing, but those are chicken-feed sports compared to golf. Golf punishes you all the time. The man on the street, how do you tell him that?'

Gary Player, Murphy's Cup, 1989

'There's not many well-adjusted people playing this game.'

Chris Moody, Desert Classic, 1990

'It's so hard to get inside the mind of a player and if you don't get inside the mind of a player then it's hard to know what he's actually there for. There's a certain superficial quality about the whole circus that doesn't enable anybody really to be very straightforward and deep down honest with anybody who's reporting on it.'

David Jones, Montpelier, 1990

'Daft game.'

Sandy Lyle, World Match Play, 1989

'When I've played in those major championships and won all those world titles I've gone into a form of hypnosis. I could never hit the ball as well as Tom Weiskopf for example, and yet he won one major championship in his life. He should have won far more than me because there's no comparison between the way I played and the way he played. But you don't get paid and win championships just by hitting the ball well. Hitting the ball is just one piece of a puzzle. Nicklaus had the complete puzzle filled in and I think I had it filled in pretty well, otherwise I couldn't have won 15 major championships.'

Gary Player, 1989

'How do I cope with pressure? I love it. My body thrives on it. It's like a drug. I would associate it with a drug. When I have pressure and I do well with pressure, it takes me a long time to get off that high.'

Mark McNulty, Epson Grand Prix, 1988

'Pressure? I enjoy pressure. One of the things I really miss most tournaments is adrenalin. It takes so much for me to get any adrenalin flowing. I'm basically fairly easy going and I think it's a bad thing when you're a golfer. It may be good when the pressure's on, but in the first and second rounds when you're playing in Tunisia or somewhere and there's no one watching, you know, it can be difficult to get going.'

Mark James, Leeds, 1989

Jose-Maria Olazabal looks like a fish out of water in the press room. He fidgets, pulls faces and betrays his age. It's pleasantly revealing. On course he seems too mature, far too composed and serious for a man of his years.

'What's wrong with your putting?' a reporter asks.

'Usually,' says Olazabal mischievously, 'when there's something wrong with your putting, it's that the ball doesn't get into the hole.'

It turns out that Olazabal is not well. In spite of his joviality, he looks flushed and exhausted. 'I'm here,' he says, 'because I love you much.' He's going straight home to bed.

'I didn't sleep well last night. I wake at 2 a.m., three and four. What I need is a nice girl.'

'So you're seeing Woosnam tomorrow?' asks Tony Greer, the owlish press officer. The joke is lost on him.

Suntory World Match Play, 1989

'But I can say this – and one thing I never do is boast about golf because it's such a tough and humbling game – but nobody's ever holed more putts from ten foot than I have. That's been a really strong point in my career. I don't think there's ever been anyone in golf that's holed more ten-footers than me.'

Gary Player, 1989

'The ones for par, 90 per cent of the time you've got to hole them if you want to win tournaments. You've got to hole the 15 to 20-footers which are for birdies. If you're having 15 to 20-footers for par every time, you might as well pack up and go and sell caravans or dog coffins.'

I look suitably mystified.

'It's Trevino's quote,' McNulty says, surprised I don't know. '"Dogs that chase cars and pros that putt for pars don't survive."'

Mark McNulty, Wentworth, 1989

'I've been doing it all my life; I'm not going to forget it before morning.'

David Feherty, on why he only hit two practice putts after his round, Gleneagles, July, 1990

'It doesn't matter how you do it, as long as you do it good. The proper technique doesn't work for some players. There are cases like Eamonn Darcy, Hubert Green and Mark James who have very unorthodox swings and who play very well. It's not how, it's how many.'

Jose-Maria Olazabal on Bernhard Langer's putting stroke, Madrid Open, 1990

'I'm a streak putter. Once I putt well, I feel like nobody can touch me . . . If you're putting well then it makes you play even more aggressively. It makes the game a lot easier.'

Greg Norman, Dunhill Cup, 1990

'Don't think they didn't work hard in the old days. I don't think that Faldo would have a prayer of working as hard as Player did.'

Simon Hobday, Murphy's Cup, 1990

'I come from a poor background. My dad was a coal miner and my grandfather was a coal miner until he became a policeman, so I always had to fight for everything I got. I was always brought up to believe that if you worked hard enough at it things would come your way. That was my approach. And I see some of the guys out there today, and I don't think that philosophy holds true. I mean, they think the world owes them a living.'

Jack Newton, Irish Open, 1989

'For £500,000 you'd play on a runway.'

Colin Montgomerie on the German Open course, August 1990

'I'm a believer that the money is very important, but you don't see any slacking off of the guys who have made half a million. They're all out there hitting balls till they're breaking them in half, and that's because there is money. That's their dream, isn't it?'

Ken Schofield, Volvo Masters, 1990

'If somebody's making more money than I am and he's doing it out of the game then I'm happy, because eventually I'm going to be making that money, right, because he's setting a precedent . . . Raymond Floyd and I were talking about it. He comes up to me, he says, "God I love it when you go and sign a big deal, because when I go and negotiate another contract I always go up!" That's what people don't understand. The majority of these guys think, "Look what he's making. It's ridiculous." And they don't look at it in the right perspective. Treat it as a big positive, not as a negative.'

Greg Norman, October 1990

In his press conference, Ballesteros is asked whether he thought about the crucial approach shot that he hit in the match against Paul Azinger in the 1989 Ryder Cup, as he came down the 18th today.

'I was thinking also about why Nick Faldo hit it in the water,' says Ballesteros with a scowl.

'That wasn't a criticism of you at all,' says the reporter hastily.

'It didn't come out the way I thought,' says Ballesteros gloomily of his own shot. 'I must say that I was very surprised that Paul Azinger was the only player out of the whole Ryder Cup team who was able to get to the green. That's the only thing I still think about. Why? I didn't put much attention to what he was doing. He was trying to drop his ball and I was concentrating on my shot, but looking back, I have the feeling that something was wrong. But that's history.'

Seve Ballesteros, English Open, 1990

'It's been very damaging to the Tour and to me personally. I think about it every day. But for the support of my senior Tour Staff, it would have driven me even more crazy than most of you probably think I am. Let's just hope it's the final end of what would be considered petty jealousies and envy.'

Ken Schofield on the infighting between the European Tour and PGA over the Ryder Cup, October 1990

'The Inner Game? I'm not so sure I want to get into that. As I say, I'm a very simple man. If I'm not feeling good I'll go in and have a bit of fun and a sing song and a few pints, and that'll do me. I'll wake up with a sore head and I know I'm going to feel better in about five hours. I'm not knocking those things. There's nothing wrong with them. But I'm a believer in hard work, and if you're working on the right lines and you know where the club is, that's all you need to know. A lot of it's baloney in my opinion. But it works for some people. Some people, all they need is a bit of a guru and off they go.'

Des Smyth, Jersey Open, 1988

'Fortunately my head's never been cluttered up with psychological stuff. I've always looked upon golf to be 95 per cent physical, five per cent mental.'

Mark James at home, 1989

'You get people who are just plain brilliant, like Ian Woosnam, Christy O'Connor and Arnold Palmer, who are incredible golfers, but they couldn't tell you how they hit the golf ball. They couldn't tell you the first thing about hitting the golf ball.'

David Jones, English Open, 1990

'I love snooker. I play a lot myself. I've watched Steve Davis and people say how lucky he is. You make your own luck. The more you practise, the luckier you get, to the extent where you become a champion. People who don't achieve anything in life are not lucky . . . Gary Player once said, "The more I practise, the luckier I get." It's not so much that I practise a lot, it's that I'm a fairly lucky person. Or it's not so much luck . . . I've just got something which enables me to get through.'

Mark McNulty, 1988

'Will you be watching the other players on television this afternoon?' Ballesteros is asked. Ballesteros shrugs, purses his lips. 'You can always learn something,' he says.

Seve Ballesteros at the World Matchplay, 1989

Two stories about Sandy Lyle:
(a) Immediately after his victory at Royal St Georges, Lyle came into the press centre to be interviewed.

'In the past you've been accused of not being able to raise your game to the occasion,' said a questioner. 'Today you've proved you can. How do you feel about that?'

'Well,' said Lyle, considering, 'it's a step in the right direction.'

(b) On his way back to Europe shortly after the 1987 Ryder Cup, Tony Jacklin flew into Houston airport. He was making his way through the building when he spotted Sandy Lyle, wandering across the concourse.

'Sandy!' he cried. 'Where are you off to?'

'Actually,' said Lyle, 'I'm just going to the toilet.'

'Anything can happen in golf and you have to be prepared for it. If you have the drive to not give up when there's nothing at stake, when you're absolutely sure that you're going to miss the cut and you're still out there trying your hardest; if you don't give up under those circumstances, there's less chance you're going to give up under any other circumstance. Just because you're in the hunt of a tournament doesn't necessarily mean that you'll be driven to do your best.'

Ron Stelton, Desert Classic, 1990

'What you've got to convince yourself is that if you string four good scores together you're going to win the tournament, whoever else is in the field.'

Wayne Player at the Murphy's Cup, August 1990

'I think some of the shit that we've handled just makes you realise how badly you really have wanted to do it, even though at the time you might have questioned yourself. Because there's no monetary rewards [when you're starting out]. Three or four years ago, not one of us was making any money really, and we'd been at it ten years then. A lot of the kids now, they have a couple of bad years and they throw the towel in.'

Andrew Murray on professional golf, Las Brisas, 1990

'There's a lot of pressure on the big players, but not as much as the guy missing cuts. I mean, if he's the type that's going to get into a little depression, he's going to get the feeling he'll never make it, which I certainly went through and lots of other players did. You almost have to go through this pain before you can get to the ecstasy at the other end.'

Des Smyth, Jersey, 1988

'I've always been told I've a lot of ability, but ability can only take you so far.'

Wayne Player, York, 1990

'It's nice to see when you get a player like Chris Moody, who's always been a struggler, who suddenly comes right. Yes, you do get a surprise, because a lot of the time even I think, "Jesus, I don't think this player is going to make it." But they turn around and shock you. So you don't quite know what's inside a person.'

David Leadbetter, PGA Championship, 1990

A typical press conference:
Jose-Maria Olazabal, explains the press officer, after going through the Spaniard's birdies and bogeys, has got a cold.

'I don't feel very well,' says Olazabal, who has nevertheless managed to shoot 67 on the West course at Wentworth. 'For quite a few holes I couldn't concentrate properly.'

'What medication are you on?' asks a tabloid reporter.

'I don't know,' says Olazabal, his voice muffled by the bowl of flowers which sits on the table and partially obscures him from view. 'Something Spanish.'

'Is it a liquid you're taking or pills?'

'Liquid,' says Olazabal, surprised at the interest.

'Big spoonfuls or little spoonfuls?'

'Big spoonfuls of orange liquid,' Olazabal tells him when he recovers. The rest of the press are falling off their chairs.

'What are you going to be thinking of this afternoon?' asks the reporter undaunted.

"I always think of nice girls,' says Olazabal with a grin. 'It's very good to relax.'

Jose Maria Olazabal at the PGA Championship, 1990

'I spoke to Olazabal yesterday. He said: "You'd won it by the 11th." I thought, "Christ, I wish you'd come and told me."'

Richard Boxall after defeating Jose Maria Olazabal in the Italian Open

'Do you think Sandy Lyle will be back?' a reporter asks Tony Jacklin.

Jacklin laughs humourlessly. 'Oh . . . That's a difficult question . . . I don't think he'll win another major if that's what "back" means . . .

'He's his own man, he's got his own individual swing. He's got his own way of doing it. But what I could never understand about Sandy is that he didn't seem to understand what he was doing. He's always rushing to somebody to see what's wrong with his swing . . . Every article I've ever read he's going back to his dad for a lesson and now he's got David Leadbetter giving him lessons. How can you need all those lessons when you've won major championships?

Why the hell you just don't get on with it and play and win while you can. Maybe he uses that as a crutch in some shape or form, I don't know. All I know is in my own game – and maybe there's an aspect of envy here, but I don't think so – I never had a coach, I never had a guru. I had me . . .'

Tony Jacklin for a record entitled,
So you think you know about golf?, **May 1990**

Open Championship quotes:
'My most common mistake at St Andrews is just turning up.'

Mark James

'How did Trevino play?' a stringer naïvely asked Willie Aitchison.
'Right-handed, I think,' came the acid reply.

'We've had it relatively easy. When it blows here, even the seagulls walk.'
Nick Faldo on the weather at St Andrews

'I don't know who designed it, but I hear he's escaped.'
Mark James on the Road Hole

'It was so far out of bounds, it landed in another time zone.'
Lee Trevino on a wayward drive

'Personally, I've always found St Andrews rather straightforward and boring as a course.'

Mark James

'I don't know and I don't give a shit.'
Defending champion, Mark Calcavecchia (who missed the cut), on being asked who he thought would win

Out on the range, warming up for the final round of the German Open, contender Eamonn Darcy is having problems. He pulls one shot left and pushes the other right. Phillip Walton has stopped his own preparations and is observing this with an impious look on his face. 'Hitting it alright, Darc.?' he asks innocently.

'No,' comes the gruff reply.

'That is so low,' chides Rick Hartmann, overhearing Walton's teasing attempt at gamesmanship.

'Hey, Phillip,' he says to Walton. 'Is that a real Taylor-Made wood you've got there, or just one of those copies?'

German Open, 1990

Rule number one in Malaysia: there are no rules. Rule number two: rule number one may be changed at the discretion of the committee.

Asian Tour maxim

'I still think that flying is one of the safest ways of travelling. It's just that when you crash it tends to be fatal.'

Gordon J. Brand, 1990

'What you've got to remember is that most professional golfers hate travelling and they're xenophobic anyway. If there's not a McDonald's down the road and they can't get ITV then they're not interested.'

Chris Moody, Dubai, 1990

'You've got to be pretty crazy to play golf for a living anyway, so everybody's got that little mad streak in them.'

Mark Roe, Dusseldorf, 1990

'Lunacy is in the eye of the beholder.'

Simon Hobday, York, 1990

'I do find, being married, that when you're away a fair bit you don't argue as much. You enjoy being home more because you're not home as much. Having said that, it's amazing how many golfers' marriages end in divorce. I think it's probably because the novelty of being married to a golf pro wears off for a lot of the wives, and they're not prepared to accept the way of life.'

Gordon J. Brand, Cannes, 1990

'If Michael and I have one contentious issue in our life, it is the lack of balance between what he gets out of it and what I get out of it, just in intellectual and emotional terms.'

Debbie Clayton on her husband, Woburn, 1989

'This life gets less carefree. The guys are under more pressure, the competition's tougher, there's more money to be made and there's more at stake. And with the wives along, there's the responsibility of keeping not only yourself happy but also your wife happy, under unusual circumstances. I think that's an added pressure on my husband. I tell him sometimes that I'm bored and unhappy, and afterwards I think, "Now really, how does he deal with that? How does he get out there and play, knowing that he's not only playing for him, but for me?" I'm lucky I have a good marriage. I really think that's the secret. If you've got a friend in your husband you'll survive. If you haven't, you won't.'

Debbie Clayton, 1989

At the Murphy's Cup, I did an exercise where I asked each player who he thought practised hardest. They were unanimous in their reply: Vijay Singh. Finally, I got around to asking Singh himself.

'Who do you think works hardest on the range?' I said.
'I don't know,' said Singh. 'Me, probably.'

York, 1990

'I don't really care how they treat me. It doesn't bother me. I'm just out there to play my game and play the best I can and beat the shit out of them. It hasn't affected me. I've been on Tour too long to let it affect me.'

Vijay Singh on racism on Tour, Cannes, 1990

'He's a streak player. When he's hot, you can't beat him.'

Mike Harwood on Peter Senior, York, 1990

'I've never been somebody to try and outdo one individual because it doesn't bother me what somebody else does. It bothers me what I do and how I do it.'

Greg Norman, October 1990

'You learn more from defeat than you do from victory.'

Chip Beck on losing to Ballesteros in 1989, World Match Play, 1990

'I think Nick's to be commended because he's obviously the best player in the world, and to stand up as a gentleman, and conduct yourself as a gentleman, and take defeat like a man, is nice to see. He is a true champion today.'

Chip Beck after beating Faldo 2 and 1 in the quarter-finals of the World Match Play

'I played crap, he played crap. He just out-crapped me.'

A disgusted Wayne Grady, after being beaten by Greg Norman at the second extra hole, World Match Play, 1990

'We both hit a bunch of skunky shots out there.'

Norman on the same match

'I think every good man is tested in the crucible of humiliation.'

Chip Beck after being beaten by Ballesteros 9 and 8 in the semi-finals of the 1989 World Matchplay

Seve Ballesteros comes into the press tent after his practice round with a bandage on his wrist. He thinks he has tendonitis.
'Have you had any treatment?' asks the press officer.
'No, I've just been taking some aspirin.'
'Have you had it long, Seve?'

'I have-a before, but he show up yesterday. I don't know why.'

'Not been to a doctor?'

'No. The doctor will give me also aspirin, so . . .'

'Woosnam's got a groin strain,' says the press officer, 'Mark McNulty has got cracked ribs, Faldo's got a stress fracture and you've got a sore wrist.'

'Good players,' explains Ballesteros. 'There's always something wrong with good players.'

'Do you think it's going to be a problem this week?'

'I hope not,' says Ballesteros fervently. 'It's all I need.'

Epson Grand Prix, September 1990

'Golf has a strange capacity to make people who actually know nothing about it think they are quite well qualified to tell the people who know everything about it how they should conduct their lives.'

David Jones, The Belfry, 1990

'If I want to enjoy my life, take weeks off, not practise as hard as I should at certain times, that's my business. That's my choice and nobody's got a right to say, if only you'd done this you'd have been a better player. I know that if I hadn't taken a club job, if I hadn't got married, if I hadn't given up the Tour for five or six years to be with my family, I would have been a better player. But look how poor my life would have been, although I would have been a great deal richer in the financial sense. So that was my choice. I made it and I have no regrets about it.'

David Jones, English Open, 1990

'As soon as you think you've got the answers to this game, somebody changes the question.'

David Feherty, Volvo Masters, 1990